W!... JRAWN BY THE
UNIVERSITY OF MICHIGAN

WITHDRAWN BY THE
UNIVERSITY OF MICHIGAN

*ALTERNATIVE DISCOURSES IN
ASIAN SOCIAL SCIENCE*

ALTERNATIVE DISCOURSES IN ASIAN SOCIAL SCIENCE

Responses To Eurocentrism

Syed Farid Alatas

SAGE Publications
New Delhi • Thousand Oaks • London

Copyright © Syed Farid Alatas, 2006

All rights reserved. No part of this book may be reproduced or utilized in any form or by any means, electronic or mechanical, including photocopying, recording or by any information storage or retrieval system, without permission in writing from the publisher.

First published in 2006 by

Sage Publications India Pvt Ltd
B-42, Panchsheel Enclave
New Delhi 110 017
www.indiasage.com

Sage Publications Inc
2455 Teller Road
Thousand Oaks, California 91320

Sage Publications Ltd
1 Oliver's Yard, 55 City Road
London EC1Y 1SP

Published by Tejeshwar Singh for Sage Publications India Pvt Ltd, phototypeset in 10/12 Goudy Old Style by Star Compugraphics Private Limited, Delhi and printed at Chaman Enterprises, New Delhi.

Library of Congress Cataloging-in-Publication Data

Alatas, Farid, Syed
  Alternative discourses in asian social science: responses to eurocentrism/ Syed Farid Alatas.
    p. cm.
  Includes bibliographical references and index.
  1. Social sciences—Asia.   2. Social sciences—Philosophy.
  3. Eurocentrism.   4. Orientalism. I. Title.

H53.A78A38   300.95—dc22   2006   2006000661

ISBN: 0-7619-3440-5 (Hb)   81-7829-586-5 (India-Hb)

Sage Production Team: Anindita Majumdar, R.A.M. Brown and Santosh Rawat

To My Son, Imad

Contents

Preface   9

Introduction   12

ONE
The Central Problem of the Social Sciences in Asia:
Critique, Diagnosis and Prescription   21

TWO
Theorizing the State of the Social Sciences   40

THREE
The Structure of Academic Dependency and the Global Division
of Labour in the Social Sciences   57

FOUR
The Definition and Variety of Alternative Discourses in Asia   80

FIVE
Nativist or Autonomous Social Science: A Clash of Orientations   108

SIX
Towards an Adequate Conceptualization of Relevance
and Irrelevance in the Social Sciences   123

SEVEN
Alternative Discourses and Power   147

EIGHT
Rethinking the Teaching of the Social Sciences   176

NINE
The Prospects and Future of Alternative Discourses in Asia 187

Bibliography 196

Index 217

About the Author 227

Preface

The ideas put forward in this book have been earlier developed in various journal articles and book chapters that have appeared over a period of about twelve years. They reflect my developing concern with the state of the social sciences in the non-Western world in the context of their relationship with the major social science powers, that is, the United States, the United Kingdom and France. While my focus is thematic rather than geographical most of my examples and illustrations are derived from Southeast, South and East Asia. The papers collected here discuss attempts to explain the state of the social sciences from various perspectives and critically assess suggestions for alternatives to what is seen as Eurocentric social science. Just what is identified as problematic and what these alternatives are depend on the orientation of those engaged in the critiques and reconstructions. While I have drawn from my previous works for the contents of this book, only Chapters Three, Six and Seven appear here in revised form. The other chapters have taken much material from previously published papers but are much reworked, reorganized and substantially revised versions, so much so that they little resemble their earlier incarnations.

I wish to thank the editors and publishers for the kind permission given to reproduce parts or wholes of the following articles and book chapters: 'On the Indigenization of Academic Discourse', *Alternatives* 18, 1993: 307–38. 'The Theme of "Relevance" in Third World Human Sciences', *Singapore Journal of Tropical Geography*, 16(2), 1995: 123–40. 'Western Theory, East Asian Realities and the Social Sciences', in Su-Hoon Lee, ed., *Sociology in East Asia and its Struggle for Creativity*, International Sociological Association Pre-Congress Volumes, María Luz Morán, general editor, 1996. 'Academic Dependency in the Social Sciences: Reflections on India and Malaysia', *American Studies International*, 38(2), 2000: 80–96. 'The Study of the Social Sciences in Developing Societies: Towards an

Adequate Conceptualization of Relevance', *Current Sociology*, 49(2), 2001: 1-19. 'Academic Dependency and the Global Division of Labour in the Social Sciences', *Current Sociology*, 51(6), 2003: 599-613. 'India and the Future of the Human Sciences in Asia', in N. N. Vohra, ed., *Emerging Asia: Challenges for India and Singapore*, New Delhi: Manohar, 2003, pp. 157-67. Comment on Immanuel Wallerstein, 'Anthropology, Sociology, and other Dubious Disciplines', *Current Anthropology*, 44(4), 2003: 453-60, pp. 460-61. 'The Meaning of Alternative Discourses: Illustrations from Southeast Asia', in Srilata Ravi, Marion Rutten and Goh Beng Lan, eds., *Asia in Europe and Europe in Asia*, Leiden: International Institute of Asian Studies; Singapore: Institute of Southeast Asian Studies, 2004, pp. 57-78. 'Indigenization: Features and Problems', in Jan van Bremen, Eyal Ben-Ari and Syed Farid Alatas (eds), *Asian Anthropology*, Routledge, 2005.

I would also like to thank the Volkswagen Foundation for a grant that enabled me to conduct fieldwork in a number of countries in Asia from 1996 to 1999 from which many ideas and materials for this book were derived. During the various fieldtrips I had the fortune of interacting with scholars such as A. Rahman, Partha Nath Mukherji, J.P.S. Uberoi, Patricia Uberoi, Yogesh Atal, Surendra Munshi, Yang Kuo-Shu, Majid Siddique, Michael Hsiao Hsin-Huang, Sun Chung-Hsing, Yeh Chi-Jeng, Ajit Singh Rye, Zeus Salazar, Clemen Aquino, Cynthia Bautista, Maria Diokno, Ambeth Ocampo, Randolf S. David, Emma Porio, Kim Kyong-Dong, Lee Su-Hoon, Park Myung-Kyu, Chang Kyung-Sup, Karl-Heinz Kohl, Karl Otto Hondrich, Ilja Srubar and Manfred Stosberg. The staff of the Central Library at the National University of Singapore have been very helpful to me throughout the years, particularly when it came to sourcing materials that seemed elusive. Numerous people, that is, colleagues at the National University of Singapore, as well as many abroad, have been part of the process of my intellectual nourishment and I am grateful to them. I would like to especially mention Vineeta Sinha, my friend and colleague at the Department of Sociology, who withstood hours and hours of conversation on many of the topics covered in this book. Another person whose friendship and advice were invaluable is Prof. Joachim Matthes who was very encouraging from the very early stages of this project. Many others from whom I greatly benefited are acknowledged in the pages of this book.

The influence on one's intellect begins at an early age. As a young teenager I had long discussions with both my father, Syed Hussein Alatas, and uncle, Syed Muhammad Naquib al-Attas. Conversations with my father had resulted in my appreciation of the seriousness of the problem of imitation and mental captivity and I came to develop an aversion to this kind of slavish mentality. Some years before the publication of Said's *Orientalism*, my uncle used to explain to me the problems of Orientalism that underlie the study of Islam in the Malay world of Southeast Asia and beyond. These influences are obvious in the present work and I am grateful for those years of intellectual nourishment that have continued right to this day.

Finally, I would like to thank my parents, Syed Hussein Alatas and S. Zahara Alatas for their unrelenting love and encouragement in matters spiritual and intellectual, to Babsy for her affection and concern, and to my wife, Mojgan Shavarebi, and children Syed Imad Alatas, Sharifah Afra Alatas and Syed Ubaydillah Alatas, for the loving and warm atmosphere that I live and work in.

Introduction

Problems Surrounding the State of the Social Sciences in Asia

This book addresses a set of problems surrounding the state of the social sciences in Asia. These problems are contextualized within the historical and continuing dominance of one particular civilizational source of knowledge, that is, the Western, over Asian social scientific discourses. The essays collected in this volume, therefore, represent an attempt to document various critiques of the state of the social sciences in Asia and critically assess the prescriptions for alternative discourses that have emerged from those critiques. Such critiques include those of Orientalism, Eurocentrism, the captive mind, academic imperialism and academic dependency and they have generated pleas for alternative and more liberating discourses, for decolonized knowledge, autonomous social science traditions, and indigenized social sciences. These pleas may be collectively referred to as the calls for alternative discourses in the social sciences, emanating mainly, but not exclusively from the Third World or the South. Yet, the calls for alternatives themselves are often problematic and require critical assessment. The organizing principles around which the critiques of the state of the social sciences in Asia and the calls for alternatives revolve, are the dual concepts of relevance and irrelevance. However, these concepts though implicit, remain unarticulated in these critiques and calls. This book, therefore, goes beyond documentation and critical assessment to the explicit conceptualization of relevant and irrelevant social science. The aim of the book however is neither to provide an exhaustive survey of the social sciences and enumerate all critiques of Western knowledge nor all attempts at creating alternative discourses. Furthermore, this work does not claim that there is no social scientific activity that is unaware of the problems of Eurocentrism and Orientalism in Asia, or that there are no works among Asian social scientists that have transcended ethnocentric divides. In fact, I do provide illustrations of a variety of attempts to produce self-consciously counter-Eurocentric social science. Despite the existence of such work, the overriding context continues to be Eurocentric.

Alternative discourses have not become mainstream even in Third World social science communities because of the number of problems they face that prevent them from becoming part of the mainstream. In this book, the aim is to raise key problems and issues surrounding the call for discourses that present themselves as alternatives to Eurocentric or Orientalist discourses. Four such issues have been singled out in this book. They are (a) the opposition between nativist and autonomous social science, (b) the need for a proper conceptualization of relevance, (c) the impact of the relationship between discourse and power on alternative discourses, (d) and teaching the social sciences along the lines of the requirements of alternative discourses. Wherever possible, illustrations and examples relevant to the arguments or points made in this book are taken from South Asian, Southeast Asian and East Asian cases. In this book, I bring together similar discourses of critique and reconstruction from different social science communities across Asia where authors often do not know each other's works even in the absence of linguistic barriers, due to their almost exclusive orientation towards the social sciences in North America, Britain and France.

It has been recognized for a long time that the process of knowledge production is not independent of the social conditions in which it takes place. This is true of both the natural and social sciences. In the case of the latter; the building of theories, the suggestion of topics for empirical studies, the prioritization of specific areas of research, and the philosophical reflection on the state of knowledge are all directly influenced by the social, or the entire web of social relations that exist in a given society. With regard to our present concern with the state of the social sciences in Asia, the web of social relations is seen to extend beyond the nation state to include other communities and regions. Of particular relevance to us is the nature and consequence of the relationship between social science communities in Asia and their colleagues and counterparts in the West, or what I identify as constituting the world social science powers (i.e., the United States, the United Kingdom and France). These contemporary social science powers are defined as countries which (a) generate large outputs of social science research in the form of scientific papers in peer-reviewed journals, books and working and research papers; (b) have a global reach of the ideas and information contained in these works; (c) have the ability to influence the social sciences of other countries due to the consumption of the works originating within them;

and (*d*) command a great deal of recognition, respect and prestige both at home and abroad. If we go a little back in history we could possibly consider Germany and Spain as social science powers. The former to the extent that it influenced sociology in Europe and North America from the nineteenth century up until the Second World War, and the latter to the extent that it dominated social thought in Latin America during the colonial period. Today, however, the global influence of German sociology is much diminished with the exception of those works that are successfully 'marketed' globally as a result of having been translated into English, and read and taught in the United States and Great Britain. It is important to make a distinction between the global dominance of certain authors on the one hand, and the global dominance of entire schools of thought or theoretical perspectives in sociology, on the other. The lesser global influence of German sociology is in this latter sense. Latin America today, is influenced more by French, German and American sociology than by Spanish ideas.

Since the latter part of the nineteenth century the rising concern in a number of Asian countries has been the problem of the dominance of European and later, American social sciences in Asian social science writing, research and teaching. This dominance exists at many levels of social science activities. At the abstract and theoretical levels, it is mainly American, British and French ideas that are imported, marketed and consumed in Asian universities and among members of the Asian intelligentsia. The very selection of topics for empirical research and the prioritization of research areas seem to take their cues from Western social science establishments. It has also been noted that there seems to be a division of labour in global social science that has serious consequences on its development in Asia. Social scientists in Asia tend to study their own societies and are generally involved in empirical and policy-related research. As a result their works lack a comparative perspective and the contribution to theory is minimal. There is, therefore, a dependence on ideas generated in American, British and French universities, books and scientific journals. This state of academic dependency is perpetuated in the teaching of the social sciences across Asian universities and is not without its consequences. Apart from the fact that it creates the tendency to ignore or assign a marginal status to indigenous, local and regional ideas and concepts, the ideas that are in turn consumed in the dependency relation are characterized by a certain irrelevancy in the Asian context.

Much of this has already been raised in critiques of Orientalism and Eurocentrism in the social sciences. Anecdotal evidence suggests that there is a tendency among some to think that such critiques constitute a spent force. Anthropologists, sociologists, historians and others, it is argued, have become aware of the need to avoid reading European meanings into non-European data and meticulously guard against homogenizing societies and communities in their teaching and research. Social scientists have become more aware of the dangers of trafficking in stereotypes when discussing non-Western topics. For example, sociologists and anthropologists are well aware and critical of the Orientalist assumptions that informs the works of Marx and Weber on India, China and Islam. But, it is vital that we realize that the critique of Orientalism and Eurocentrism in the social sciences cannot stop here. The social sciences have generally failed to take such critique to its logical conclusion, that is, the building of theories and research programmes founded on the discovery and development of non-Western categories and concepts. Let me explain what I mean by this.

In the West, discussions on the state of the social sciences do not focus on problems plaguing the Asian social sciences. This is due to the different historical and cultural circumstances in which the social sciences emerged there. For example, the long-standing concern in the West is in reconciling the search for structural continuities with continuous historical change (Wallerstein, 2003: 455). Without meaning to suggest that the above should not be a concern of Asian social scientists and historians, it must however, be pointed out that this is not the only reconciliation that is needed in the social sciences. For instance, there is a need to reconcile the cultural specificity of concepts with the self-understanding of the people being studied. There is something of a cultural divide in the social sciences that can be seen in the very concepts employed by the various disciplines. The nature of this cultural divide is as follows. Many concepts in the social sciences originated from a Greco-Roman, Latin-Christian and European tradition, which in itself does not pose a problem if these concepts evolve to become universal or plural. The problem, however, is that most of the concepts are passed off as universal when in fact they derive their characteristics from a particular cultural tradition. This wreaks havoc on our understanding of social phenomenon as can be illustrated by referring to the example of the concept of religion.

While 'religion' is presented as a universal concept, the understanding of what makes up religion in phenomenological, historical and sociological terms is often derived from Christianity, in what Joachim Matthes (2000) while referring to Islam, calls the '"hidden" cultural Christianisation' of the Muslim world since it started to think of Islam as a 'religion'. This raises the interesting question of the extent to which 'religions' such as

Buddhism, Hinduism and Islam have been intellectually reconstructed after the image of Christianity due to the very concepts employed by the disciplines that study religions such as, 'church', 'sect', 'denomination', 'secularization' and 'religion' itself. A case in point is a table presenting statistics on 'Church membership in the United Kingdom' in Anthony Giddens' *Sociology* (1997: 461). The religions included in the table are not just Christianity but Hinduism, Islam, Judaism, Sikhism and others, thereby giving the impression that the temple, mosque and synagogue are all, sociologically speaking, 'churches'. The term 'church' is generalized without the concept being rendered universal or plural. What should be considered is the possibility that other concepts of religious organization can be derived from other belief systems. Another example, furnished by Nandy (1983: 25), is the issue of the Christianization of Hinduism, that is, the attempt to fashion Hinduism after the image of Christianity with church and priesthood. As a result, writing about Hinduism poses a problem from the outset because the term and its *European* equivalents such as *hindouisme*, *Hinduismus* and *induísmo* are all European constructions. The danger of reading into 'Hinduism' meanings associated with the term 'religion' in the West has been cautioned against (Madan, 1977: 261).

Religion is a much discussed phenomenon in sociology, anthropology, history, psychology and philosophy. Yet, theoretical discussions surrounding religion have been unable to develop conceptualizations of religion that are derived from religions other than Christianity. The field of the sociology of religion, for example, is founded on a conceptual vocabulary almost wholly derived from Christianity. An approach that moves away from parochialism would not merely study non-Christian religions but attempt to develop an alternative conceptual vocabulary that is derived from various religions. The term 'alternative' is used here not to indicate that indigenous or local concepts are to replace Western ones, but to suggest that there is a need for thinking in universal terms, for taking seriously non-Western sources of ideas and concepts in the social sciences, and for considering a more critical assimilation of Western theories and concepts. For example, Marriott (1989: 2-3) points out that Durkheim's definition of religion as the separation of the sacred from the profane is inadequate for understanding the Hindu concept of Dharma in which these categories are merged. As long as the study of religion does not start looking at its objects as potential sources of concepts rather than just data, it will remain backward as it downplays the objects' conceptualization of itself and denies the culturally plural origins of ideas in the social sciences. The plea for alternative concepts, theories and whole discourses, then, is simultaneously a plea for a culture of plural concepts.

What are the prospects of such a culture emerging in academia? As noted above, in Asia and in other parts of the world usually termed collectively as the Third World, the South, or developing societies, there is a high degree of dependence of social science practitioners and institutions on their counterparts in the United States, Great Britain, France and a few other nations. This takes the form of dependence on ideas, theories and concepts, the media of ideas, technologies of education, and aid and investment in education. This state of what we might call academic dependency is perpetuated by certain features of the global division of labour in the social sciences. This is seen in the division between theoretical and empirical intellectual labour, other country studies and own country studies, and comparative and single case studies. As long as academics in the South continue to do predominantly empirical work that is largely confined to single cases in their own countries or localities and therefore lack a comparative perspective, the prospects for theoretical or conceptual innovation are bleak. Even if the social sciences were to successfully reconfigurate as historical social sciences and extricate themselves from the petty squabbles carried out between the nomotheticists and ideographers (Wallerstein, 2003), the global division of labour as I have described it would still remain intact and culturally plural concepts and theories would remain the exception. Therefore, the reconstruction of the social sciences must simultaneously involve conceptual pluralizations in the context of the dismantling of the current global division of labour in the social sciences.

Theorizing the State of the Social Sciences and the Call for Alternatives

This book seeks to understand those aspects of the state of the social sciences in Asia that allow for the continuing dominance of one particular civilizational source of knowledge. While the problem sketched here has been recognized for a long time, yet, to date there have been no systematic studies in Asia that document theoretical explanations of the state of the social sciences as well as critically assess the prescriptions for alternatives that have emerged over the decades. I have introduced the term 'alternative discourses' as a category that subsumes the works of various authors from a wide variety of disciplines in the social sciences, most of which are concerned with the task of liberation from academic colonialism, with the problem of the irrelevance of Euro-American social sciences and have expressed the need to create the conditions under which alternative social sciences in non-Western societies may emerge. This discourse itself has not been critically assessed as a whole. The absence of systematic studies on the social sciences in Asia itself is a reflection of the problem that this book is raising. As research agenda are generally influenced by debates, research projects and publications in the West, the lack of attention to the problem of academic dependency in the West is also replicated in Asia.

The concern regarding the state of the social sciences has been critically expressed by various Asian scholars during the last 150 years or so. Chapter One introduces the central problem addressed in this book through a broad overview of the critique of Western social science and by surveying Asian diagnoses of the problem as well as the calls for alternative discourses. The Asian diagnoses of the state of the social sciences is taken up systematically in Chapter Two. Here, the focus is on the various theories of the social sciences that address themselves to understanding the state of the social sciences in Asia, demonstrating the plurality of concerns and approaches that have developed in the Asian region and beyond. These theorizations are logical outcomes of the identification of the problems discussed in Chapter One. A typology of these theories is presented in Chapter Two. Chapter Three discusses in detail the academic dependency theory of social science. This theory provides a critical view of the state of the social sciences in Asia by suggesting that academic dependency is a crucial structural dimension of the problem of the domination of Western ideas in the social sciences. It extends an answer to the question of why alternative discourses remain marginal. Chapter Four discusses a variety of positions that emerged as a result of the theoretical reflection on the state of the social sciences in Asia discussed in Chapters One to Three. These positions can be collectively referred to as calls for alternative discourses. The definition and traits of alternative discourses are presented here. The reasons behind these discourses being marginal are also discussed in this chapter.

Chapters Five to Eight raise a number of key issues and problems surrounding the call for alternative social sciences discourses. Each of the Chapters from Five to Eight discuss a problem faced by alternative discourses that has a bearing on these discourses becoming more influential and less marginal. Chapter Five examines the opposition between nativist and autonomous social science. Chapter Six shifts the attention to a more theoretical critique of the emerging alternative discourses in the Asian social sciences through the conceptualization of relevance and irrelevance. Chapter Seven raises the issue of understanding the obstacles faced by alternative discourses in terms of the relationship between discourse and power. Chapter Eight takes us into the teaching arena and suggests ways in which alternative discourses, stated in terms of overcoming irrelevance and academic dependency, can be tackled in the classroom. Chapter Nine concludes with some remarks on what remains to be done for the social sciences in Asia.

Once again, this book does not claim that there are no cases of non-Eurocentric, counter-Orientalist and autonomous social science in Asia. In fact, the existence of such social science in all its varieties and at its creative best is documented with the help of illustrations and examples in Chapters One, Four and Five. Yet, the reality is that these success cases of alternative discourses in Asia remain on the margins of global social science (Chapter Three). In many instances, they are even on the margins of the social sciences within Asia itself (Chapter Eight). The poor state of libraries in Asia or its linguistically plural nature are far too simplistic explanations for the current state of the social sciences. Most Filipino or Singapore-based social scientists read English fluently but do not discuss the works of Indian social scientists, which are predominantly in English, in their classes. The university libraries of Malaysia and Singapore are superior in terms of funding and facilities to those of India and the Philippines. Yet, alternative discourses thrive more in India and the Philippines. Clearly, the reasons as to why non-Eurocentric, counter-Orientalist, alternative discourses remain marginal are to be found in more sophisticated explanations. This book attempts to provide such explanations.

1

The Central Problem of the Social Sciences in Asia: Critique, Diagnosis and Prescription

The Implantation of the Social Sciences in Asia

The development of the various disciplines of the social sciences and the institutions in which they were taught in much of Asia was initiated and sustained by colonial scholars and administrators since the eighteenth century; other Europeans also contributed to this development, directly and indirectly, in vicariously colonized areas.

In Afghanistan, political economy, sociology, economic geography and political history were taught since 1939 at Kabul University. While the foreign teaching staff there were mainly Turkish (Rahimi, 1984: 28), Turkish social science itself was very much influenced by the French and German traditions. In the Indian subcontinent the three presidency capitals of Bombay, Calcutta and Madras established universities in 1856 and these were modelled after British centres of higher education (Dube, 1984: 233). Set up in 1921, Dhaka University in Bangladesh was modelled on Calcutta University and offered courses in economics, political science, sociology, anthropology and geography (Karim, 1984: 84-87).

In Burma, the University of Rangoon was established in 1920 in the images of Oxford and Cambridge universities, and teaching encompassed the disciplines of economics, history, political science, psychology, anthropology and sociology (Kyi, 1984: 100-1). In Nepal, the first social science, economics, was introduced in 1943 at Tri Chandra College, which was itself established by the British in 1918 (Rana, 1984: 354-55).

In the Netherlands Indies, Dutch and Dutch-trained Indonesians were teaching the social sciences since the 1920s (Bachtiar, 1984: 253). In Malaysia and Singapore, social science disciplines were formally introduced with the formation of Raffles College in 1929, with the primary function being to produce second-level manpower for the colonial administration while serious research, especially in anthropology, history, law and linguistics, was conducted by colonial scholars and administrators (Chee, 1984: 297). Raffles College and King Edward VII College of Medicine, both in Singapore, were amalgamated to become the University of Malaya in 1949, and subsequently, in 1958, two autonomous divisions of the University of Malaya were established in Kuala Lumpur and Singapore. These eventually became two separate national universities, the University of Malaya and the National University of Singapore.

In the Philippines, the first social science to be taught—history—was introduced as early as the seventeenth century, with anthropology, economics, political science, psychology and sociology emerging during the American colonial period (Feliciano, 1984: 469). The Philippine system was patterned along the lines of the American educational system. In the early part of the twentieth century many Filipinos were sent to the United States for graduate studies, further strengthening the American influence in social science education (ibid.: 1984: 470).

In Japan, the social sciences were introduced from the West[1] in the nineteenth century and in China at the beginning of the twentieth century. Although not formally colonized, the mode of implantation of the social sciences in these societies was not very different from the colonies. The social sciences were introduced into Japan during the Meiji period (1868–1912) (Watanuki, 1984: 283) and influenced above all by the Germans and Americans. The social sciences began their career in China with a partial translation of Herbert Spencer's *Principles of Sociology* by Yen Fu, with a complete translation appearing in 1902 (Hsu, 1931: 284; Huang, 1987: 111–12). Since the communist takeover, Chinese sociology can be divided into its Marxist (Maoist) variant in the People's Republic of China and American sociology in Taiwan (Huang, 1987; Maykovich, 1987; Schmutz, 1989: 7).

Social Science as a Western Phenomenon

The fact that the humanities and social sciences in developing societies mostly originated in the West had raised the issue of the relevance of these arts and sciences to the needs and problems of Third World societies. Non-Westerners have at times been recognized as precursors of the various disciplines in the human sciences, which underwent their formative stages in the West and were then implanted in the non-West.

A prominent example of such a precursor is 'Abd al-Rahman Ibn Khaldun (733-808/1332-1406), the Arab scholar, often referred to as the 'Father of Historiography' and sometimes regarded as the true founder of sociology before Comte as well as the precursor of ideas in many other fields such as economics, political science, anthropology, and historical geography (Barnes, 1917; Gumplowicz, 1899; Ibn Khaldun, 1981; Toynbee, 1935: 321-28). Taking geography as a case in point, it is clear to many that Ibn Khaldun's theory of historical development, which incorporated the role of climatic factors and topography, built the foundation for historical geography. He was, therefore, the discoverer of the 'true scope and nature of geographical inquiry' (Kimble, 1938: 180) and the first scholar to take notice of man-ecology relations (James & Martin, 1972: 53). There are a fair number of studies that have attempted to establish similarities between the works of Ibn Khaldun and the classics of post-enlightenment Western thought (Baali & Price, 1982; Faghirzadeh, 1982; Newby, 1983; Stowasser, 1983; Turner, 1971).

Therefore, while it is not true that there was nothing approximating social scientific theory in Asian and other non-Western societies prior to its introduction by the West, it is certainly worth noting that no indigenous schools or traditions in sociology or any other social science discipline ever came into being autochthonously in non-European societies.[2] What I am referring to here is a general problem of knowledge even in countries like India, Egypt, Turkey, Korea and the Philippines where the social sciences are relatively more developed. In Korea in the 1970s, for example, scholars were 'awakened' to the need to establish a more creative Korean sociology (Shin, 1994).[3] For all the justifiable attacks against the Eurocentrism of Western scholarship, we cannot speak of a modern Khaldunian, Gandhian or Confucian school in, say, sociological theory. A Khaldunian school in geography, sociology or any other discipline never came into being autochthonously in the Arab world. A qualification to this statement is that there has been some attempt at the integration of Ibn Khaldun's theory into existing 'so-called' Western theories, with the field of application being the Middle East (Alatas, 1993b; Carre, 1988; Cheddadi, 1980; Gellner, 1981). It is not surprising that many scholars since the nineteenth century have questioned the relevance and validity of truth claims of the social sciences for the countries of Asia and Africa.

The lack of home-grown or indigenous theories, concepts and methods in the human sciences is not an issue peculiar to the Arab world. It is true of the general condition of knowledge in the Third World. We have yet to see the emergence of indigenous alternative theoretical traditions outside of the West. As noted by Madan (1966), the Indian sociologist 'has been content to live the life of an intellectual imitator: he has assiduously sought to apply techniques learnt from English and American books to obtain empirical answers to questions mostly suggested by the content of Western sociology' (ibid.: 10). To this it can be added that the issues and problems that social scientists in Asia 'take up for study are either fashionable in the "developed" world or the "developed" world is interested in them' (Misra, 1972: 91). This statement still holds for the social sciences in much of Asia. In East Asia there has been a strong awareness of a lack of fit between Western theory and East Asian realities, but there has been little work that has been successful in creating indigenized, nationalized or distinctively East Asian schools of thought in the social sciences. The social sciences here continue to be dominated by the West and this is partly due to the degree to which general theory has been valorized, thereby making classical and contemporary Western theory the focal points of theoretical debates (Lie, 1996: 65).

Parekh's (1992: 535) verdict that no contemporary non-Western society has produced original political theory rings true of other fields and disciplines as well. Even an intellectually lively society such as India has generally failed to Indianize the social sciences. For example, questions such as the nature of the state, state-society relations, secularism and political morality, all of which have been frequently debated in parliament, Gandhism, the conservatism of Bipan Chandra Pal, Aurobindo Ghose and Swami Vivekananda, have all not been worked upon as materials for a distinctly Indian brand of political theory in terms of ideas and problem-raising. Neither have Indians reinterpreted or reworked the theories of Marx against the back-drop of Indian history and experiences (ibid.: 546-47). The list of under- or non-achievements can be extended to cover various periods of the nineteenth and twentieth centuries throughout the non-West, when the social sciences began to be implanted in these societies.

This general lack of creativity and originality is in no small measure a result of the wholesale adoption of Western educational systems and philosophies in both formally as well as vicariously colonized nations. The social sciences, as they were introduced in the colonies and other peripheralized regions of the world from the nineteenth century onwards, were implanted without due recognition given to the different historical backgrounds and social circumstances of these societies, the awareness of which would have warranted modified and revamped theories and methods. To be sure, part of the problem has to do with the fact that the social sciences in much of Asia, Africa and Latin America were introduced by colonial powers and failed to be sufficiently indigenized, domesticated, or nationalized in order that they could be more relevant than they are.[4] This is due in part to the lack of continuity between the European tradition of knowledge and indigenous systems of ideas (Watanuki, 1984: 283) and the non-existence of an organic relationship with the cultural history of the colony (Kyi, 1984: 94).

Despite political emancipation, the intellectual dependence of the former colonies on Western models continued. Although the leading theoretical perspectives originating in Europe and America have not stood the test in an alien milieux, their continuing presence in university syllabi and journal article bibliographies in the non-West are testimony to the process of adaptation to the 'rules of the dominant caste within the Euro-American social science game' (Kantowsky, 1969: 129) that world social science has been undergoing (Kantowsky, 1969; Kazmi, 1993; Nandi, 1994).

This intellectual dependence can be seen in terms of both the structures of academic dependency as well as in terms of the relevance of the ideas derived from alien settings. Academic dependency can be gauged from the relative availability of First World funding for research, the prestige attached to publishing in American and British journals, the high premium placed on a Western university education, and a host of other indicators. Intellectual dependency on ideas may be understood from a survey of theoretical perspectives that are in vogue across a range of disciplines in the Third World. For example, geography in former British colonies is fashioned along predominantly Anglo-Saxon theoretical traditions.

Ramstedt's (1997) observation of Indonesian anthropology as being hegemonized by colonial discourse, American anthropology and state nationalization agenda, is true of anthropology in most other countries. The interesting thing about Japanese anthropology is that while it was introduced from the outside, its development received further impetus during the Japanese colonization of China in the nineteenth century, resulting in a dramatic accumulation of ethnographic knowledge on China (Eades, 1997: 6).

The introduction of the social sciences in the context of colonial expansion, had defined the subsequent development of these disciplines during the postcolonial period in a number of ways. This has been captured by the Asian diagnoses of the problem, to which we turn in the next section.

Asian Diagnoses of the Problem

In Asia, it was the Indians who led the movement against Eurocentric knowledge. Having grown up under colonialism, many Indian thinkers of the eighteenth and nineteenth centuries were familiar with the works of Comte, Spencer, Marx, Weber and Durkheim. But, as noted by Yogendra Singh, it would not be correct to understand their thinking as being Western-oriented. They were responding to Western ideas concerning rationalism, positivism and historical materialism and yet, their thought was rooted in the nationalist consciousness that was emerging among leaders of the Indian social reformation. Among the pioneers of Indian social thought and sociology were Rammohun Roy, B.N. Seal, Benoy Kumar Sarkar, G.S. Ghurye, Radhakamal Mukherjee, D.P. Mukerji, S.V. Ketkar, B.N. Dutt, and K.P. Chattopadhyay (Singh, 1986: 5).

Among the earliest to counter Eurocentric thinking was the Indian thinker and reformer, Rammohun Roy (1772-1833). Roy lived during a period of intense proselytization by British missionaries among the Hindus and Muslims of India. Roy was critical of the derogatory attitude of the English missionaries towards Hinduism and Islam. Replying to British objections against the literary genres of the Vedas, *Puranas* and *Tantras*, Roy argued that the doctrines of the first were more rational than Christianity and that the teachings of the last two were not more irrational than what is found in Christianity (Roy, 1906, cited in Sarkar, 1937/1985: 622).

Less cited but a very important early sociologist, Benoy Kumar Sarkar (1887-1949), systematically critiqued various dimensions of Orientalist Indology. Writing in the early part of the twentieth century, Sarkar was well ahead of his time when he censured Asian thinkers for having fallen 'victim to the fallacious sociological methods and messages of the modern West, to which the postulate of an alleged distinction between the Orient and the Occident is the first principle of science' (Sarkar, 1937/1985: 19). He attacked such Eurocentric notions as the inferiority of Hindus in matters of science and technology, the one-sided emphasis on the otherwordly and speculative dimension of the Hindu spirit, and the alleged dichotomy between the Orient and the Occident (ibid.: 4, 18, 35). He was also critical of the methodology of the prevailing Indology of his times on three grounds: (*a*) it overlooked the positive, materialistic and secular theories and institutions of the Hindus, (*b*) it compared the ancient and medieval conditions of India with modern and contemporary European and American societies, and (*c*) it ignored the distinction between existing institutions on the one hand and ideals on the other (Sarkar, 1937/1985: 20-21).

D.P. Mukerji (1955) was critical of the intellectual culture of his time. He said: 'I have seen how our progressive groups have failed in the field of intellect, and hence also in economic and political action, chiefly on account of their ignorance of and unrootedness in India's social reality' (Mukerji, 1955: 240, cited in Madan, 1994: 17).

The generation of sociologists that began their work in the 1950s, 1960s and 1970s, included scholars such as M.N. Srinivas, Kapadia, A.K. Saran, N.K. Bose, J.P.S. Uberoi, T.N. Madan and Yogendra Singh, who focused on the idea of a 'sociology for India'. The debate was carried out in the journal, *Contributions to Indian Sociology*, initially edited by the Europeans, L. Dumont and D.F. Pocock, but continued in the *Contributions to Indian Sociology (New Series)* under the editorship of T.N. Madan. Under the special rubric entitled 'For a Sociology of India' (Singh, 1986: 23), numerous papers appeared with the aim of helping Indian sociologists reach a certain level of self-awareness regarding the state of their discipline and the central question of what an Indian sociology would look like.

In 1966, *Contributions to Indian Sociology* ceased publication and was succeeded by *Contributions to Indian Sociology (New Series)*. In the last issue of the older *Contributions*, T.N. Madan (1966: 9) wrote an article entitled 'For a Sociology of India' in which he lamented that Indian sociologists paid less attention to the theoretical assumptions underlying their work, exemplified by their lack of interest in the controversy started in the first issue, also under the heading of 'For a Sociology of India'.[5] He went on to state that:

> modern Indian scholars had from the very beginning regarded the theoretic foundations of their subject as 'given' and therefore not a basic concern of theirs. Sociological theory was imported into India along with much other intellectual baggage from the West, particularly Britain, and received here enthusiastically and uncritically (ibid.: 10).

In 1968, the well-known Indian periodical, *Seminar*, devoted an issue to the topic of academic colonialism, which was understood in terms of two aspects. One referred to the use of academically generated information by overt and covert North American agencies to facilitate political domination of Afro-Asian countries. The other refers to the economic, political and intellectual dominance that North American academics themselves exercise over academics elsewhere (Saberwal, 1968: 10). According to Saberwal, the 'dependence on North American sponsors is pathetic; its consequences for problem selection, research design, and modes of publication are disastrous' (ibid.: 13).

Indians continued to debate the problem of academic imperialism, academic colonialism (Singh, 1984), the servitude of the mind (Misra, 1972; Saberwal, 1983), and on the related issue of Western representations of Indian society (Madan, 1994).

In China, in the 1940s, Fei (1947/1979) was critical of the way debates among sociologists were being carried out. According to him:

> The positions taken by professors in their debates were for the most part based upon facts and theories derived from Western sociology. The various schools of Western sociology were each introduced into China by its followers. That which made Chinese sociology less identical with Western sociology lay in its relationship to the real society. Whatever the particular one, the various schools of Western sociology each reflected a portion of social phenomena, but when they were brought into China, they became empty theories divorced from social reality. This can be seen in the professors' debates at the time because their criticisms of each other always ended up in appeals to logic, and not in appeals to the facts (ibid.: 25).

Korean sociologists too have been questioning the relevance of sociology in terms of its impact on Korean society and have called for a revamping of the sociology curriculum (Lee & Jung,1994: 57-63; Yang, 1994: 31-32). The need was felt for sociology to have its own identity, to be used to improve the quality of life, and to have a predictive value (Yang, 1994: 33-34). The year 1970 was a landmark for Korean sociology, when the conference entitled 'Contemporary Sociological Theory and Methodology: Relevance and Applicability to Korean Society' was held. It was in this decade that the trend to explore the problem of the relevance and applicability of Western sociology to the Korean context was established (Kim, 1985: 101).

A persistent characteristic of Japanese sociology today is defined by *nihonjinron* (theories of Japanese people), which constitute essentialized views on Japan, emphasizing cultural homogeneity and historical continuity. Such culturally deterministic theories of society continued the tradition of Western scholarship on Japan in the tradition of auto-Orientalism (Lie, 1996: 5) so typical of non-Western social science.

Since the nineteenth century Southeast Asian and other scholars have been addressing the state of the social sciences in the region. Their assessments often involved a critique of Eurocentrism and the wholesale adoption of American and European social sciences in Southeast Asia. Many of these works have come out of Singapore, including the writings of Syed Hussein Alatas (1956, 1969, 1972a, 1974), M.L. Blake (1991),

Syed Farid Alatas (1993b, 1995a, 1995b, 1998a, 1998b), and Vineeta Sinha (1997, 1998). Also in Singapore there was a growing interest in feminist alternatives to mainstream sociological discourses (see, for example, Chung, 1989; PuruShotam, 1992, 1993, 1998; Sinha, 1999; Wee, 1988; Wee, Heyzer & Kwa, 1995).

Among the first critics of the state of knowledge in Southeast Asia was the Filipino thinker and reformer, José Rizal (1861–1896). An example of an alternative discourse can be found in Rizal's annotated re-edition of Antonio de Morga's *Sucesos de las Islas Filipinas* which first appeared in 1609. Prior to producing this work Morga served eight years in the Philippines as Lieutenant Governor General and Captain General as well as a Justice of the Supreme Court of Manila (Audiencia Real de Manila) (de Morga, 1890/1991: xxxv). Rizal believed that Spanish colonization had virtually wiped out the pre-colonial past from the memory of Filipinos and presented his annotated re-edition in order to correct false reports and slanderous statements to be found in most Spanish works on the Philippines (Rizal, 1890/1962: vii). This includes the destruction of pre-Spanish records such as artefacts that would have thrown light on the nature of Filipino pre-colonial society (Zaide, 1993: 5). Rizal found Morga's work an apt choice as it was the only civil history of the Philippines written during the Spanish colonial period, other works mainly being ecclesiastical histories (Ocampo, 1998: 192). The problem with ecclesiastical histories, apart from the falsifications and slander, was that they 'abound in stories of devils, miracles, apparitions, etc., these forming the bulk of the voluminous histories of the Philippines' (de Morga, 1890/1962: 291). For Rizal, therefore, existing histories of the Philippines were both false and biased as well as unscientific and irrational.

Similar problems were raised in Indonesia at first, not by Indonesians themselves, but by Dutch scholars. One of the first among the Dutch in particular, and Europeans in general, to challenge Eurocentrism in the social sciences was Jacob Cornelis van Leur, a scholar who tragically died at a young age in the Battle of the Java Sea against the Japanese. (van Leur, 1937, 1940a, 1940b) was critical of the Eurocentric tendencies found in Dutch scholarhip on the Netherlands Indies. He wrote in Dutch but several of his essays were translated into English (van Leur, 1955). Van Leur is well known for having written against a perspective arrived at from 'the deck of the ship, the ramparts of the fortress, the high gallery of the trading house' (ibid.: 261), although he himself had not achieved such a level of objectivity in his assessment of, for example, the Islamization of Indonesia (Alatas, 1962: 225–26). For example, he questioned the appropriateness of the eighteenth century as a category in the history of the Netherlands Indies, as it was a category borrowed from Western history (van Leur, 1940a).

Gradually, Indonesians themselves began to write on the problem of Eurocentrism and other biases evident in the writing of Indonesian history (for example, Pané, 1951). Soedjatmoko (1960: 13) was critical, among other things, of the one-sided India-centric view of the history of the Hinduization of Java as it failed to yield any understanding of the nature of the Indonesian society which absorbed Hindu elements.

Some scholars also highlighted the question of intellectual imperialism and related ideas. In the 1950s, Syed Hussein Alatas from Malaysia referred to the 'wholesale importation of ideas from the Western world to Eastern societies' (Alatas, 1956) without due consideration of their socio-historical context, as a fundamental problem of colonialism. It was further suggested that the mode of thinking of colonized peoples was akin to political and economic imperialism. Hence, the expression academic imperialism (Alatas, 1969).

In the Philippines about the same time, Catapusan (1957) lamented that while sociology as a discipline existed and empirical studies were carried out, a distinctive Filipino cultural perspective had yet to emerge. Tham Seong Chee (1971), writing from Singapore, described such colonial thinking or the colonial mentality as being informed by 'a false consciousness about values, person and goals. It is a mode of seeing one's society—its workings and the direction of its movement—by super-imposing on it another reality, that is to say, the reality of a foreign society' (ibid.: 39).

The idea of the colonial mentality was developed by Syed Hussein Alatas (1972a, 1974) in the form of the concept of the captive mind. The captive mind merely extends the application of the American and European social sciences to its own setting without the appropriate adaptation of imported ideas and techniques to the Asian setting, an indication of continuing intellectual domination. There is a high demand for knowledge from the West among Asian scholars due to the need to maintain self-esteem independent of the objective utility of such knowledge (Alatas, 1972a: 9–10). The global spread of the social sciences, because it 'takes the form of an uncritical demonstration effect, introduces many defects and shortcomings' (ibid.: 11). The uncritical imitation of Western social science pervades all levels of scientific enterprise including problem-setting, analysis, abstraction, generalization, conceptualization, description, explanation, and interpretation (ibid.: 11–12). Such defects in the social sciences include the prevalence of redundant propositions, highly abstract and general statements, inadequate familiarity with local facts, and the neglect of pertinent problems.

The captive mind lacks creativity and the ability to raise original problems, is characterized by a fragmented outlook, is alienated both from major societal issues as well as its own national tradition, and is a consequence of Western dominance over the rest of the world (Alatas, 1974: 691). One dimension of this Western dominance is academic imperialism which was first discussed by Syed Hussein Alatas (1969, 2000) some 30 years ago as well as more recently.

Academic imperialism can be said to exist within the context of the structure of academic dependency, a notion developed by Syed Farid Alatas (1995a, 1995b) writing out of Singapore. The idea of academic dependency links Western and Third World social scientists in ties that bind unevenly and unequally. Third World social scientists are dependent on their counterparts in the West for concepts and theories, research funds, technologies of teaching and research, and the prestige value attached to publishing in Western journals (ibid.). Nevertheless, not all the woes of the social sciences in Asia can be blamed on academic dependency. There is a transnational flow of social science in the global market place of ideas. Within the structures of academic dependency lies a market of theories and concepts that gain currency in Asia partly due to their marketability, which in turn is determined by successful rhetorical programmes that permeate the social sciences. For example, the proliferation of a new set of vocabulary and terminology accompanying the rise of a new perspective in sociology may be complicit in successfully peddling 'novel' ideas (Alatas, 1995b, 1998b).[6]

The result of mental captivity and academic dependency is the perpetuation of what Shamsul Amri Baharuddin (1999) refers to as colonial knowledge. Using the example of Malay ethnicity, Shamsul demonstrates how colonial knowledge continues to be the most powerful form of knowledge in post colonial societies, having been responsible for inventing the ethnic category 'Malay' which has since become internalized by Malaysians themselves.

Defining the Problem of the Social Sciences

From the above account, the various problems identified by a number of Asian social scientists and thinkers can be broken down into the following traits:

1. There is a Eurocentric bias in that ideas, models, problem selection, methodologies, techniques and even research priorities tend to originate exclusively from American, British, and to some extent, French and German works.[7]
2. There is a general neglect of local literary and philosophical traditions. While there may be studies on local literature or philosophy, these traditions remain objects of study and are not considered as sources of concepts in the social sciences.
3. The lack of creativity or the inability of social scientists outside of the Euro-American cultural area to generate original theories and methods (Sinha, 1998: 19). There is a lack of original ideas in terms of the generation of novel concepts, new theoretical perspectives or schools of thought, or innovations in research methods.
4. Mimesis refers to the uncritical adoption or imitation of Western social science models (Sinha, 1998: 19). Eades (1997) provides an example of this by referring to the theorizing of a Chinese anthropologist well grounded in Sahlins, Firth and Mauss as being largely irrelevant to the Chinese case as a result of the poor ethnography on which the work is based (ibid.: 41-42). Related to this is the problem of auto-Orientalism, i.e., the internalization of Orientalist ideas developed in the West and then consumed in those areas that are the object of such Orientalist constructions.
5. European discourses on non-Western societies tended to lead to essentialist constructions of these societies, 'confirming' that they were the opposite of what Europe represented, that is, barbaric, backward, and irrational (Sinha, 1998: 11-12).
6. The absence of minority points of view. For example, Evans (1997) notes that in the multitude of materials gathered by Chinese, Vietnamese and Lao ethnographers there is 'no tradition of recording minority "voices"' (ibid.: 10). If we understand by 'minority' not just ethnic minorities but all other disadvantaged and underprivileged groups, then we may define such social science as dominated by an elitist perspective.
7. Alignment with the state. The role that disciplines such as anthropology and geography played in the colonial period continues to define them in the present day. For example, anthropology is in the service of the state as far as the promotion of national integration, control over state policies, and the creation of a national

culture are concerned (Evans, 1997: 8; Pieke, 1997: 6; Ramstedt, 1997: 15).
8. The above problems can be seen to exist within the context of academic or intellectual imperialism (Alatas, 2000a), that is, the intellectual domination of the Third World by the social science powers (United States, Britain and France).

As a result of such problems a number of theories of social science emerged. These sought to theorize the state of the social sciences and humanities in postcolonial societies and include the theory of Orientalism (Said, 1979, 1990), the theory of mental captivity (Alatas, 1972a, 1974), pedagogical theories of modernization (Al-e Ahmad, nd; Freire, 1970; Illich, 1973), the colonial critique of Césaire (1972), Memmi (1967) and Fanon (1968), and academic dependency theory (Alatas, 1995b; Altbach, 1977; Altbach & Selvaratnam, 1989; Garreau, 1985) and others. A more detailed discussion of each of these theories will be taken up in Chapter Two.

The Call for Alternative Discourses

The call for alternative modes of thinking in the past had generally fallen on deaf ears. Therefore, in the interest of historical accuracy and out of the moral responsibility to acknowledge the contributions of our predecessors that mention must be made of a few early pioneers of alternative discourses.

The understanding that the social sciences in Asia have been plagued by problems such as those listed and discussed above had led to intellectual reactions among both Western and non-Western scholars. What these reactions have in common is not just the critique of the Eurocentric, imitative, elitist, and irrelevant social science they find in their societies but also the call for alternative discourses. The call for alternative discourses may be seen to originate in the second half of the twentieth century when in fact they began in the nineteenth century. The call to indigenization is a more recent manifestation of earlier efforts towards more relevant social science. As noted by Sinha (1998),

> the by now common-place critique of essentialist tendencies in 'European'/ 'Western' orientalist discourses about 'other' peoples and places, launched by

feminist, post-colonial, post-orientalist and deconstructionist theorists, was in a very serious way already anticipated/prefaced/embedded in the discourse about 'decolonising' the social sciences (ibid.: 18).

It would be accurate to say that the notion of indigenization appeared *avant la lettre* in the minds of those who in the nineteenth century came to be critical of Orientalist language and culture studies.

Sarkar (1937/1985: 28-29) was very explicit about his call for a new Indology that would function to demolish the *idolas* of Orientalism as they are found in sociology. The need, therefore, for alternative discourses in India was keenly felt and did result in a critical tradition of scholarship in the social sciences and historical studies. One has only to mention the example of Subaltern Studies to realize this.

As noted by Pieke (1997), China in the 1930s and 1940s came close to establishing an anthropological tradition of its own. A case in point is the work of Fei Xiaotong who introduced British functionalist anthropology in the study of Chinese villages and towns (ibid.: 7). One of his finding, namely that 'the way the Chinese person defines him/herself is fundamentally different from Western individualism' (ibid.: 8), attests to the need for a judicious application of Western theories to non-Western realities. What was laudable in Fei's (1947/1979) view, were the efforts to extend or revise existing theories. This went beyond making descriptive statements on Chinese society and the systematic application of Western concepts to Chinese realities. Rather, he attempted to apply Western theories to the observation and analysis of social life in China with a view to generating explanations for problems in Chinese society (ibid.: 29).

Another interesting example is from Rabindranath Tagore's *The Home and the World* (1919). Tagore challenged commonplace notions and attempted to transcend ideas founded on an East-West dichotomy. An example of his undermining or calling into question this dichotomy can be seen in *The Home and the World*. Though fictional, it also serves to function as a theoretical reflection on history. Standard Marxist accounts would tend to view the aristocrat as oppressive and seeking to advance the interests of the old order while the patriot and nationalist may be portrayed in a more positive and progressive light. It is partly for this reason that Georg Lukacs' (1983) review of *The Home and the World* was highly unfavourable, being based on a Eurocentric-Marxist reading of Tagore (Nandy, 1994: 15-16).

In the Malay world of Southeast Asia, an early proponent of alternative social science in a non-academic mode was probably Abdullah bin Abdul Kadir Munshi (1796-1854). Among his several works is the *Kesah Pelayaran Abdullah* of 1838. Abdullah (1838/1965) was a keen observer of the problem of Malay backwardness in his time, which he attributed to the prevailing feudal order. Abdullah was in favour of utilizing the Malay language as the medium for developing the consciousness of the Malays. While he was certainly not against the art of Qur'anic recitation, he regarded as irrational the study of the Qur'an without understanding its contents (ibid.: 15). He lamented that the Malay elite did not play a leading role in patronizing learning among the Malays in order that they would be able to produce works in the various branches of knowledge (ibid.: 15-16). Abdullah goes on to assess the impact of feudalism on the Malay mind, which he saw as opposing Islamic values. His is the first critical account of Malaysian feudalism which offered a perspective that broke both the prevailing feudal and colonial viewpoints.[8]

However, more profound than Abdullah and a thinker in his own right was José Rizal (1861-1896). Rizal pioneered the notion of an International Association of Philippinists, the object of which was to study the Philippines from a 'historic and scientific point of view' (Rizal-Blumentritt, 1992: 229). Ocampo (1998: 106) has noted that while Rizal is often referred to as rewriting Philippine history, he was in fact the first to write that history from the viewpoint of the colonized. The task of such a history was to correct the biases of the Spanish historical works on the Philippines, to establish which sources were reliable and, thereby, present an Indio point of view of Philippine history. Such an attempt was made by Rizal in his annotation of Morga's history, which was mentioned earlier. For this, a more than casual acquaintance with the conditions of the inhabitants of the Philippines was necessary. Rizal was critical of a work on the Philippines by the friar Casal. He regarded Casal as not being knowledgeable about the Philippines as he 'is a happy man and he has only mingled with the happy and powerful' (Rizal-Blumentritt, 1992: 234). This suggests that the point of view of the oppressed was also a feature of the new Indio history as Rizal saw it.

This critical tradition initiated by Rizal continued in the Philippines in the form of the indigenization movement that influenced the three areas of psychology, historiography and Philipinology. In all cases, the aim is to deconstruct the Eurocentric epistemological legacy by bringing to the fore indigenous ways of knowing, whether this involves subverting the universalist claims of Western psychology, developing a new framework for historiography, or conceiving of a new academic discipline such as Philipinology (Mendoza, 2002: 11-12).

In Indonesia, it was the Dutch colonial scholars and then later the Indonesians themselves who discussed the question of alternatives in the study of Indonesian history. While the notion of Indocentric history remains vague as a concept and appears to be 'more successful in conception than in execution' (Kartodirdjo, 1982: 30), it is possible to make some remarks on these early attempts.

The Dutch scholar, J.C. van Leur, had questioned the appropriateness of the eighteenth century as a category in the history of Indonesia.[9] The eighteenth century is a category borrowed from Western history signifying aspects specific to the West. Furthermore, it was not legitimate to consider the history of Indonesia as the history of the Dutch East India Company. Moreover, historians had made the error of assuming that 'Oriental' states were in decay in the eighteenth century as was the case in Europe prior to the Industrial Revolution. Therefore, what was needed was a new system of categories which could only be generated through familiarity with Indonesian history as a history in its own right and not as a history of the Dutch overseas.

The Indonesian scholar Armijn Pané (1951) published an essay containing an outline for an Indocentric history of Indonesia. This does not involve setting aside foreign works or sources but rather recasting them in the light of Asian and Southeast Asian, rather than European history (Pané, 1951). Indocentrism can be understood as correcting the history of Indonesia as a mere extension of the history of the Dutch overseas, by focusing on Indonesians as playing a role in history. The implications of this include attention to regional and local histories. Such micro-histories in turn would lead to the call for a more multidimensional approach not found in the more conventional approaches to history (Kartodirdjo, 1982: 38-39). While the need for this would seem obvious, much of Southeast Asian history has yet to be rewritten in this spirit.

The 1960s saw several discussions for and against the possibility of a Southeast Asian point of view in the writing of history. These discussions were characterized by the two extremes of subjectivism and objectivism. John Bastin (1959) regarded the possibility of a new type of Southeast Asian history written from a Southeast Asian point of view as bleak. He noted that the type of Asian and Southeast Asian history that was written by Asians themselves, was history in the Western tradition and what was usually passed off as history from an Asian point of view turned out to be propogandistic history (ibid.: 12). Bastin was suggesting that neither the Western nor Asian historian could write history from an Asian point of view as neither could escape the conditioning of Western thought patterns and cultural influences (ibid.: 10, 11). Adding to the problem is the fact that the bulk of the source materials for Asian history are to be found in Western languages, which can only be comprehended within a Western historical framework. As noted by Syed Hussein Alatas (1964: 250–57), the possibility of what Collingwood calls 'emphatic understanding' or what Windelband, Dilthey, Rickert and Weber call *verstehen* as a means to understand history from a Southeast Asian point of view, was not entertained by Bastin (1964: 250–51).

Smail (1961), goes to the other extreme in criticizing Bastin, by saying that there is only one thought-world and, as a result, 'whatever the modern Asian historian can achieve in the way of an Asia-centric perspective can equally be achieved by the Western historian' (ibid.: 75–76).[10] Southeast Asia has come within the fold of a single world civilization with a single universal history and all that is meant by an Asian-centric history is a history in which the 'Asian, as a host in his house, should stand in the foreground...' (ibid.: 76, 78). For Smail, the notion of an Asian-centric history is not a philosophical problem but rather a practical one (ibid.: 76). Little significance is attached to Western cultural hegemony over the 'single world culture' that he posits.[11]

Nevertheless, the dominant view in these debates was in favour of a Southeast Asian point of view in the writing of history and called for the reconstruction of history. An example is the work of the Malaysian, Syed Hussein Alatas, (1962: 22; 1964) which puts forth proposals for the reconstruction of the history of the Malay-Indonesian Archipelago that pertain to methodology and the philosophy of history. He noted that the thirteenth to sixteenth century in Malay-Indonesian history was a neglected period in the study of Southeast Asian history and should be treated as a subject in its own right (ibid.: 219). Alatas suggests that this period should be treated as an Islamic period with an individuality of its own as it was a period of intensive proselytization, and raises a number of historiographical problems such as periodization, unit of analysis and historical viewpoint (ibid.: 224).

Another early work on reconstruction is that of Alatas' brother, Syed Muhammad Naquib al-Attas (1969), followed by another work along similar lines in Malay (1972). These works provide a general theory of the Islamization of the Malay-Indonesian Archipelago based on the history of ideas. Al-Attas accomplishes this by examining the 'changing concepts of key terms in the Malay language' in the sixteenth and seventeenth centuries. The evidence that forms the basis for this general theory was derived from primary literary sources in Malay, Arabic and Persian, and the methods employed were those of 'critical, commentative, interpretation' of texts as well as the 'methodological concepts and approach of modern semantic analysis' (al-Attas, 1969: 1–2). Also of importance with regard to the study of Islam in the Malay World of Southeast Asia is al-Attas' (1970) *The Correct Date of the Trengganu Inscription*, which was the first serious attempt to settle the controversy surrounding the authenticity of the famous Trengganu stone inscription of the eighth Muslim century. Other critical works of al-Attas (1968, 1971, 1975) that assess and correct Orientalist constructions include his writings on the origin of the Malay *syair* (a Malay form of poetry) and on Sufism in the Malay World.

Here, it may be interesting to note that Singapore has had a tradition of producing alternative discourses since the 1970s. Examples include the historical sociological research on colonial ideology that had been carried out by Syed Hussein Alatas with a focus on (*a*) the political philosophy of Raffles (1971) and (*b*) the myth of Malay, Javanese and Filipino laziness (1977), and (*c*) his call for an autonomous social science tradition in Asia (1979, 1981), as well as other works by Shaharuddin Maaruf (1984, 1989, 1992) and Sharifah Maznah Syed Omar (1993). A further example includes the call by Wang Gungwu (2001) for Asian perspectives in the social sciences. Also along these lines is an essay by Vineeta Sinha (2001) which critically assesses the project *Open the Social Sciences* (Wallerstein et al., 1996) which is itself aimed at rethinking and restructuring the social sciences.

To sum up, social scientists across Asia have been engaged in a critique of the state of the social sciences in their respective societies. These critiques cover various dimensions but are all to be understood within the context of the relationship between the Asian social sciences and Western social science establishments. The term 'alternative discourses' is a collective term referring to a wide variety of often unrelated attempts to address the problems raised in the critique of the state of the social sciences in Asia. This involves addressing Western ideas in the social sciences that are otherwise regarded as unproblematic, as well as generating alternative concepts and theories. This chapter has merely introduced the two central issues concerning the state of the social sciences in Asia. One is the assessment of the state of the social sciences in Asia, including the critique of Eurocentric and Orientalist social science and academic dependency. The other is the call for alternative discourses that see themselves as correctives to Eurocentrism, Orientalism, academic dependency and other problems. Chapters Two and Three theoretically extend the discussion on the state of the social sciences. Chapter Two provides a typology of meta-analyses of theories of the social sciences, while Chapter Three discusses in detail the theory and reality of academic dependency. Chapter Four takes the discussion of alternative discourses further by providing a formal definition and classification and also furnishes numerous illustrations of what alternative social science is.

Notes

1. As this book is concerned with the state of the social sciences outside of the cultural milieu of the West, particularly in those areas usually designed by the terms 'developing' or 'emerging areas', or 'Third World', 'West' is used here purely in a descriptive sense. It is not used in any Occidentalist mode but as a convenient category to refer to a largely Anglo-Saxon and, to some extent, a Continent (particularly French and German) dominated social science tradition.
2. Non-European precursors of the social sciences have frequently been identified, a notable example being that of the Arab historical sociologist 'Abd al-Rahman Ibn Khaldun (Ibn Khaldun, 1377/1981). Nevertheless, neither the Arabs nor others have reinterpreted or reworked the theories of Marx, Weber or Durkheim against the backdrop of Arab historical experiences and cultural practices, or attempted to integrate modern Western theories with those of Ibn Khaldun. For exceptions see Alatas (1993a), Cheddadi (1980) and Gellner (1981).
3. I am grateful to Kwon Eun-Young for translating some passages from Shin (1994) for me.
4. On the concept of relevance see Alatas (2001).
5. Madan was referring to three articles. See Dumont & Pocock (1957: 7–22; 1960: 82–89) and Bailey (1959: 88–101).
6. See also Altbach & Selvaratnam (1989).
7. For a discussion on various dimensions of Eurocentrism in the social sciences see Wallerstein (1996).
8. For an excellent discussion of Abdullah's thought, see Shaharuddin (1988: Chap 2). I have relied on this work for the above account.
9. This account on van Leur is taken from Hall (1959: 7–8) who discusses van Leur's review (1940a) of Stapel (1938–1940).
10. For another critical comment on Bastin, see Singhal (1960). This is a comment on Bastin's 'The Western Element in Modern Southeast Asian History', an abbreviated version of his inaugural lecture cited above.
11. For another assessment of Bastin, see Singhal (1960).

2

Theorizing the State of the Social Sciences

Even though there is a considerable body of work on the state of the social sciences in much of the non-Western world, such attempts at meta-analysis have yet to constitute a well defined area of inquiry within the philosophy or sociology of social science. This is partly because meta-analysis itself, particularly within the discipline of sociology, had come under severe attack during the 1980s and has yet to come of age as a subfield (Ritzer, 1988). Furthermore, the relative poverty of theory in most of the non-Western world also contributes to the underdevelopment of the philosophy and sociology of social science in these parts of the world. The theoretical study of the state of the social sciences in Asia (to the extent that they involve excursive accounts of and calls for the decolonization, nationalization, indigenization and globalization of knowledge) is generally viewed as being peripheral and, sometimes, oppositional to established areas of inquiry such as sociological theory, the sociology of knowledge, and the philosophy of social science. On the other hand, no progress can be made in the human sciences as long as the various disciplines do not inform, and are not informed by the problems of the relevance of knowledge beyond its spatio-cultural origins in the West, the relationship between knowledge and power, and a host of other questions that have been raised by scholars in the Third World, in developing societies and in the South.

Part of the reason for the peripheral status of these studies is their highly rhetorical and polemical nature, as well as their inadequate conceptualization upon which they are founded. This chapter contributes to the systematic study of the state of the social sciences in Asia by providing a preliminary meta-analytical framework to approach the topic.

Meta-analysis and its Varieties

Ritzer (1988: 188) defines meta-analysis as the reflexive study of the underlying structure of a discipline which involves not only the study of its theory and concepts (metatheory) but also methods (meta-methods), data (meta-data analysis), and substantive fields within a discipline. A distinction in the literature has been made between meta-analyses that aim to work out the principles and prerequisites for doing analysis and meta-analyses that take developed bodies of work (theories, concepts, methods, data, sub-fields within a discipline) as their subject matter (ibid.).

One type of meta-analysis within sociology is metatheory which studies 'theories, theorists, communities of theorists, as well as the larger intellectual and social contexts of theories and theorists' (Ritzer, 1988: 188). The reflexive study of the non-Western social sciences is a broader project that has not been confined to the study of theory in these societies but to the social sciences in general. These varieties of meta-analyses, therefore, are directed to the study of theories, concepts, methods, data, sub-fields within a discipline, as well as the intellectual, social and political contexts of social science in general. Nevertheless, what gives such meta-analyses a specific orientation in the case of the present study is its concern with the state of the social sciences.

Theories of Social Science: A Typology of Meta-analyses

The concern with the questions of relevance and irrelevance, notwithstanding their implicit or explicit nature, led to the formulation of a number of theoretical perspectives on the state of the social sciences in the Third World. It must be stressed that these various theories, in providing critical assessments of Western social science, do not consciously address themselves to the problem of relevance and irrelevance, although they point to problems that clearly imply some form of irrelevance on the part of theories and methods that originate in one socio-historical context and are applied in another.

Furthermore, these theories fall under one variety of meta-analysis or another. Therefore, these theories of social science, are seen as meta-analyses of the social sciences, as they exist in non-Western or peripheral areas of the world. The reflexive nature of these studies covers the entire range of social science—theory, empirical studies and data collection, methodology, and applied social science.

A typology of such meta-analyses can be developed by utilizing the two dimensions of *internal–external* and *cognitive–institutional*.[1] *Internal* refers to factors which relate to research, theory construction, methodology, empirical studies, and applied social science. *External* refers to factors that are external to discourse but nevertheless influence the social sciences. *Cognitive* relates to the ideal aspects of the social sciences such as ideas, theories, concepts and values. *Institutional* refers to the structural components both within and without the social sciences which determine social scientific activities.

Internal-Cognitive

Internal–cognitive meta-analytical approaches to the state of the social sciences in developing societies include the theories of Orientalism, Eurocentrism, postcolonialism and rhetoric.[2] What all these approaches have in common is the critique of ideas internal to social scientific discourse such as the notion of progress, the superiority of Western civilization and its inherent paternalism.

Orientalism

Edward Said's work on Orientalism (1979) was instrumental in bringing to focus the discursive dimensions of colonialism. The study of Orientalism in view of its lingering influence as a particular construction of the Orient, is not merely of historical interest but must be further developed as a theory of modern social science, particulary in the Third World.

The theory of Orientalism as espoused in the works of Edward Said (1979) is well known. Perhaps not as well known is the fact that several others had discussed the problem independently of Said's *Orientalism*. For example, Abdel-Malek (1963: 107–8) had discussed how non-Europeans were portrayed as unheard objects whose points of view were communicated only when the narrators saw fit. These objects are passive, non-participating, non-active, non-autonomous and non-sovereign beings. Tibawi (1979: 37) noted the 'persistence in studying Islam and the Arabs through the application of Western European categories..'.[3] In 1975, Ahmad Ashraf described Orientology as that corpus of work produced by Western scholars that attempts to 'comprehend and delineate the Asian communities and history, as well as constructing models for its directed economic, social and political change…' (Ashraf, 1976: 113). He divided Orientological works into four categories (ibid.: 114):

1. Historical and historiographical works undertaken during the period of Western penetration into Asia in the nineteenth century.

2. Reports on current situations and problems during the same period undertaken by missionaries, government officers and military officers.
3. Social-scientific works on Asia which expanded during the Cold War era.
4. Works on development models, development policies and planning and case studies on development in Asia.

Said (1979: 3) himself critically examines the manner in which Orientalism as a discourse produced the Orient 'politically, socially, militarily, ideologically, scientifically, and imaginatively'. The academic manifestation of Orientalism is a phenomenon based on the economic and political expansion of Europe. This expansion involved not only new institutions and organizations but a corpus of theory founded on certain assumptions, beliefs and ideologies which were to underlie a set of disciplines which studied the Orient. In the name of scientific research and objectivity Oriental economies, societies, cultures, religions and languages were studied to understand the 'pathologies' afflicting these societies and to yield techniques of intervention in order to normalize these societies.

A central feature of Orientalism is the Occident–Orient divide in which Western societies, cultures, religions, and languages are superior to Eastern ones. Orientalism is a 'style of thought based upon an ontological and epistemological distinction made between "the Orient" and (most of the time) "the Occident"' (Said, 1979: 2). Imaginative geographies, such as that of the Orient as created by Europe, disregard, essentialize and denude the humanity of another culture or geographical region (ibid.: 108). Arbitrary geographical distinctions help to maintain the difference between a familiar 'our' space and an unfamiliar 'their' space (ibid.: 54). For example, Chinatown in North America designates more than just a spatial location of people originating from China, it is also an evaluative term which has framed the western mindset (Anderson, 1991: 31).

For example, Orientalist assumptions had made their way into Marxist scholarship on the history of Arab political economy. The notion of a static 'Asiatic' Arab society was contrasted with that of a dynamic Europe. The notion of a static Arab society precluded any further discussion that would reveal a different dynamic of Arab history that might arise from the application of, say, Ibn Khaldun's theory of state formation. The Orientalist perspective remains important to the extent that its assumptions linger in the works of both Western and non-Western thinking alike. Concepts of development and progress also have their roots in

Orientalism and ethnocentric biases are difficult to discard even in contemporary scholarship on the Third World. For British geographers, for example, the Commonwealth is the 'entry point' and is invaded and conquered with theories of development and underdevelopment (Bell, 1994: 183). Here, the Occident/Orient dualism takes the form of spatial dualisms such as North/South, core/periphery, and developed/developing (ibid.: 184). Poverty, technological backwardness and other indicators of economic underdevelopment are seen to connote deprivation while the solutions to these 'problems' are seen in positivist terms (ibid.). The Orientalist dualism of progress/backwardness is perpetuated and the result is the promulgation of economic theory and policy that prepares the natural and cultural landscape of developing societies to be recepients of First World commodities, aid and ideologies.

In the case of India it was noted, furthermore, that the idea of a superior Western civilization was expressed in 'recurrent attempts to link all fundamental changes in Indian society and history to Western intervention in some form'. Also, in

> patronizing and/or contemptuous reviews of Indian publications, allusions to personal hardships while working in India, refusal to acknowledge Indians as 'agents of knowledge', or even blatant arrogance which makes one wonder if the civilized values of Western academia have not left its Indology mostly untouched (Chakrabarti, 1997: 1).

Another example of Orientalism from the Indian context is furnished by Madan's exposé of representations of Indian society in the works of American cultural anthropologists, from Kroeber to Marriott. For example, the great American anthropologist, Alfred Louis Kroeber (1876-1960) issued a verdict in his *Configuration of Culture* (1944) that Indian culture had been dead for a thousand years (Madan, 1994: 87-88). Ralph Linton (1893-1953) continued along these lines to construct an image of India as a static culture (Linton, 1955). It was only British colonial rule that began a process of change in Indian society towards drastic reform, thereby, introducing India to the modern world (Linton, 1955, cited in Madan, 1994: 89-90). David Mandelbaum's two-volume *Society in India* (1970) views India as not static but structurally stable where change is practically an illusion (cited in Madan, 1994: 91).

Eurocentrism

Eurocentrism is defined as a theoretical construction of world history according to which Europe, owing to its uniqueness, superiority and 'manifest destiny', had to bear 'the white man's burden' of expansionism. Some years after the appearance of *Orientalism*, Samir Amin's (1989) *Eurocentrism* was published. This work sought to illustrate how Eurocentrism was a systematic and important distortion influencing social theories and ideologies in the contemporary world. Amin defines Eurocentrism as a theory of world history which posits Europe as unique and superior. Politically, it involves the legitimacy of European expansionism through such notions as 'manifest destiny' and 'the white man's burden'. These notions live on in contemporary scholarship as is seen in the works on American foreign policy that justify the intervention in Vietnam and other parts of the world on the basis of the moral superiority of the US.

The rise of capitalism in Europe before it appeared elsewhere, was traced to the Greek heritage which predisposed Europe to rationality. Greece gave rise to rational philosophy while the Orient was never able to extricate itself from metaphysics (Amin, 1989: 91). That is why, Arabo-Islamic philosophy was relegated to the function of transmitting the Greek heritage to Europe. The impact of the Greek heritage was the creation of an honest bourgeoisie, free from medieval religious prejudice (ibid.: 91–92).

A fundamental part of Eurocentrism is the ideological construct of the 'Orient'. But Amin (1989: 101–2) criticizes Said's work on Orientalism for 'not having gone far enough in certain respects, and having gone too far in others'. Said is faulted for denouncing Eurocentrism without having suggested another explanation to account for the facts that Eurocentric theory puts forth. Said is also seen to be guilty of provincialism in that he denies the right of a European Orientalist to declare Islam as an Arian heresy (Amin, 1989: 103; Said, 1979: 62–63).

The Eurocentric ideology of development is a prop for the capitalist expansion and the centralization of surplus, both of which constitute obstacles to the progress of peoples who are the victims of development. The solution is in delinking the analyses and appraisal of Third World prospects on the basis of Eurocentric yardsticks (Amin, 1989: 115).

Postcolonial Criticism

Postcolonial criticism offers a theory of social science that is directed towards revealing how discourses on development wield power not merely in the sense that they legitimize an order but through discursive practices that lead to the normalization and disciplinary control of persons. We therefore shift our attention to the relations of knowledge production rather than commodity production. This requires a study of subjects in the Third World as an 'objective of control...[to be] examined, measured, categorized, made the target of policies of normalization...' (Taylor, 1985b: 158).

The various disciplines in the field of development studies are designed to portray a positive image of development so that developing societies can be normalized accordingly (e.g. the infusion of Western values, how to silence tradition/religion to facilitate development, by reducing the problems of underdevelopment to general, anonymous forces such as market size, terms of trade, direct foreign investment penetration, etc.). The goals of normalization are ostensibly to raise the standards of living, increase productivity, improve the distribution of income, raise educational levels, and so on. And while some of these aims are fulfilled in some areas, the processes of normalization and disciplinary control can still be discerned in development processes (Alatas, 1993b: 326).

Rhetorical Theories of Social Science

Another kind of meta-analysis is focused on the text of social scientific discourse and is founded on the notion that the truth is evoked via rhetoric. Knowing is 'only through engagement in rhetorical activity' (Weimar, 1977: 19). Rhetoric is, therefore, epistemic (Scott, 1967).

The rhetorics of social science is interested in, among other things, the way words are deployed to mislead, misinform and persuade, rather than expose and clarify. The recognition of the social sciences as textual activity implies that there are rhetorical techniques employed by authors to evoke responses to truth claims. A successful discourse is one that resorts to metaphors, metonyms, irony and the like, in order to present its version of reality as 'attractive, edifying, obvious, compelling' (Baehr & O'Brien, 1994: 62). The study of the relationship between the sociologist and his audience through the persuasive dimension of sociological discourse has been referred to as the 'poetics of sociology' (Brown, 1977; Peters, 1990; Simons, 1989).

This means that the assessment of social theories need not be restricted only to their logical or empirical dimensions. In other words, social theories are not only constructed logically and empirically, but rhetorically as well. The rhetorical construction of social theory involves the employment of rhetorical techniques that function to 'persuade' the audience to accept a particular version of reality. The success of this deployment partly depends on the 'common concerns, common places in their cognitive charts' (Davis, 1986: 286) of the audience to which the sociologist-rhetor speaks. In other words, apart from the factual concerns and the truth value of theory, the ability of social theorists to get their audience to consider their utterances seriously has a lot to do with how well they address such audience concerns. In rhetorical theories of social science, the Third World or non-Western societies are seen as fields on which various rhetorical techniques are deployed that function to evoke the desired responses to the truth claims of the social sciences (Alatas, 1995b). To the extent that rhetorical techniques define the utility of Western social science in the Third World, the study of rhetorics is an important area at the level of meta-analysis.

External-Cognitive

This set of approaches examines the manner in which ideas, attitudes, values and mentalities from outside the social sciences impinge upon their activities. Such approaches include the theory of mental captivity, pedagogical theories of modernization and modern colonial critique.

The Theory of the Captive Mind

According to the theory of mental captivity, the captive mind is a victim of Orientalism and Eurocentrism and is characterized by a way of thinking that is dominated by Western thought in an imitative and uncritical manner. Uncritical imitation permeates all levels of scholarly activities, affecting problem-setting, analysis, abstraction, generalization, conceptualization, description, explanation and interpretation (Alatas, 1972a: 11–12).

The concept of the captive mind was first discussed by the Malaysian sociologist, Syed Hussein Alatas (1974) and led to the conceptualization of the nature of scholarship in the developing world, particularly in relation to Western dominance in the social sciences and humanities. The captive mind is defined as an 'uncritical and imitative mind dominated by an external source, whose thinking is deflected from an independent perspective' (ibid.: 692). The external source comes from the Western social sciences and humanities whose uncritical imitation influences all the constituents of scientific activity such as problem-selection, conceptualization, analysis, generalization, description, explanation, and interpretation (Alatas, 1972a: 11). Among the characteristics of the captive mind are; the inability to be creative and raise original problems, the inability to devise original analytical methods, and alienation from the main issues of indigenous society. The captive mind is trained almost entirely in the Western sciences, reads the works of Western authors, and is taught predominantly by Western teachers, whether in the West itself or through their works available in local centres of education. Mental captivity is also found in the suggestion of solutions and policies. Further, it reveals itself at the levels of theoretical as well as empirical work.

Alatas (1972a; 1974) elaborated the concept in two papers published in the early 1970s but had originally raised the problem of mental captivity in the 1950s. He had referred to the 'wholesale importation of ideas from the Western world to eastern societies' without due consideration of their socio-historical context, as a fundamental problem of colonialism (Alatas, 1956). He had also suggested that the mode of thinking of colonized peoples paralleled political and economic imperialism. Hence, the context within which the captive mind appears is that of academic imperialism (Alatas, 1969).

While the phenomenon of the captive mind is important, discourse on the concept as developed by Alatas has been limited to citations in works of scholars sympathetic to the type of critique undertaken by him. There have been no systematic expositions or rebuttals of the concept and it seems to be largely ignored, particularly by Western social science establishments (Interview with Syed Hussein Alatas, 29 August 2004).

Alatas begins his conceptualization of the captive mind with a parallel idea of the demonstration effect as developed by James Duesenberry (1949) in connection with consumer behaviour. According to the idea of the demonstration effect, rising incomes would lead to higher levels of consumption as consumers attempt to match the consumption patterns of those whose life-styles they wish to imitate. Alatas suggests that the thinking of Third World social scientists can be understood in terms of the demonstration effect. According to this interpretation the consumption of social science knowledge from the West arises from the belief that such knowledge is superior. This kind of consumption is seen to parallel the economic demonstration effect primarily because of traits like: (*a*) the frequency of contact with Western knowledge; (*b*) the weakening or erosion of local or indigenous knowledge; (*c*) the prestige attached to imported knowledge; and (*d*) that such consumption is not necessarily rational and utilitarian (Alatas, 1972a: 10–11).

Alatas provides illustrations of how the captive mind works, from development studies. The dangerous consequences of the captive mind lie in the weaknesses exhibited in the thought pattern, as is evident in the imitation of Western development studies. The captive mind is found in the various areas of scientific activity such as abstraction, generalization, conceptualization, problem-setting, explanation, and the understanding and mastery of data (Alatas, 1972a: 12). For instance, in the area of abstraction and generalization, Alatas discusses the work of Tinbergen (1967) on development planning as being marred by general and abstract propositions that are redundant (Alatas, 1972a: 12–13). In another illustration, this time from the work of Kuznets (1966), Alatas criticizes some of the propositions for being so general that they lack any utility for meaningful analysis. This problem could have been avoided had the work attempted to derive propositions and conclusions directly from historical and comparative data (ibid.: 14). Another problem in development studies discussed by Alatas is that of erroneous judgment as a result of the unfamiliarity with data or an ignorance of the context. The example given is Hagen's view that digging with the Southeast Asian hoe is an 'awkward process', but the spade, which is a better instrument, can only be of limited use in low-income societies because shoes are not widely used (Hagen, 1962: 31–32, cited in Alatas, 1972a: 15). Alatas suggests that Hagen did not comprehend the function of the hoe in its proper context. In the Southeast Asian context, the hoe is actually the more efficient instrument because of terrace cultivation on mountain slopes. Hagen's failure to judge the efficiency and utility of the hoe with reference to its context is a violation of an important anthropological principle (Alatas, 1972a: 15).

In development studies as well as the social sciences in general it is problems such as the above that are imitated and assimilated by the captive mind and result in ill-conceived development plans. Dominated by Western thought in a mimetic and uncritical way, the captive mind lacks creativity and the ability to raise original problems, is characterized by a fragmented outlook, is alienated both from major societal issues as well as its own national tradition, and is a consequence of Western dominance over the rest of the world (Alatas, 1974: 691). The problem of the captive mind is unique to the non-Western world. While uncreative, imitative, fragmented and alienated minds are to be found in the West as well, the context in which these occur is not the same. Alatas (1974: 692) argues that the counterpart of the captive mind does not exist in the West because there we do not find people who are trained in non-Western sciences, in non-Western universities, or by non-Western professors, and assigned works of non-Western scholars in non-Western languages. The captive mind is a phenomenon peculiar to the developing world seen in the existence of uncritical and imitative thought in the context of the domination by an external civilization, the West (Alatas, 1976b).

The spread and development of the social sciences in Third World countries takes the form of an 'uncritical demonstration effect', that is, the driving force behind the assimilation of Western theories, concepts, interpretations, and whole research agendas is the belief in their utility and superiority (Alatas, 1972a: 10-11). Nevertheless, what is imitated turns out to be of inferior quality because only that which is within reach will become the object of imitation. As a result, the construction that is the desirable target of imitation is not the 'impressive intellectual palace but the hut around the corner' (ibid.: 18). The problem of mental captivity is all the more serious when it is 'unconscious of its own captivity and the conditioning factors making it what it is', (Alatas, 1974: 691) such as those of Orientalism, Eurocentrism, and academic dependency. The concept of the captive mind is not political or ideological but a phenomenological concept (ibid.: 692). For example, an Asian scholar may adopt French poststructuralism in a creative way by successfully domesticating it and not necessarily be a captive mind, while another may be a Gandhian but may intellectually be dependent upon metropolitan academe.

Pedagogical Theories of Modernization

Pedagogical theories of modernization include, for example, the works of the well known writer of educational theory, Ivan Illich (1973), known for his idea of the *hidden curriculum*. To begin with, he was critical, of the way modernization severed people from their traditional skills which previously enabled them to be self-sufficient. Today, people are reliant on a host of modern devices and institutions, including doctors for health, television for entertainment, employers for a living, and teachers for education. Illich called this *passive consumption* or the uncritical acceptance of the social order. Formal education through the school system achieves this not through the formal content of lessons but through the discipline and regimentation so typical of schools. In this way, the dominant values of the social order are inculcated in children. Children learn to 'know their place in life and to sit still in it' through the hidden curriculum (ibid.).

The Iranian literary artist, teacher and political activist, Jalal Al-e Ahmad also had a particular interest in education. He is well known for his essay on Weststruckness (*gharbzadegi*) which first appeared in 1962 (Al-e Ahmad, nd). He defined this concept as a condition defined by the existence of cultural forms and mentalities in the East which are not rooted in history or tradition but are the results of the introduction of the machine (ibid.: 34-35). The machine, of course, symbolizes the kind of modernization which had sealed the fate of Iranian political economy and culture in the hands of Western governments and transnational capital (Al-e Ahmad, nd: 77). Education perpetuates this state of affairs because it creates technicians who merely operate the products of Western technology, whether in science, engineering or administration, and are dependent on their Western consultants and advisors (ibid.: 171–77).

Modern Colonial Critique

The manner in which education does this is elaborated by Paulo Freire (1970) through his 'banking' concept of education. Education suffers from narration sickness because the teacher fills students with the contents of his narration, which are divorced from the reality and surroundings of the students. The words of the narration then become objects to memorize. The student's scope of action does not go beyond receiving, filing and storing such deposits, with the resulting effect of minimizing the creativity of the student. This serves the interests of the oppressors who are more inclined towards changing the mentality of the oppressed, rather than change oppressive conditions (ibid.: 57–61).

Modern colonial critique is important for its investigation into the subjective experience of the consequences of colonialism. These consequences continue to manifest themselves after the era of formal colonization (Césaire, 1972). What are often regarded as mere diatribes against the West often turn out to be helpful in lending insights into the nature of the psychology of the colonized and the neo-colonized. A lot of what is said about the colonized applies to the neo-colonized as well. To a great extent, the ideology of the colonizers is adopted by the colonized. It is this that makes oppression tolerable to the oppressed. But the adherence of the colonized to colonization and their conformity with the roles assigned to them are the result of colonization, and not its cause (Memmi, 1967: 88). Colonization removes the colonized from history in the sense that he is no longer the subject of history but more its object. Memories of freedom become faint, the interest and feeling for control fade away, and the possibilities of being agents of change in history do not even occur to the colonized (ibid.: 91–95). Furthermore, colonialism does more than just denude the mind of the colonized. It also 'turns to the past of the oppressed people, and distorts, disfigures, and destroys it...The effect consciously sought by colonialism was to drive into the natives' heads the idea that if the settlers were to leave, they would at once fall back into barbarism, degradation, and bestiality' (Fanon, 1968: 210–11).

Perhaps it is the resultant inferiority complex that may explain the extent to which the world division of academic labour, referred to later, is not exclusively due to structural imperatives but also due to the acceptance of this order by Third World scholars themselves. This had not gone unnoticed in the 1960s when Worsely (1964) wrote of the 'colonization of personality' and the 'infantilization of adults', but remains insufficiently researched.

The works of the modern colonial critiques such as Frantz Fanon, Albert Memmi, Aimé Cesairé, Ali Sharia'ati, Malik Bennabi, and others are important because they reveal the lingering psychological dimension of colonialism among the colonized, i.e., the need to emulate the West by remaining in a strategically subservient position.[4]

Internal-Institutional

Internal-institutional approaches are concerned with the impact that structural components within a social science have upon its activities in developing areas. These approaches are best represented by the theories of intellectual imperialism and academic dependency.

The Theory of Intellectual Imperialism

This perspective, first elaborated by Syed Hussein Alatas in 1969, recognizes that imperialism is not confined to political or economic dimensions. He discusses six main traits of imperialism, that is, exploitation, tutelage, conformity, relegation of the dominated to a secondary role in society, intellectual rationalization of imperialism, and the inferior talent of the imperialist rulers. These characteristics of imperialism are operative when a people are subjugated politically, economically and socially by another people. These characteristics also apply to intellectual imperialism which is 'the domination of one people by another in their world of thinking' (Alatas, 1969; Alatas, S.H., 2000: 24). Intellectual imperialism does not allow for the critical and selective assimilation of knowledge from foreign sources and results in the neglect of the local intellectual tradition (Alatas, S.H., 2000: 27). As a result, in Asia, for example, few foundational courses in the universities pay attention to Asian thinkers. It is quite common to find that introductory courses on sociological theory cover theorists such as Marx, Weber, Durkheim, Simmel, Tocqueville and others, but leave out a host of Asian thinkers such as Wang An Shih, José Rizal, Rammohun Roy and B. K. Sarkar. There is an intellectual alienation engendered by imperialism.

Alatas makes the distinction between intellectual imperialism and the phenomenon of the captive mind discussed above. The captive mind, 'one that is imitative and uncreative and whose thinking is based on Western categories and modes of thought', allows for the implantation of intellectual imperialism (Alatas, S.H., 2000: 37). In other words, the six traits of imperialism effect intellectual domination to the extent that the captive mind is pervasive and there is less resistance to intellectual imperialism.

Academic Dependency Theory: Ideas and the Media of Ideas

The existence of such cultural problems as Orientalism, Eurocentrism and mental captivity is not to deny the existence of structures of academic dependency that link core and peripheral social scientists. Mental captivity exists within this context of dependency. Academic dependency highlights the structure of relations between academicians in the core and periphery when the former dominates the latter in an intellectually imperialist mode. Academicians in the periphery are dependent on their counterparts in the core for research and development funds. Scholarly journals are controlled mainly by academic institutions in core countries. The various aspects of academic dependency have been discussed by others (Altbach, 1977; Weeks, 1990).

It is not only economies but organized education systems which are in a state of dependency vis-à-vis industrialized nations. In this sense, dependency reflects the current inequality in wealth and power distribution not only in economic and military terms but in education as well. This is particularly true in the design of curricula, and the production and distribution of knowledge. Speaking of foreign aid in science, Uberoi (1968: 120) emphasized that it 'upholds the system of foreign dominance in all matters of scientific and professional life and organization...It subordinates the national science of the poor to the national and international science of the rich. It confirms our dependence and helplessness and will not end them'. Developing countries, therefore, are at the periphery of the world's educational and intellectual systems, the latter being concentrated in the core. The result is that 'industrialized nations dominate the world's research production, mass media, information systems, and advanced training facilities' (Altbach, 1977: 188).

A case in point is the marginalization of research on or from the Third World as reflected in the parochialism of British geography (Sidaway, 1993: 299). The South accounts for 75 per cent of the world's population but this is not reflected in the percentage of geographers specializing in

Third World regions in British geography departments (Potter, 1993: 292). Among the main papers appearing in the *Transactions of the Institute of British Geographers* between 1989 and 1992, there were 14 out of a total of 122 that dealt with Third World issues (Potter, 1993: 292).

The structure of academic dependency[5] can be understood in terms of a number of dimensions. Relevant to the internal-institutional approach are two forms of academic dependency—the dependence on ideas and the media of ideas. Although the ethnocentric biases in the Western social sciences had been long identified, the imagination needed for the emergence of alternative theoretical traditions outside of the world social science powers of the United States, Britain, France and a few other countries, is yet to be seen. Meanwhile, the dependence on theories and concepts generated in the context of Western historical backgrounds and cultural practices continues.

External-Institutional

External-institutional approaches are concerned with the structural components that lie outside of the social sciences which impact upon social scientific activities in developing areas. Like internal-institutional approaches, they are also represented by academic dependency theory.

Academic Dependency Theory: Technology, Aid and Investment

The three remaining dimensions of academic dependency—technology, aid and investment—which lie outside of the social sciences, nevertheless impinge upon them.

The technology dimension is a crucial aspect of the dependency relation in the social sciences. For example, instructional materials such as films and laboratory instruments are imported because there is little innovation in the creation of curricula and instructional materials. This has partly to do with the lack of funds and partly with the fact that many educationists in the Third World went through a Western education and find it more convenient to draw upon the West for their resources.

There is also a dependence on aid for research and teaching. Various governmental organizations as well as corporate foundations in the United States, Britain, France and Germany play crucial roles in the training of Third World scholars by providing scholarships and fellowships, funding social science research, and providing expert personnel for research and teaching institutions in the developing world—training which would otherwise be hard to come by.

Finally, we have dependence on investment in education. Educational institutions in industrialized nations do invest in education in the Third World.

There is, therefore, a core-periphery relationship in academe. The division of labour in world scholarship seems to be such that core scholars perform theoretical, cross-national, comparative, and other country studies, while peripheral scholars limit themselves to empirical, single-case and own-country studies.

The Need for Meta-Analysis of the Social Sciences in Asia

Meta-analysis of the social sciences in Asia is necessary for a number of reasons. First, in order that the kind of concerns raised in this book regarding the relevance of knowledge generated in the West and applied in Asia become more widespread, there have to be more studies of the meta-analytical kind. The various theories of social sciences detailed above are all varieties of meta-analyses that look at knowledge in terms of its intellectual and social bases in the context of the relationship between the West and Asia. But these meta-analyses emerged among different disciplines, both in the West and in Asia, in differing contexts. It is often the case that scholars in different Asian countries are unaware of their counterparts' works, including those from neighbouring countries. There are few comparative studies on the state of the social sciences in Asia. Meta-analyses of the social sciences provides us with the opportunity to bring together similar experiences of diverse social science communities in Asia under common theoretical constructs. For example, academic dependency theory can bring together the diversity of Asian data relevant to its understanding, thereby uniting those across the region who wish to combat the problem.

Second, such exercises in metatheory building as the one above are necessary as they give us tools with which to cognitively manage the diversity of perspectives across Asia that criticize the state of the social sciences. Finally, it is studies at the meta-analytical level, particularly those that seek to understand the underlying structure of theories and concepts (metatheory), methods (meta-methods), data (meta-data analysis), as well as those which study the intellectual, social and political contexts of knowledge, that will help to give a place to issues such as those raised in this book in the fields of the philosophy of social science, the sociology of knowledge and the history of ideas. This is an important prerequisite to draw attention, both within and outside Asia, to the problems being faced by the social sciences in Asia.

The next chapter focuses on the academic dependency theory, detailing its structure and function in the global division of labour in the social sciences.

Notes

1. The idea of typologizing meta-analyses along the lines of two dimensions comes from Ritzer's (1988) typology of metatheory in sociology. However, the two dimensions utilized in this paper correspond only superficially to Ritzer's two dimensions of *internal-external* and *intellectual-social*. By internal-external Ritzer is referring to 'things that exist within sociology' and 'phenomena that are found outside of sociology but which have an impact on it', respectively (1988: 190). By intellectual-social Ritzer is referring to the 'cognitive structure of sociology—theories, metatheoretical tools, ideas borrowed from other disciplines' and the 'sociological structure of sociology—schools, the effect of individual background factors on sociologists, the impact of the larger society, etc.' (ibid.: 190).
2. Some of these theories have been discussed in Alatas (1995a), though not in the context of the typology given in the present work.
3. See also Tibawi (1963).
4. 'One's cognition and awareness about problems have a nauseating predictableness about it. This false consciousness is found in every level of society, from a *jaga kereta* who 'prefers' to open the car door of a European vis-à-vis a local, to the highest level of the decision making process when a choice between using local expertise to that of the foreign is preferred', in Tham (1971: 39-40).
5. For some variations of this theory see Alatas (1995b); Altbach (1977); Altbach & Selvaratnam (1989); Garreau (1985).

3

The Structure of Academic Dependency and the Global Division of Labour in the Social Sciences*

This chapter attempts a political economy of the social sciences in order to assess the state of the social sciences at the global level. The focus will be on the relations between the social sciences in the First and Third Worlds. The political economy approach utilized for this purpose is the academic dependency theory. The global division of labour, I argue, plays a significant role in maintaining the structures of academic dependency.

The literature in the social sciences and humanities of the last two hundred years and of the last 50 years in particular, has deplored the state of knowledge in the arts in the Third World, highlighting various problems that can all be subsumed under concepts, expressions and movements such as the critique of colonialism (Césaire, 1955; Memmi, 1957), academic imperialism (Alatas, 1969; 2000), decolonization (of knowledge) (Fanon, 1968), critical pedagogy (Freire, 1970), imitation and the captive mind (Alatas, 1972a, 1974), deschooling (Illich, 1973), academic dependency (Alatas, 1999; 2000a; Altbach, 1977; Garreau, 1985), Orientalism (Said, 1979; 1993), and Eurocentrism (Amin, 1989; Wallerstein, 1996). These were discussed as theories of social science in Chapter Two. The problems that these theories raise are seen to be a part of the larger context of relations between the former Western colonial powers and the ex-colonies, including those societies that were vicariously colonized. The recognition and assessment of these problems led to various calls for the indigenization of the social sciences (Atal, 1981; Fahim, 1970; Fahim & Helmer, 1980), deschooling (Illich, 1973), endogenous intellectual

---

*This chapter was previously published in American Studies International, vol. 38 (2), June 2000.

creativity (Alatas, 1978), an autonomous social science tradition (Alatas, 1979), postcolonizing knowledge (Chakrabarty, 1992; Prakash, 1990, 1992), globalization, decolonization, and nationalization of the social sciences. All these may be collectively referred to as calls for alternative discourses in the social sciences (discussed in greater detail in Chapter Four).

In the present chapter I focus on the problem of academic dependency and the related question of the global division of labour in the social science. Here, I delineate the structure of, and suggest measures towards the reversal of academic dependency.

The Definition of Academic Dependency

Any attempt to define academic dependency would benefit from a prior discussion of the related idea of intellectual or academic imperialism. Academic imperialism is a phenomenon that is analogous to political and economic imperialism. Generally, imperialism or empireism is understood as the policy and practice of the political and economic domination of colonies by more advanced nations since the sixteenth century, through military conquest and subjugation. Defined in this way, imperialism is equivalent to colonialism. To the extent that the control and management of the colonized required the cultivation and application of various disciplines such as history, linguistics, geography, economics, sociology and anthropology in the colonies, we may refer to the academe as imperialistic. In fact, it is possible to cite numerous examples of scholars from the last five hundred years who directly or indirectly researched and taught for the imperialist cause. Research has documented that the work of social scientists, among them anthropologists and geographers, served colonial interests like divide and rule. Having said that, however, it should be noted that not all colonial social scientists were simply driven by colonial aspirations. As far as academic imperialism is concerned it is not the intentions and motivations of social scientists that interest us but rather the structure of academic dependency within which ideas in the social sciences are marketed and deployed.

One of the most notorious and most expensive social science research projects ever conceived is Project Camelot. Project Camelot was the creation of the Special Operations Research Office (SORO), attached to the American University in Washington, D.C., but financed by the United States Department of Defense with a grant of about US$ 6 million

(Horowitz, 1967: 4, 17). On 4 December 1964, the Office of the Director of the Special Operations Research Office (SORO) released a document describing the project. This is worth quoting at length:

> Project CAMELOT is a study whose objective is to determine the feasibility of developing a general social systems model, which would make it possible to predict and influence politically significant aspects of social change in the developing nations of the world. Somewhat more specifically, its objectives are:
> *First*, to devise procedures for assessing the potential for internal war within national societies;
> *Second*, to identify with increased degrees of confidence those actions which a government might take to relieve conditions which are assessed as giving rise to a potential for internal war; and
> *Finally*, to assess the feasibility of prescribing the characteristics of a system for obtaining and using the essential information needed for doing the above two things.
> The project is conceived as a three to four-year effort to be funded at around one and one-half million dollars annually. It is supported by the Army and the Department of Defense, and will be conducted with the cooperation of other agencies of the government. A large amount of primary data collection in the field is planned as well as the extensive utilization of already available data on social, economic and political functions. At this writing, it seems probable that the geographic orientation of the research will be toward Latin American countries. Present plans call for a field office in that region.
> By way of background: Project CAMELOT is an outgrowth of the interplay of many factors and forces. Among these is the assignment in recent years of much additional emphasis to the US Army's role in the over-all U.S. policy of encouraging steady growth and change in the less developed countries in the world. The many programs of the U.S. Government directed toward this objective are often grouped under the sometimes misleading label of counter-insurgency (some pronounceable term standing for insurgency prophylaxis would be better)....
> Another major factor is the recognition at the highest levels of the defense establishment of the fact that relatively little is known, with a high degree of surety, about the social processes which must be understood in order to deal effectively with problems of insurgency....
> Project CAMELOT will be a multidisciplinary effort. It will be conducted both within the SORO organization and in close collaboration with universities and other research institutions within the United States and overseas.[1]

The project was terminated before it ever took off after the above memorandum was posted to a select list of scholars worldwide (Horowitz, 1967: 4). One of the scholars invited to join the project was Johan Galtung.

He was invited to participate in a June 1965 conference that aimed to draw up a preliminary research design for the study of the potential for internal wars and the role of government action. The basis of this proposed conference was the 4 December 1964 memorandum. Galtung's reply of 22 April 1965 stated that he could not participate in Project Camelot for a number of reasons, one of them being the 'imperialist features' of the research design (Horowitz, 1967: 12–13). Numerous other examples can be cited here but the point is that social scientists may be involved in research that directly serves the imperialistic or hegemonic interests of a power.

Project Camelot may have been the most famous of such projects but was certainly not the first. Project Sierra, for instance, commenced in 1954 by the RAND corporation 'to examine possible limited war situations in Southeast Asia, the Far East and the Middle East, with particular reference to Air Force effectiveness' (Weiner, 1960: 4, cited in Said, 1995: 212). After Camelot, there were other projects. The Institute for Defense Analysis (IDA) conducted research on the problem of literacy among conscripts in underdeveloped countries, which was applied to the ground forces of a Middle Eastern country (IDA, 1968: 18, cited in Said, 1995: 212). Another IDA study conducted for the U.S. Joint Chiefs of Staff looked at military and political problems facing the United States in the Mediterranean and the Middle East (IDA, 1969: 27, cited in Said, 1995: 213). Millions of dollars had been spent on these and dozens of other similar projects.

The use of these examples is not to suggest that most research projects in the United States have the aim of counter-insurgency or that there is a conscious academic imperialist policy on the part of United States funding organizations and American social scientists. However, it cannot be denied that the nature of world social science is such that the development and expansion of social science in developing societies is influenced by and is a reflection of its development in the United States, and to a lesser extent in Great Britain, France, Germany and Japan. It is this structure of dependency in the social sciences that I attempt to delineate later in this chapter.

There is another sense in which we may understand academic imperialism. In addition to considering the role of social scientific research and scholarship in the service of political and economic imperialism, we may also think of it as analogous to these two kinds of imperialism, that is, the 'domination of one people by another in their world of thinking' (Alatas, 2000: 24). In other words, academic imperialism is a phenomenon analogous to political economic imperialism. There are imperialistic relations in the world of the social sciences that parallel those in the world of international political economy.

Academic imperialism in this sense began with the setting up and direct control of schools, universities and publishing houses by the colonial powers in the colonies. It is for this reason that the 'political and economic structure of imperialism generated a parallel structure in the way of thinking of the subjugated people' (Alatas, 2000: 24).[2] These parallels include the six main traits of exploitation, tutelage, conformity, secondary role of dominated intellectuals and scholars, rationalization of the civilizing mission, and the inferior talent of scholars from the home country specializing in studies of the colony (ibid.: 24-27).

Today, academic imperialism is more indirect than direct. If, under political economic imperialism the colonial powers had direct control over the political systems, production and marketing of goods from the colonies—today that control is indirect via international law, the power of major commercial banks, the threat of military intervention by the superpowers, and covert and clandestine operations by various governments of advanced nations. Similarly, it can be said that in the post colonial period what we have is academic neo-imperialism or academic neo-colonialism as the West's monopolistic control of and influence over the nature and flows of social scientific knowledge remain intact even though political independence had been achieved.

If in the colonial past, academic imperialism was maintained via colonial power, today academic neo-colonialism is maintained via the condition of academic dependency. The West's monopolistic control of and influence over much of the Third World social sciences is not determined by colonial power only but rather by the dependence of Third World scholars and intellectuals on Western social science in a variety of ways.

The Structure of Academic Dependency

Marxist, dependency and world-system theories of development generally look upon culture, including social science, as reflecting global economic hierarchies. The spread of Western culture and modes of knowledge, or cultural imperialism, help perpetuate global inequalities to the extent that Third World peoples are culturally and ideologically prepared to receive Western goods, services, technology and aid (Chase-Dunn, 1989: 88-105; Meyer, 1987; Meyer & Hannan, 1979; Szymanski, 1981: 257-88). Such a perspective does not necessarily view consciousness, ideology, norms and values as dominant institutions that integrate the modern world-system. Indeed, the view that culture plays a secondary role in the reproduction of global capitalism is partly responsible for the neglect of the study of the internal dynamics of global social science. Nevertheless, there have been attempts to understand the political economy of social science not merely in terms of 'base-superstructure' arguments, but also by way of the application of the market analogy. Such an approach either takes its cues from classical economics with its emphasis on the free market, or from the concerns of dependency/world-system analysis with the hierarchical nature of the capitalist world economy. According to the former, social science operates according to the principles of *laissez-faire*. Scientific (and by extension, social scientific) communities are seen to function on the basis of perfect competition (Storer, 1970, cited in Garreau, 1991: 303). Academic dependency theory, however, recognizes an imbalance in the production of social sciences across societies and in the resultant division of labour between the producers and consumers of such knowledge (Oommen, 1991: 67). Thus, it is no coincidence that the great economic powers are also the great social science powers (Chekki, 1987; Garreau, 1985: 64, 81, 89), although the case of Japan would suggest there are exceptions to the rule.

Academic dependency is a theory on the global state of dependence amongst the social sciences. It originated in Brazil in the 1950s with its proponents recommending that Latin American social scientists should cut their ties with the social science powers of the West and instead develop autonomous or indigenized social sciences (Garreau, 1985: 114–15). From this perspective, Third World social science communities are seen to be dependent to the extent that the definition of problem areas, methods, and standards of excellence come from another social science community (Lamy, 1976: 107). Kuwayama speaks of the 'world system' of anthropology in which the three core countries, that is, the United States, Great Britain and France, determine the nature of the discourse in anthropology (Kuwayamma & van Bremen, 1997: 54). It would be pertinent to mention here that academic dependency theory has much in common with Kuwayama's world system of anthropology in which there is a dominance of the core over the periphery. The situation is characterized by '"scientific colonialism", in which the center of gravity for acquisition of knowledge about a people is located elsewhere' (Kuwayama & van Bremen, 1997: 54).

However, while the phenomenon of academic dependency has been identified, there have been few works that attempt to delineate its structure, a notable exception being the works of Altbach (1975, 1977) and

Garreau (1985, 1988, 1991). The aim in this section is to do just that. Now that the parallel between academic dependency and economic dependency theory is clear, it would be logical to attempt a definition of the former by beginning with a definition of economic dependency. The oft-quoted definition of economic dependency as given by Theotonio Dos Santos (1970) is as follows:

> By dependence we mean a situation in which the economy of certain countries is conditioned by the development and expansion of another economy to which the former is subjected. The relation of interdependence between two or more economies, and between these and world trade, assumes the form of dependence when some countries (the dominant ones) can expand and can be self-sustaining, while other countries (the dependent ones) can do this only as a reflection of that expansion, which can have either a positive or a negative effect on their immediate development.[3]

Keeping in mind the shared parallels with economic dependency, academic dependency may therefore, be defined as a condition in which the social sciences of certain countries are dependent on the development and growth of the social sciences in those countries to which the former countries are subjected. The relations of interdependence between two or more social science communities, and between these and global transactions in the social sciences, assumes the form of dependency when some social sciences communities (those located in the social sciences powers) can expand according to certain criteria of development and progress, while other social science communities (those in the Third World, for example) can only do this as a reflection of that expansion, which can have mixed effects (positive and negative) on their development according to the same criteria. There is a psychological dimension to this dependency whereby the dependent scholar is a passive recipient of research agenda, methods and ideas from the social science powers. This is due to a 'shared sense of... intellectual inferiority against the West'.[4]

There is, therefore, a centre-periphery continuum in the social sciences that roughly corresponds to the North-South divide (Lengyel, 1986: 105). Von Gizycki (1973: 474, cited in Lengyel, 1986: 105) defines the centre as 'constituted by the fact that works produced there command more attention and acknowledgement than works produced elsewhere. A center is a place from which influence radiates' (ibid.). While von Gizycki was making this statement with respect to the international social science community of the nineteenth century, it continues to apply to the situation today. In fact, as noted by Wallerstein, et al., the institutionalization of the social sciences took place in mainly five locales—Great Britain, France, the Germanies, the Italies and the United States, mainly because of the international prestige and numerical weight of their universities (Wallerstein, et al., 1996: 14). For a variety of reasons that I shall not get into here, Italy and Germany are no longer social science powers.

The mode of conditioning and subjection of the social sciences in academically dominated countries depends on the dimensions of academic dependency that are operating. In two earlier publications (Alatas, 1999: 167-70; 2000a: 84-89), I listed the dimensions of academic dependency and provided empirical examples of each. These dimensions can be listed as follows:[5]

1. Dependence on ideas.
2. Dependence on the media of ideas.
3. Dependence on the technology of education.
4. Dependence on aid for research as well as teaching.
5. Dependence on investment in education.
6. Dependence of Third World social scientists on the Western demand for their skills.

Dependence on Ideas

The first dimension refers to the dependence on the various levels of social scientific theory, that is, metatheory, theory, empirical social science and applied social science. Both teaching and research knowledge at all these levels overwhelmingly originated from the United States and the United Kingdom and in the case of the former French colonies, France. There is hardly any original metatheoretical or theoretical analysis emerging from the Third World. While a significant amount of empirical work is generated in the Third World, much of this takes its cues for research agenda, theoretical perspectives and methods from research in the West. Dependence on ideas is the general condition of knowledge in the Third World. Although scholarly communities in developing societies have tirelessly pointed out ethnocentric biases in the Western social sciences, the emergence of autonomous and alternative theoretical traditions are yet to be seen. The dependence on theories and concepts generated in the context of Western historical backgrounds and cultural practices continue.

This problem of dependence is linked to the pervasiveness of imitation. In the case of India, as elsewhere, mimesis may involve not only theories and concepts but also the internalization of ethnic and cultural prejudices

(Nandi, 1994). For example, although many Indians are dark, phrases such as 'black sheep,' 'black heart' or 'black eye' have found their way into Indian discourse with all their negative connotations (ibid.: 23).

Related to the dependence of ideas from the West is the assumption that there is nothing to learn from Asian works. Syed Hussein Alatas (1976b) refers to the widely prevailing but unstated assumption that there is little to learn from earlier Asian thinking on the conditions of progress because many such works are ignored or remain unknown. As a result, credit for uncovering or focusing attention on certain issues is usually given to Western scholars or their 'Asian imitators who have a limited historical perspective' (ibid.: 63). Dependence on ideas is the most important dimension of academic dependency. The other dimensions discussed below facilitate in one way or another, the flow of ideas from the social science powers, but are in, and of themselves meaningless without this first dimension.

Dependence on the Media of Ideas

The second dimension refers to dependence on the media of ideas such as books, scientific journals, proceedings of conferences, working papers and electronic publications of various kinds. The degree of academic dependency in this case can be gauged from the structure of ownership and control of publishing houses, journals, working paper series and websites. Take scientific journals as an example. The greatest numbers of social science journals are published in the United States together with France, Germany, Italy and the United Kingdom. Over 80 per cent of articles in the political science journals in these countries were contributed by scholars who belonged to a professional organization of the same nationality as that of the journal (Garreau, 1988: 173).

The bulk of the world's intellectual output is from the industrialized nations, particularly the United States, Britain, France and Germany. As early as the 1970s, a survey of social science journals reported that more than 60 per cent of them were published in the United States, Britain and France (Line & Roberts, 1976: 133). Where books, journals and other periodicals are concerned, the better established publishers and distributors are located in the West, with the Third World being net importers of foreign reading materials. The distribution networks between core and periphery have come to be well developed over the years while those among Third World countries are lacking. Consequently, in a place like Malaysia or India it is much easier to obtain works published in the United States and Britain than works from each other's countries.

While there are efforts to develop a publishing industry in several Third World countries, publishing and distribution are still dominated by the social science powers. As a result, Third World scholarship in terms of the selection of problems, the language of communication and the choice of research methods are often tailored to the requirements of the global market.

Dependency on the Technology of Education

There is also the technology dimension to the dependency relation in the social sciences. Western embassies, foundations, and other non-governmental institutions often set up resource centres in Third World countries, which are equipped with the latest information retrieval systems that are may be generally absent in local universities and institutions. While such resources are able to provide data and knowledge that would not otherwise be available, the choice in the selection of data would naturally be the prerogative of the foreign organization providing these services. The technology relation is, therefore, a very important dimension of the dependency relation in the social sciences. At one time, in the 1960s and 1970s when many major journals in the social sciences were publishing articles utilizing advanced statistical methods, richer countries tended to have a comparative advantage because of the lack of computing facilities in many Third World countries. While this may not be true today because of the relative ease with which such facilities can be acquired, the dependency upon the technology of education continues in other ways. Instructional materials such as films and laboratory instruments are imported because there is little innovation in the creation of curricula and instructional materials. This has partly to do with the lack of funds but also with the fact that many educationists in the Third World went through a Western education and continue to draw upon the West for their resources.

An example of this form of dependency is the Lincoln Resource Center at the Embassy of the United States of America in Kuala Lumpur which provides useful resources to academicians, journalists and other interested members of the public. It is well equipped with video-conferencing and CD-ROM facilities. Books and documents are lent out while a periodical list of articles covering American international relations, social issues, and the arts is maintained from which one can make selections and order free-of-charge. While many materials of interest, unavailable elsewhere in Malaysia, can be obtained through the Lincoln Center, the choice of selection is understandably governed by the Americans.

Dependence on Aid for Research as well as Training

The fourth dimension refers to aid dependence in the form of foreign funds and technical aid originating from governments, educational institutions and foundations in the United States, Great Britain, France, Germany, the Netherlands and Japan, which routinely find their way to scholars and educational institutions in the Third World. These funds are used to sponsor research, purchase books and other instructional materials, finance the publication of local books and journals, and buy expertise in the form of visiting scholars.

Various governmental organizations as well as corporate foundations in the developed world play crucial roles in the training of Third World scholars. They provide scholarships and fellowships, fund social science research and provide expert personnel for research and teaching institutions—training that would otherwise not be available, in the developing world.

The United States, for instance, has been very active in providing foreign assistance in the field of education. Land grant colleges based on an American model have been established in India, Indonesia, Nigeria and Latin America (Altbach, 1977: 198). Huge amounts of funds and technical aid have been provided to develop these universities.

The United States, Britain, France and Germany have also sponsored the study of their languages and cultures in developing countries. The French are particularly active in this regard, both in terms of promoting French in the Third World and further developing the language in former French colonies. The Americans have been active in establishing management training institutes in the developing world. However, it has been suggested that the American orientation of such institutes results in their graduates being unable to find jobs because the training they underwent was unrelated to local conditions (Altbach, 1977: 200).

Foreign aid in books and published materials is also crucial in fostering academic dependency. One aspect of this is foreign aid in publishing. Book programmes are another, in which the Americans are the most organized and widespread. A case in point would be the Asia Foundation that provided books free-of-charge to organizations and individuals on a regular basis, covering both the social and natural sciences. The United States Information Agency provided funds for the production of 80 million copies covering some 9,000 works in 51 languages (Benjamin 1964: 72). The Book Translation Program is still active in a number of countries such as Indonesia, Thailand, Vietnam and China.[6] The British also have their subsidized book programmes, such as the English Language Book Scheme (Altbach, 1977: 201). Foreign aid programmes and private foundations also make it possible for libraries in Third World countries to receive Western academic journals.

Even in the case of locally published journals the funding often comes from abroad. An example is the Congress for Cultural Freedom that sponsored the publication of several leading journals in India and other countries. In fact, some of these funds came from the Central Intelligence Agency and the Ford Foundation (Lasch, 1969: 61-114). Today, many American, British, German and French organizations continue to provide assistance to Third World journals that would otherwise have to cease publication. While it is true that foreign funds do bring benefits to the social sciences in the Third World, it must be noted that the funding is ultimately linked to the interests of the donors and their countries of origin in terms of research agenda and the identification of themes of debate (Hadiz & Dhakidae, 2005: 4).

Dependence on Investment in Education

The fifth dimension of academic dependency refers to the direct investment by Western educational institutions in the Third World. An example would be the various degree programmes offered by North American, British and Australian universities in Asia, sometimes involving joint ventures with local organizations. Without such direct investment there would be fewer opportunities for tertiary education and fewer teaching jobs available in Asian countries.

This dimension of academic dependency is derived by drawing a parallel between multinational corporations and the knowledge industry (Garreau, 1985: 60). Educational institutions in industrialized nations do invest in education in the Third World, for instance, the various degree programmes being offered in Malaysia by various North American, British and Australian universities. These involve joint ventures between foreign and local institutions. In one particular variant, known as the twinning programme, students spend a large portion of their academic career in Malaysia, taking courses whose credits are transferable to the university that is twinned with the Malaysian counterpart. In this way, the financial burden of studying abroad is greatly reduced. At the same time, Western universities are more or less guaranteed contingencies of foreign students who otherwise may not attend foreign universities because of prohibitive costs.

The dependence of Third World academic communities on First World social science establishments and institutions along these five dimensions constitute the vertical relations on which global social science is founded. An important feature of these vertical relations is the flow of information between the periphery and the core, and the lack of communication among peripheral social science communities (Garreau, 1985: 107; 1991: 300–301). These vertical relations are seen to obstruct the flow of independent and original ideas, promote pro-capitalist ideologies and subject Third World countries to development policies supportive of the globalization of capital (Toh 1983).

Dependence of Third World Scientists on the Western Demand for Their Skills

The brain drain is the final dimension of academic dependency in the sense that Third World scholars become dependent on the demand for their expertise in the West. Brain drain may not necessarily result in the physical relocation of these scholars in the West, but it occurs in terms of the using up of mental resources and energy of Third World personnel as junior research partners for research projects conceived in the West.

Here it would be interesting to speculate on how academic dependency may be affected by shifts in the balance of economic power. It is not uncommon in Asia to hear optimistic views to the effect that if Asian economies overtake the West, Asian culture will become more dominant globally. The global hegemony of Western culture is a result of two centuries of economic and political domination. It is reasonable to suggest that as Asia gains more economic strength, Asian cultural influence will as well. However it is doubtful that any Asian nation or Asia as a whole would become dominant in the social sciences on a global scale. The case of Japan is instructive in this regard.

Japan is a world economic power but it is not a social science power by any means. While Japanese social science is not dependent on the social science powers in terms of the technology of education, aid for research and teaching, investment in education, and demand in the West for their skills—there is some degree of dependence on Western ideas and media of ideas. At the same time, Japanese social science wields some international influence, not through its ideas but via its provision of funding for research in the Third World through organizations such as the Japan Foundation and the Toyota Foundation. But for all its economic might, Japanese social science has not challenged the position of the three reigning social science powers. This is not the place to go into the reasons for this. Nevertheless, the Japanese case shows that economic power alone does not bring about social scientific dominance. There has to be a conscious effort on the part of social scientists and the administrators of research and teaching institutions to formulate and implement policies designed to help social science communities to break out of the current division of labour. The Japanese case illustrates one possible avenue. Generally, the Japanese social science establishment, while very much influenced by Western models, does not gauge academic success according to publications in Western periodicals and in Western languages. There is, in a sense, an opting out of that game. The same is true of the German social sciences. In both cases, great prestige is to be derived from publishing in the national language in nationally recognized periodicals.

It is important to point out that while all the social science powers are Western, this is not to suggest that the centre-periphery continuum corresponds to a West/non-West divide. There are many Western social science communities which do not have the features of a social science power and are dependent on the latter for ideas. They may not suffer from the other dimensions of academic dependency, but they also do not exert any global influence in the social sciences like the United States, British and French social science communities do. This suggests the need for a third category, that of the semi-peripheral social science power. This may be defined as a social science community that is dependent on ideas originating in the social science centres, but which themselves exert some influence on peripheral social science communities through the provision of research funds, university degrees for postgraduate students, postdoctoral fellows from the Third World, the funding of international conferences, and so on. Australia, Japan, the Netherlands and, possibly Germany, are examples of semi-peripheral social science powers.

The Global Division of Labour in the Social Sciences

As discussed earlier, academic neo-colonialism is maintained by the condition of academic dependency, which we have detailed in terms of six dimensions. The claim that academic neo-colonialism is an existing phenomenon that defines the relationship between academic communities, in the First and Third Worlds suggests that there is a relationship of inequality between the social sciences in the West, on the one hand,

and the Third World on the other. The nature of this inequality can be understood by scrutinizing the global division of labour in the social sciences. This division of labour is historically a direct consequence of academic colonialism and dependency, but in turn also functions to perpetuate academic neo-colonialism and dependency. The global division of labour in the social sciences was originally determined by the colonial mode of knowledge production. The subsequent inequalities in relations between First World and Third World social science communities in the form of academic neo-colonialism and academic dependency are in turn maintained and even exacerbated by specific features of the current division of labour in global knowledge. This division of labour has three characteristics:

1. The division between theoretical and empirical intellectual labour.
2. The division between other country studies and own country studies.
3. The division between comparative and single case studies.

The evidence to empirically verify that this division of labour is in operation in today's global social science is not difficult to provide. For example, data can be gathered from social science and area studies journals, textbooks, and encyclopaedias. One can also cite personal and anecdotal evidence.

The first characteristic refers to the phenomenon of social scientists in the social science powers engaging in both theoretical as well as empirical research, while their counterparts in the Third World do mainly empirical research. A glance at several issues of a leading theory journal in the discipline of sociology, *Sociological Theory*,[7] will reveal this. Volume 20 (2002) of this journal carried 20 articles authored by a total of 28 authors all of whom were based in universities in the United States, despite the fact that the journal calls for submissions in all areas of social thought and theory without specifying any particular theoretical or geographical area of interest. Volume 32 (2002) of the journal, *Philosophy of the Social Sciences*,[8] carried 23 articles, discussions and review essays and the breakdown of authors by country of residence was as follows—14 of the authors came from the United States, Britain and France, while other countries such as Canada, Italy, Israel, New Zealand, Spain, Belgium, Germany and South Africa were represented by either one or two authors. Three countries from the social science powers account for more than half of the articles published in this volume. Volume 31 (2002) of *Theory and Society*[9] published a total of 16 articles. Among the 20 authors of these articles, 15 were based in the United States, two in Germany, one in Canada, one in France and one in Singapore.

The second characteristic refers to the fact that scholars in First World countries undertake studies of both their own as well as other countries, while scholars in the Third World tend to confine themselves to research on their own countries. Scholars located in the Third World rarely study societies other than their own or undertake research on the West. Notable exceptions of Third World scholars who did not restrict their writings and research interests to their own societies are Surajit Sinha, Satish Saberwal, J.P.S. Uberoi, T.N. Pandey, R.K. Jain, Tapan Raychaudhuri (Srivastava, 2000: 10) and Syed Hussein Alatas.

The third characteristic refers to the far greater frequency of comparative work in the West as compared to generally single case studies which almost always coincide with own country studies in the Third World. The distribution of authors by country of residence in the journal, *Comparative Studies in Society and History*,[10] shows trends along the lines of the second and third characteristics described above. The 2002 volume of this journal (vol. 44) carried a total of nineteen articles. Out of the 34 authors in this volume, 20 are based in the United States, four in the United Kingdom and one in France, the rest being in Second and Third World countries. What is striking is that the vast majority of articles written on Second and Third World areas such as Cuba, Romania, Bangladesh, Ottoman Damascus, China and so on, were authored by people based in one of the social science powers. Furthermore, a study of various issues of this journal reveal that articles with a comparative perspective tend to be written by those based in one of the social science powers.

Area studies journal are too numerous to be reviewed here in their entirety. But, it would be obvious to anyone who surveyed them that most of the articles on non-Western topics are authored either by scholars based in one of the social science powers or by scholars who are nationals of the country being written about.

If progress in the social sciences is defined in terms of the development of original concepts, theories, models and methods that are creatively applied to a wide range of historical, comparative and empirical situations in the context of research agendas independently drawn up according to certain criteria of relevance—then it will be readily understood that the division of labour in the social sciences actually hinders such progress. The division of labour, therefore, functions to perpetuate academic dependency and academic neo-colonialism.[11]

The Prospects for Academic Dependency Reversal

Amongst the many problems faced by the social sciences in the Third World, some are management and administration-related. Other problems are of a more intellectual nature and are concerned with the history and development of the social sciences in the Third World, as well as certain philosophical and epistemological problems plaguing the social sciences. These problems have been identified in various theoretical studies on the state of the social sciences in developing societies as seen in the examples of—Orientalism (Said, 1979, 1993), Eurocentrism (Amin, 1979), the theory of the captive mind (Alatas, 1972a, 1974), rhetorical theories of social science (Alatas, 1998b), pedagogical theories of modernization (Al-e Ahmad, nd; Freire, 1970; Illich, 1973) colonial critiques (Césaire, 1955; Fanon, 1961; Memmi, 1957), and, of course, academic dependency theory (Alatas, 1999, 2000a; Altbach, 1975, 1977; Garreau, 1985, 1988, 1991).

What are the prospects for academic dependency reversal? The problem is structural and the partial dismantling of this structure requires concerted action on the part of social scientists all over the world. However, before this can be done, more basic problems need to be addressed.

1. The social sciences should not merely be regarded as facilitators to economic growth. This would result in an unbalanced support for those areas in the social sciences that are deemed more practical. The overriding concern should be with a broader conception of development that values the contribution of all the social sciences to the process of development in the broader sense of the term.
2. Social science communities in the Third World, particularly those with more resources, should consider various means of attracting a critical mass of post doctoral students and researchers so that they may carry out their research work there. Various incentives should be provided to achieve this.
3. The development of a vibrant and creative social science community cannot take place without a well developed tertiary education sector. There should be serious efforts towards rationalizing and

upgrading universities in a number of areas including the following: (a) international benchmarking of research output and facilities; (b) competitive remuneration packages to stem the tide of brain drain and attract local scientists working abroad; and (c) expansion of research facilities, especially libraries and scientific equipment.

Assuming that the necessity of the above is recognized, what other measures are required to block developments in the direction of academic dependency? A few suggestions can be made here. First, there is a need for more serious theoretical and empirical research on the problems of academic dependency and academic colonialism. This research should be communicated to students and academicians via teaching, publications and international conferences. Beyond this, it is vital that the public is made aware of the problem.

However, there have been few works that deal with the problem of delineating the structure of academic dependency in both the social science powers as well as academically dependent social science communities. This is partly due to the very structure of academic dependency in force. Many conceptual and practical problems peculiar to the social sciences in developing societies like—academic dependency, the problem of relevance, the problem of mental captivity and others—have not become the subject matter of social science research in the developing world because the social scientists here mainly take their cues from the social science powers in the drawing up of research agenda. They do this in ways consistent with the global division of labour outlined above.

Second, beyond just discussing the problem, social scientists should consider measures to deal with each dimension of academic dependency. For example, the dependence on ideas from the social science powers can be lessened by attempts to rewrite classical sociological theory textbooks featuring not only European thinkers such as Marx, Weber and Durkheim but also non-European contemporaries such as Sarkar and Rizal.

Third, the above efforts can be significantly aided by greater interaction among the social scientists of the Third World. However, such interaction cannot be left to chance. While there are ample opportunities for scholars from the Third World to meet each other, they tend to gravitate to the West for conferences and research opportunities. It is necessary, therefore, to form regional associations. For example, there is a need for an Asian sociological association. Such a regional association could consciously strive to organize events that bring together Asian scholars from all over the world with similar concerns about academic dependency and focus on research and activism around this theme.

Education in the humanities and social sciences in developing societies should not be downplayed. It must be realized that the Chinese, Indian and Islamic civilizations made seminal contributions to the sciences by having a strong foundation in philosophy and theology which aimed to develop the creative instinct. To the extent that the arts and humanities may play this role today, quality education in these areas must be provided too.

The Demerits of Academic Dependency Theory

Academic dependency theory provides an interesting structural approach with which to understand the relationship between First World and Third World social science. While many ideas pertaining to academic dependency theory took shape in the 1960s and 70s, there is a continuing concern with the problem both in India and Malaysia, as revealed by contemporary publications (see, for example, Alatas, S.H., 2000; Mukherji, Aikara & Sengupta, 1997). However, academic dependency theory is not without its weaknesses. The analogy with economic dependency theory for instance, is not always appropriate.

For example, with regard to dependency on ideas and the media of ideas, the problem is less structural and more a question of lack of interest. In many Third World countries, there are sufficient number of books, both foreign and local, to enable a theorist to develop some interesting and researchable ideas, assuming that his/her reflection is carried out against the backdrop of local conditions. A collection of—Western social science classics, local reading materials and the empirical field of the researcher's society—are the right ingredients for an autonomous social science tradition.

Regarding dependency on the technology of education, this would be a problem only to the extent that educational technologies are crucial to the development of social science. But it is quite clear that there are many areas of interest in the social sciences for which state-of-the-art technology is not crucial. Nevertheless, even in these areas the social sciences in the Third World lag behind that of industrialized nations.

On the dependency on aid for research and teaching, the analogy with economic dependency is not entirely appropriate because there is nothing equivalent to World Bank or International Monetary Fund (IMF) conditionality in the funding of research by international foundations or government organizations. In other words, the terms and conditions of grants are sufficiently flexible for Third World researchers in exercising autonomy in deciding upon areas of research and methods to be used.

Finally, foreign investment in education does not necessarily foster unoriginality. Twinning programmes in Malaysia and elsewhere, for example, could easily be modified in such a manner as to offer courses more relevant to local situations while at the same time satisfying the requirements of the foreign 'twin'.

This is not to suggest that academic dependency theory is without merit. It is useful in providing a structural account of the transnational flow of ideas whose understanding, however, cannot be limited only to structural aspects. The billions spent on advertising is due to the realization that it takes more than economic power to sell products and services worldwide. Similarly, it takes more than academic power to 'sell' ideas worldwide. A more compelling explanation for the spread of ideas from core to periphery comes from enumerating the 'selling strategies' resorted to by social science discourse, even if these are deployed within the context of the structures of academic dependency. These selling strategies are the rhetorical devices internal to the social sciences.

The Rhetorical Element in the Global Spread of the Social Sciences

The success of the rhetorical programme of social science is dependent upon its ability to capture the attention of its audience. What are the rhetorical techniques that the social sciences resort to, or should resort to, in order that their implantation in Third World countries is seen as a legitimate and necessary project? The answer to this depends upon the 'conditions of the speakers, as well as the speech, in order to achieve conformity with all the requirements of a given situation' (Ibn Khaldun 1958: 335). The given situation refers to the worldview of the audience of Western social science in the Third World. What then is the worldview of this audience?

These can be provisionally listed as positivism and counterism. Due to their intellectual upbringing and ancestry, most Third World scholars generally operate within the bounds of positivist science. In addition to that, particularly since the 1970s, there has emerged in much of the Third World, an apparent oppositional stance against the Western social sciences that can be labelled as counterism. This stance is not to be confused with indigenization or the call for an autonomous social science tradition in the Third World. Counterism opposes Western modes of knowledge at the rhetorical level but nonetheless succeeds in incorporating Western assumptions, theories and concepts. Positivism and counterism each make social science audiences in the Third World responsive to rhetorical techniques deployed in the global spread of the social sciences.

Positivism

The influence of positivism can be gauged from the success of the quantification rhetoric. Numbers and other forms of quantification are pervasive in the social sciences. By attributing mathematical order to the objects of social reality, results are often projected differently through the use of various kinds of comparisons and by switching between absolute numbers and percentages (Potter, Wetherell & Chitty, 1991: 335). Perhaps the bias for statistical techniques, survey research methods and other forms of quantification can be understood in this light.

Positivism had also predisposed scholars in the Third World to being receptive to a rhetorical technique that may be termed the technicization of development. Faith in the notion that life is a machine and that the 'study of man will reveal nothing except what is adequately describable in the concepts of mechanics and chemistry' (Lashley, 1923) had resulted in the discursive reduction of development problems to purely technical ones. For example, the problem of development in Egypt is seen to be due to 98 per cent of the population crammed onto 4 per cent of land along the Nile. The problems, therefore, are technical ones such as natural limitations, topography, and overpopulation (Mitchell, 1991, cited in Escobar, 1995: 47).

Counterism and the Proliferation of Terminology

The oppositional tide against Western social science, sometimes very rational and cosmopolitan, but when insular, unwittingly works in favour of the inflow of Western theory. For example, the body of literature that has come to be known as Islamic economics, grounds itself on a theory of rational man and a hypothetico-deductive methodology while adorning itself with a fine array of Islamic terminology. It has merely substituted

Islamic terms for neo-classical ones, all the while retaining the same assumptions and methods. The proliferation of new terminology, Islamic ones in this case, enables foreign ideas to be smuggled in and given pre-eminence while at the same time preserving the aura of Islamization of knowledge. The proliferation of indigenous terminology enables one to have her cake and eat it too.

By way of a summary of the above, the rhetorical construction of knowledge is only successful to the extent that a problem is formulated and a concern addressed. This concern must be of an issue of vital importance to the addressed audience. What general concerns must social science speak of in order to be taken seriously in the Third World? First, the social sciences must formulate a problem. The problem formulated here is that of underdevelopment. Second, the concern of the audience addressed is with the role of the scholarly community in solving the problems of underdevelopment. Third, the problem so formulated implies that there is a need to offer a solution. The solution presented is that of the universalization or internationalization of the social sciences, which means its acceptance in the Third World. The purpose of highlighting the rhetorical dimension of social scientific discourse is to urge us to consider that 'internationalization inspired from the West would necessarily be a search for an enlarged market for Western sociology [for sociology read social science and for Western read American]' (Oommen, 1991: 82).

The prominence of American and Western social sciences in the Third World depends not only on their ability to present a better fit between theory and practice (which may in fact be irrelevant), but on their ability to capture the attention of their audience of social scientists in developing societies. Rhetorical construction in social science activities constitutes the subjective dimension of the structures of academic dependency. In the context of academic dependency, the rhetorical techniques outlined above facilitate the acceptance of the social sciences in the Third World.

Chapters Two and Three have discussed a variety of theories that are concerned with explaining the state of the social sciences in Asia. The next chapter, on the other hand, shifts attention to the definition and variety of alternative social science discourses in Asia. These are discourses that emerged as a result of the theoretical criticism of the state of the social sciences detailed in Chapters Two and Three. What are being presented in Chapter Four as alternative discourses see themselves as correcting and transcending the problems identified in the previous two chapters.

Notes

1. The complete text is printed in Horowitz (1967: 47–49).
2. This theme was first discussed by Syed Hussein Alatas in a lecture to the History Society, National University of Singapore, in 1969. See Alatas, S.H. (1969).
3. This is taken from Dos Santos' original Spanish. See Dos Santos (1968: 6).
4. This point was made by Lie (1996) for Japan but applies to other social science communities as well.
5. This centre-periphery continuum or structure of academic dependency applies equally to the humanities, particularly those areas concerned with the theoretical or conceptual study of literature and the arts as opposed to the generation of literature and art per se. What is being said here about academic dependency and the global division of labour in the social sciences applies to the sciences as well. For a strong case made in this regard, see Rahman (1983).
6. See the following websites <http://jakarta.usembassy.gov/; <http://bangkok. usembassy.gov, <http://www.usia.gov/abtusia/posts/VN1/www husis.html>; <http://www.beijing.usembassy-china.org.cn
7. Published by Blackwell Publishing for the American Sociological Association (2002).
8. Published by Sage Publications (2002).
9. Published by Kluwer Academic Publishers (2002).
10. Published by Cambridge University Press.
11. Data gathered from periodicals published in the Third World would yield similar results.

4

The Definition and Variety of Alternative Discourses in Asia

In Chapter Two, various perspectives that diagnose the state of the social sciences were enumerated. In addition to such works that carried out critical assessments of the state of knowledge in Asia, there have also been prescriptions of varieties of alternative discourses that serve as correctives to the type of social sciences introduced during colonial times and which have been criticized by the theories outlined in Chapter Two.

This chapter has two objectives. One is to provide a formal definition of alternative discourses. The second is to document and discuss the variety of alternative discourses in Asia in terms of the different ideas and intellectual movements that have emerged. As this chapter shows, there has been a great deal of critical and creative thinking, much of it in a counter-Eurocentric mode among Asian social scientists. This book does not claim that such works do not exist, but that they have not been able to become dominant or more influential than they are in teaching and research because of a number of obstacles faced by alternative discourses, such as academic dependency and others discussed in the following chapters. For example, while the works of D.D. Kosambi have been recognized as being innovative and critical of received Western knowledge, his radical views on Indian history have not been integrated into textbook versions of Indian history (Chattopadhyaya, 2002: xxix). The same can be said of many of the thinkers that are referred to in this book.

Towards a Definition of Alternative Discourses

The discussions on the state of the social sciences in Asia do not arise from an intellectual movement but rather from a diverse group of scholars, both Asian and Western, from the various disciplines of the social sciences. Prescriptions range from calls for endogenous intellectual creativity and an autonomous social science tradition to the decolonization of knowledge, the indigenization of the social sciences and others. The general concern has been with the problems of Eurocentrism—the uncritical imitation of ideas, concepts and theories from the West—as well as the context of academic dependency and intellectual imperialism within which these take place. The call for alternative social sciences has been in existence since the late nineteenth century. It was and continues to be a response to what many Asian and other non-Western social scientists perceive as the inability of Euro-American social science to constitute a relevant and liberating discourse in the context of Asian, African and Latin American societies. This problem was exacerbated by the fact that much of such social science was assimilated uncritically outside of their countries of origin among students, lecturers, researchers and planners.

The various works referred to in Chapter Two in the section on 'The Call for Alternative Discourses', all provide alternative readings of history and society and call for revision and reconstruction which in turn necessitates reconceptualization and the innovative use of methods in the social sciences. The works of earlier British, Dutch, Indian, Indonesian and Malaysian scholars cited in Chapter Two as well as many others not cited, were pioneering attempts at alternative discourses and it is unfortunate that little attention is paid to them today. While they come under different names, what they have in common is the concerted effort towards countering the Eurocentric and Orientalist bias in the social and historical sciences. The label 'alternative discourses', therefore, is appropriate because they set themselves in opposition to what they understand as constituting the mainstream, which are largely Euro-American oriented discourses that continue to dominate the arts and social sciences of most Asian societies.

Alternative discourses constitute a revolt against intellectual imperialism. Pertierra (1997) recognizes the role of indigenized social science (read alternative discourses) as a weapon in neo-colonial struggles as long as the social sciences 'act as the counter-point between the state and society' as opposed to becoming an instrument of the state's colonization of civil life (ibid.: 10, 20). Sinha (1998) views the call for indigenization (read alternative discourses) as arising out of the need to '"purge" the social sciences of Eurocentrism and thus register a crucial break from the hegemony of a colonial past...' (ibid.: 16).

As a preliminary statement on the nature of alternative discourses, we may itemize some of their features as follows:

1. Their starting point is the critique of Eurocentrism and Orientalism in the social sciences.
2. They raise methodological and epistemological problems relating to the study of society, historiography or the philosophy of history.
3. They are implicitly or explicitly concerned with an analysis of the problems presented by the world division of labour in the social sciences in which the Asian social sciences find themselves to be in a state of conformity, imitation and unoriginality.
4. They are committed to the reconstruction of social and historical discourses which involve the development of concepts, categories and research agenda that are relevant to local/regional conditions.
5. They are committed to raising original problems in social and historical studies.
6. They recognize all civilizations and cultural practices as sources of ideas for the social sciences.
7. They are not in favour of the rejection of Western social science *in toto*.

These traits are true of most of what is presented as critical discourses of Eurocentric social science, although, there are exceptions, as discussed later in Chapter Five.

I can then formulate a definition of alternative discourses as those which are informed by local/regional historical experiences and cultural practices in Asia in the same way that the Western social sciences are. Being alternative means a turn to philosophies, epistemologies, histories, and the arts other than those of the Western tradition. These are all to be considered as potential sources of social science theories and concepts, which would decrease academic dependence on the world social science powers. Therefore, it becomes clear that the emergence and augmentation of alternative discourses is identical to the process of universalizing and internationalizing the social sciences. It should also be clear that alternative discourses refer to good social science because they are more conscious of the relevance of the surroundings and the problems stemming from the discursive wielding of power by the social sciences—and with the need for the development of new ideas. Alternative is being defined as that which is relevant to its surroundings—is creative, non-imitative and original, non-essentialist, counter-Eurocentric, autonomous from the state and autonomous from other national or transnational groupings. As such, alternative discourses could be advocated for Western social science itself.

The search for alternative discourses is a contribution to the universalization of the social sciences to the extent that alternative civilizational voices are added to the ensemble of ideas and works. But there are varying levels of alternatives (and all the things this entails such as creativity, originality, non-essentialism, autonomy, and relevance to the surroundings) and, therefore, universality. At the lowest level, good social science in the Third World would insist on a cautious application of Western theory to the local situation. Here we cannot yet speak of an alternative discourse. At a higher level, alternative and universal discourses refer to both local and Western theories applied to the local context. At yet another level, local, Western and other indigenous theories and concepts (that is, indigenous to other non-Western societies) are applied to the study of the local setting. I have in mind as an example, the application of the Khaldunian theory of state formation to the Mongol conquest of China. The highest level among alternative and universal discourses is achieved with the application of locally-derived theories from within and beyond one's own society to areas outside. Whatever the level of universality, there is in principle a commitment to the universal source of theories, concepts and ideas in general, although the extent to which ideas from without the locality are brought in and domesticated varies from one level to another.

Therefore, it is difficult to understand why some are not in favour of the project of alternative discourses. What is being advocated here is not a school of thought nor a particular theoretical or metatheoretical perspective, but simply good social science.

The Varieties of Alternative Discourses

Indigenization: A Plurality of Calls

A consequence of the critique of the state of the social sciences in Asia was the call for the indigenization of the social sciences. This was more prominent in the case of the disciplines of anthropology in India and some other Asian countries, and psychology in the Philippines. While there has been a great deal of discussion on indigenization, there has been little actual practice of indigenized social science. As a result, there are few examples of what indigenous knowledge constitutes from the theoretical, methodological and empirical points of view. It is in this context that the project of the indigenization of anthropology and psychology must be seen.

The numerous works on indigenization present a wide range of definitions for the same. These are useful to work with for the aim of enumerating a list of traits which capture the essential features of the notion. Evans' (1997) essay is appropriate to begin with, because his discussion on indigenous and indigenized anthropology in Asia provides a definition of indigenization that is at odds with most other definitions as well as with the dominant thinking on the subject.

Evans suggests that communism in Asia indigenized anthropology. In Vietnam, for example, for a long time anthropological research was conducted largely by indigenous anthropologists whose research agendas were defined by the developmental aims of the state. These anthropologists subscribed to an ideology according to which national minorities were backward and in need of the kind of development as was defined by the state (Evans, 1997: 5). The theoretical basis of this indigenized anthropology was derived from a 'Stalinist-Maoist version of Marxism' (ibid.: 6). Here, indigenized anthropology is defined in terms of having 'forced Marxism through their [Chinese, Vietnamese, North Korean] own cultural sieve, and rationalised this in all sorts of ways' (ibid.: 6). Further (Evans, (ibid.: 8) compares the works of these anthropologists to a high form of colonial anthropology because they had aligned themselves to the state in its bid to control the national minorities.

Ramstedt (1997:2) is tempted to understand the amalgamation of Western anthropological theory with Indonesian state philosophy (*pancasila*) as a form of indigenized Western anthropology. Although such anthropologists may see themselves as indigenizing Marxist or Western theories, this understanding of indigenization is antithetical to existing definitions.

Indigenization has generally been understood to constitute a revolt against intellectual imperialism as a component of the revolt against politico-economic domination (Bennagen, 1980: 7). Pertierra (1997: 10, 20) sees the indigenized social sciences as weapons wielded in neo-colonial struggles only to the extent that the social sciences are autonomous and resist becoming an instrument of the state.

For Sinha, (1998: 16) the indigenization of anthropology and the other social sciences are consequences of the move to counter Eurocentrism and mark a crucial break from the intellectual hegemony of the colonial past. She further elaborates this as a need to 'articulate and theorize global politics of academia and its complex role in perpetuating the traditional intellectual division of labour: non-Western scholars as gatherers of empirical material, which forms the grounding for theoretical arguments advanced by Western scholars' (Sinha, 1998: 35). An analysis of the problems presented by the structure of the world system of anthropology where the dominant discourse of the core social science powers of the United States, Great Britain and France result in conformity, imitation and lack of originality in the periphery (Kuwayama & van Bremen, 1997: 54–55)—is seen to be a central task of the indigenization of anthropology project.

Another feature of indigenized anthropology is its problematization of the epistemological and methodological underpinnings of the social sciences (Sinha, 1998: 33). This would involve exposing the Eurocentric and Orientalist bias that undergirds much of the social sciences.

The indigenization of anthropology can not simply be understood in negative terms of delinking from metropolitan, neo-colonialist control. It is also understood in a more positive way, in terms of the contribution of non-Western systems of thought to anthropological theory (Evans, 1997: 17). Non-Western thought and cultural practices are to be seen as sources of anthropological theorizing, while at the same time Western anthropology is not to be rejected *in toto*. The indigenization-of-anthropology-projects are not conceived to be a 'categorical rejection of all "Western" input in theorizing' and does not 'seek to replace "Eurocentrism" with "nativism" or any other dogmatic position' (Sinha, 1998: 34). Here, there is an explicit claim that theories and concepts can be derived from the historical experiences and cultural practices of the various non-Western cultures, whether culture is defined as coterminous with the nation-state or otherwise (Alatas, 1993b, Enriquez, 1994a; Fahim & Helmer, 1980; Lee, 1979).

Pieke (1997) suggests, with reference to China, that one can speak of mature, indigenous anthropology only when it has generated a corpus of knowledge that is comparative and cross-cultural. The need for comparative and cross-cultural research is based on the idea that an indigenized anthropology 'autochthonously generates its own ideas, concepts, and debates that are informed by an ongoing hermeneutics between one's own and other cultures' (ibid.: 23). In the absence of such a hermeneutics existing ideas would simply be recycled and new ones imported from the usual Western sources. While this point is well taken, the role of comparative and cross-cultural research can have the desired effect of indigenizing anthropology only if such research is carried out by people already conscious of the problems of academic imperialism, mental captivity and relevance. Only then would comparative research yield original ideas and concepts.

The call for indigenization has often been heard in Asia[1] but attempts at conceptualizing it are rare. An exception would be Sinha (1997: 176–78), who suggests a research agenda for those wishing to begin the process of indigenizing the social sciences rather than simply talk about it. This is as follows:

1. To question the epistemological status of social science concepts, including those of 'indigenous', 'native', 'West', and 'non-West'.
2. To ground social theory in the socio-cultural and political conditions of a locality, without necessarily rejecting Western social science.
3. To theorize the global politics of academia with a view to uncovering its role in the perpetuation of a world division of labour in the social sciences, whereby non-Western scholars are the collectors of empirical data and Western scholars the theorists.
4. To recognize multiple centres and sources of social theory, that is, to regard all civilizations as potential sources of social science theorizing.

I could then formulate a definition of indigenous anthropology as that which is based upon indigenous historical experiences and cultural practices in the same way that Western social sciences are. Indigenization requires the turn to indigenous philosophies, epistemologies, histories, art and other modes of knowledge, which can all be potential sources of social science theories and concepts. Such knowledge leads to decreased intellectual dependence on the core social science powers of the North Atlantic. Nevertheless, most observers and proponents of indigenization do not understand it as con-stituting a rejection of Western social science.

The generation and use of indigenous viewpoints can be approached in two broad ways (Enriquez, 1994b). Indigenization from within refers to the process by which key indigenous concepts, methods and theories are semantically elaborated, codified, systematized, and then applied. On the other hand, indigenization from without refers to the modification and translation of imported materials which are ultimately assimilated theoretically and culturally (ibid.: 22).

Atal (1981), on the other hand, made a distinction between indigenization and endogenous development:

> Taken literally, endogenous development signifies development generated from within and orthogenetically, which would, thus, have no place for any exogenous influence... Indigenization, by contrast, at least honestly alludes to outside contact by emphasizing the need for indigenizing the exogenous elements to suit local requirements; whether this is done by the 'indigenous' or by 'outsiders' is mere detail (ibid.: 193).

Indigenization as understood by Enriquez and by other authors also includes both of what Atal refers to as endogenous development and indigenization. It has been widely recognized and accepted that if serious efforts are to be made to bring about more 'relevant' social sciences, the selective assimilation of exogenous (Western) elements should be considered as a vital part of endogenous intellectual activity (Alatas, 1981: 462).

It should, therefore, be apparent that the projects involving indigenization of knowledge around the world seek to contribute to the universalization of the social sciences by not only acknowledging but insisting that all cultures, civilizations and historical experiences be regarded as sources of ideas. Indigenous social scientists should contribute on an equal basis with their Western colleagues to international scholarship (Fahim, 1970: 397). Referring to the indigenization of development thinking, Hettne (1991: 39) suggests that the solution to academic imperialism is not to altogether do away with Western concepts but to adopt a more realistic understanding of Western social science as reflecting particular geographic and historical contexts. By and large, proponents of indigenization recognize that the Western social sciences are also indigenous to the extent that they arose in answer to the concern with problems developed on the basis of indigenously generated research agenda, and supported by indigenous academic institutions.

In line with the view that indigenization and universalization are one and the same thing, indigenizers of knowledge do not wish to discard Western social science, but wish to open up the possibilities for indigenous philosophies, epistemologies, and histories to become bases of knowledge.

If we understand indigenization in this way, it becomes clear that it is a prerequisite to the universalization of the social sciences and to the maintenance of internationally recognized standards of scholarship. In fact, indigenization has been defined in precisely these terms. In Korea, for example, indigenization (to-chak-hwa) refers to proceeding from research on the historical development of Korean society to universal theory

(Shin, 1994: 21) and to 'the extent to which we can digest and profitably assimilate things foreign...against the specific cultural and social backgrounds of the country' (Kwon, 1979: 21). Without indigenization projects throughout the world, only one set of indigenous (Western) discourse would dominate. Furthermore, the project of indigenization has to be carried out at the level of ontological assumptions, epistemology and axiology, and empirical theory (Kim, 1996b).[2]

> Indigenization is 'not about a counter-parochialisation of native social science to offset parochialism of Western social science. Indigenisation is a step forward from the contextualisation of our understanding of social phenomena. At a time when competing social science paradigms in the West are engaged largely in comprehending their own internal contradictions, it is important that we do not get restricted to debates and disputations within the parameters of the Western paradigms, for comprehending our social realities' (Mukherji, 2004: 31–32).

In spite of the repeated clarifications regarding the universality of indigenization projects, there continues to be indifference or even hostility towards the various projects of indigenization of social sciences around the world. Some of this may have to do with the term indigenization itself, which has its pitfalls. There is a pernicious rhetoric associated with 'indigenization'.

First of all, the term carries within it a notion of indigeny which itself has been mutilated to some degree (Benjamin, 1995). Indigeny refers to a concrete place, not abstractly defined states and provinces. Forms of consociation based on indigeny are 'bound up in the physical and biotic details' of the place of abode (ibid.: 3–4). The term indigeny, then, connotes insularity. The adjective, indigenous, is equally unattractive because it connotes tribal, ethnic, native or race identity (ibid.: 2–3).

Second, it has been argued by Syed Hussein Alatas that the term indigenization assumes a local or indigenous social scientific tradition as a base from which original theories may be constructed, which is generally not the case.[3]

Third, there is a view that indigenization implies the universality of Western knowledge, which simply needs to be localized or domesticated because there is nothing endogenous worth contributing to the social sciences.[4]

Fourth, another reason for the negative reactions to the term indigenization has to do with the way it has been used in political discourse.

For example, during his rule in South Korea, Park Chung-Hee had justified authoritarian rule with a Confucian basis by referring to it as the indigenization of democracy.[5]

The above do not refer to the logical or conceptual problems of the idea of indigenization but rather to rhetorical properties of the term. For strategic reasons, some may choose to distance themselves from the term but not from the ideas couched in it and the programmatic action encouraged by it.

The Call for an Autonomous Social Science

There are those works that call for an autonomous social science tradition that is rooted within the Third World context. While this idea had been around in Asia for more than thirty years, it has not been the basis of a dominant tendency in Asian social sciences. In the case of Southeast Asian history, there were some reactions to the views of John Bastin (1959) who was pessimistic about the possibility of writing Southeast Asian history from a Southeast Asian point of view. This would require a 'revolutionary reappraisal of existing historical methods and techniques, and of existing historical concepts and periodization. But that particular task, which is so often talked about, is fraught with so many difficulties and hazards that it remains unattempted' (ibid.: 22). Smail (1961: 102), on the other hand, believed in the possibility of an Asian-centric history in which Asians should be in the foreground and attention should be displaced from the colonial relationship to domestic history.

Here the question of an autonomous approach was misunderstood. The call for an autonomous approach in history and the social sciences should not be confused with the suggestion to merely highlight local problems with the appropriate methodology. It refers to the formation of a social science tradition which involves the raising and treatment of original problems and new research questions as well as the generation of new concepts (Alatas, 1979: 265). It also involves the critique of positivist social science to the extent that models of society epistemologically founded on the physical sciences obstruct the interpretive understanding of local situations. Phenomenology as part of the anti-positivist tradition has made its way into the disciplines of psychology, sociology and geography. The idea of autonomous social science will be taken up in more detail in Chapter Five where it is juxtaposed with nativist social science.

The Call for Endogenous Intellectual Creativity

The subject of the 'Asian Symposium on Intellectual Creativity in Endogenous Culture', was the call for endogenous intellectual creativity in Asian social sciences (jointly sponsored by the United Nations University and Kyoto University and held in Kyoto, Japan from 13-17 November, 1978) (Abdel-Malek & Pandeya, 1981). Endogenization refers to the effort involved at intellectual creativity in the context of original problem raising, the generation of new concepts and theories, and the synthesis between Western and non-Western knowledge. For example, the creative application of both Marx's theory of the Asiatic mode of production (Wiegersma, 1982) and the Khaldunian theory of social change (Alatas, 1993b) to the study of Asian history should be seen as part of endogenous intellectual creativity. The 'endogenous' here is 'understood as referring to the effort at intellectual creativity rather than to the constituent elements of the accomplished result' (Alatas, 1981: 462) or the materials used. The selective assimilation of exogenous elements should be considered as part of endogenous activity as both the exogenous and the endogenous are required in the effort to address the problem of the dominance of Euro-centric knowledge. In this sense, endogenous intellectual activity is not any different from the idea of the indigenization of the social sciences discussed earlier in the chapter. Indeed, the works of many scholars can be considered as coming under this category of work even though they themselves do not use the term endogenous intellectual creativity. Two examples of such works from India are those of T.K. Oommen and Sudhir Kakar.

Oommen's work, entitled *Alien Concepts and South Asian Reality* (1995) consists of 12 chapters covering various topics but which are united in the purpose of confronting what he calls alien, by which he means Western or Marxist concepts and theories. For example, Oommen takes Erving Goffman to task for confining his analysis to Anglo-American society and ignoring Afro-Asian society despite the radical differences between the two in empirical terms. In Anglo-American societies, face-to-face interactions are shifting and short-lived and the presentation of the self often takes place in anonymous and impersonal contexts. On the other hand, in the predominantly rural Afro-Asian societies, face-to-face interactions are often with the same set of persons everyday, for decades. One significant difference between Anglo-American and Afro-Asian societies, therefore, is that the self as presented and perceived is a fragmented entity in the former and a total entity in the latter (Oommen,

1995: 171). Oommen's attempt to critique and extend Goffman's analysis while applying it to the empirical field of everyday protests by the rural poor in Kerala, South India (ibid.: Chapter Nine)—is an example of endogenous intellectual creativity.

Another example comes from the work of the Indian psychoanalyst, Sudhir Kakar. In his *Shamans, Mystics and Doctors* (1982), Kakar states that a major objective of the work is to compare indigenous mental healing networks against Western assumptions and practices (ibid.: 5). He notes that psychoanalysis is marginal to Indian culture because its concepts of person and reality are deeply rooted in Western philosophical traditions which do not have the same connotations in Indian cultural traditions. As a result, the Indian psychoanalyst may reject or withdraw from his cultural tradition (Kakar, 1982: 8) and, presumably, fail to take indigenous healing philosophies and practices seriously. Kakar, on the other hand, seriously considered the limits of various mental healing traditions, Western as well as Indian. Kakar's work is rich in the presentation of empirical case studies, which are skilfully discussed in the context of both Western and Indian concepts of mental health and illness. The results are interesting conceptual developments. An example is the concept of the 'person'. The Hindu dividual, an idea Kakar derived from the anthropologist McKim Marriott, is contrasted to the Western individual. The dividual is fluid and temporarily in integration, open, dyadic rather than monadic, and has an internally heterogeneous structure. While Kakar is conscious of the need to avoid overemphasizing the difference between Western and Indian persons, his work does support the need for a radical rethinking of the sciences concerned with mental health.

The Decolonization of the Social Sciences

In many former European colonies, there was a need for the colonial administration to have broad-ranging and detailed information of the civilizations and societies they dominated. The social sciences were an indispensable element of colonial capitalism. Whole societies were literally catalogued, with information on cities and villages, tribes and ethnic groups, religious orders, historical origins, statecraft, and economy—all meticulously noted. As the colonialist nature of the social sciences did not disappear upon independence, the first task postcolonial intellectuals were called upon to perform was the decolonization of the cultural domain, including academia (ben Jelloun, 1985: 70). Decolonization implies independence from the science of the former colonial master and a critical scientific policy founded upon the comparative study of 'underanalysed (or rather badly analysed) countries' (Khatibi, 1967).

As long as the social sciences were not decolonized, postcolonial societies would only participate in the development of the social sciences as objects of research undertaken largely by Americans and Europeans. The decolonization of the social sciences meant, therefore, a rupture with Western culture. This necessitated, first of all, that postcolonial scholars not only took charge of their reality but examined and challenged the scientific and political foundations of the work on their own societies undertaken by colonial or colonized minds (Zghlal & Karoui, 1973).

In geography this meant, among other things, critiquing the fundamental concept of diffusionism. Diffusionism, or the belief that culture changes only through contact with an outside source, resonated with modernization theory's emphasis on the diffusion of transnational capital and its associated ideology, attitudes and political culture from the West to underdeveloped regions as the prescription for development (Blaut, 1994: 174). Both diffusionism and the ideological underpinnings of modernization theory have been critiqued by geographers (Blaut, 1970, 1973, 1977, 1994; Brookfield, 1975). Such critiques take their cues from the political economy literature that includes both the 'circulationist' and 'productionist' schools (Higgot, 1980, cited in Forbes, 1981: 70). Circulationists (Amin, 1974, 1975; Emmanuel, 1972; Wallerstein, 1974, 1979, 1980) focus on the mechanisms of exchange of the world-economy, while productionists (Godelier, 1974; Meillassoux, 1972; Rey, 1975) look at the structure of production within the periphery.

These counter modernization theories are, in Blaut's words, 'intensely geographic', although few of their adherents are geographers (1973: 22). He suggests that the theory of underdevelopment redraws the *mappa mundi* in that it presents an alternative world historical atlas since 1492. In contrast to modernization theory which views the causes of underdevelopment as internal and cultural, and in need of First World external aid and investment—the theory of underdevelopment postulates that it is due to the evolution of a global system of exploitation, which has been growing and spreading since 1492. He isolates the significant moments of this evolution represented through plates in a revised edition of the historical atlas. Plate I depicts a traditional, feudal Europe in 1492. Plate II shows the Europe of 1789 when European merchants are gaining political control over their societies and spearheading industrialization. Plates III and IV are the New World in 1820 and the Old World hundred years later, respectively. They both display the classical colonialist form of exploitation. Finally, Plate V is the present, depicting the newest phase of underdevelopment, i.e, neo-colonialism (Blaut, 1973: 23).

In Tunisia, decolonization was expressed in the desire of researchers to direct the changes which the social and political structures were undergoing (ben Jelloun, 1985: 71). The decolonization of sociology in North Africa and the subsequent birth of Maghrebi sociology meant that research was to be directed more towards local situations without commitment to institutionalized theories, such as functionalism, which serve to legitimize the established order. It also meant that the researcher had to avoid voluntary incarceration in the ivory tower in order to be continuously in touch with social reality. As a result, sociologists became suspect as a potential challenge to the state (ibid.: 72). Thus, the decolonization of sociology meant that sociology was to become politicized if it was to become relevant.

The resistance to colonialist discourse also takes place in the humanities. Recognizing that literary discourse is a great seducer, Zawiah Yahya (1994: 17-19) calls for a resistance that provides an alternative reading of European texts by seeking to demystify colonialist power, resist the colonialist writer's marginalization of the native voice and destabilize the ideological structure of the text. Arguing that the most effective way of deconstructing Western discourse is by using its own tools of critical theory, Zawiah wants not only to dismantle colonialism's signifying system but also to articulate the silences of the native by liberating the suppressed in discourse (ibid.: 27). As in the human sciences, in the arts and humanities also one sees the use of 'the language of the oppressor' while at the same time rejecting colonialist definitions and transcending the boundaries of colonialist discourse (Boehmer, 1995: 105-6).

The Globalization of the Social Sciences

A good example of the discourse on the globalization of social science comes from geography. Ron Johnston (1985: 325) argues for the globalization of geography and against its myopia and parochialism. Globalization here refers to the presentation of the world in its full diversity for the aim of creating international awareness and peace (Johnston, 1985: 334; Taylor, 1993: 182). Nevertheless, the globalization that is argued for here must be distinguished from the global view that arose within the imperialist context (Hudson, 1977).The origins of the modern discipline of geography lie in the exploration and trade activities of the Europeans in the sixteenth century, when much of the non-European world was 'discovered', visited, explored (Taylor, 1993: 182-83) and, finally, colonized.

European political and economic superiority was reflected in the geographical monologue in which Europe 'told the rest who and what they were in its new world' (Taylor, 1993: 184). By the end of the nineteenth century as geography began to consolidate itself as a university discipline it founded itself on the social theory of environmentalism (ibid.: 185). Such a globalized discipline was to be an imperialistic tool in terms of, for example, mapping regions of the world by economic value (Herbertson, 1910). This presupposed a division of the world into a white, civilized core and a non-white barbaric periphery (Taylor, 1993: 186-87).

If the formative period of the first globalized geography belonged to the end of the nineteenth century, the second globalized geography was being thought through at the end of the twentieth century. The beginnings of this are to be seen in the interest geographers are taking in global issues such as the food problem, transnational corporations and the international division of labour (Dicken, 1986; Grigg, 1985; Tarrant, 1980; Taylor & Thrift, 1982). The 'geo' in geography was rediscovered in the 1980s (Taylor, 1993: 191).

While this new geography is still in its formative stage, whatever its content might be, it would no longer be a discipline in which Europeans were the subject and the rest of the world the object. The geographical monologue would be replaced by a dialogue between many geographies as there would not be one objective description of a place but alternative geographies (Taylor, 1993: 194). These alternatives shy away from the spatial dualisms of North/South, core/periphery and developed/developing which tend to 'impose a negative uniformity upon non-Western societies' (Bell, 1994: 184). Therefore, what is needed are alternative historical and contemporary geographies and, more generally, social sciences that are able to transcend these dualisms and can account for the diversity in political economy within the Third World (ibid.: 188).

Furthermore, alternative geographies and other social sciences also question fundamental concepts, tenets, and processes of modernity such as the superiority of industrialization and technological progress, and highlight varieties of indigenous knowledge utilized by communities coping with ecological change. The goal of alternative theories is to reveal the diversity in historical, social and geographical contexts of the Third World. There are alternatives to the established corpus of theories, concepts and methods that can be indigenously generated.

Sacralization of the Social Sciences

The project of sacralization of knowledge is to be found in many of the religious traditions of the world including Christianity and Islam. The challenge of secularism had led Christian social theory to make a compromise with secular rationality in terms of accepting the readings of reality provided by the human sciences and then transposing them into theology and social ethics (Milbank, 1991; Troeltsch, 1931). Sacralized social theory, by way of a political theology, challenges the direct relationship between the state and the individual by calling for the decentralization of power. Such a mode of thinking, when transferred to the Third World, emerges as liberation theology, which attempts to both rediscover the social meaning of the Gospel for Third World countries waging wars against injustice as well as combine theology with a materialist interpretation of history (Boff, 1985; Guttierez, 1983).

The Islamization of knowledge aims to restore religious experience and spirituality to its rightful place in knowledge seeking activities by means of the sacralization of the human sciences. These are understood to have been desacralized or secularized in the West. Sacralized knowledge or *scientia sacra* is knowledge that 'lies at the heart of every revelation and is the center of that circle which encompasses and defines tradition' (Nasr, 1981: 130). The relative insignificance of sacred knowledge today points to the need for a science which can 'relate the various levels of knowledge once again to the sacred' (Nasr, 1993: 173).

The idea of the 'Islamization of knowledge' first made its appearance at a conference held in 1977 in Mecca and was conceived of by Syed Muhammad Naquib al-Attas who raised the issue in the context of his discussion on the concept of education in Islam.[6] At the same conference, the late Ismail R. al-Faruqi presented a paper on the Islamization of the social sciences.[7] The idea of Islamic science and, in particular, Islamic methodology were themes in the works of Seyyed Hossein Nasr,[8] who had spoken of the need for all knowledge originating from without the Muslim world to be integrated into the Islamic world view and 'Islamicized'.[9] Al-Faruqi established in the United States the International Institute of Islamic Thought and Civilization (ISTAC) in the 1980s. The activities of the institute are not only restricted to the dissemination of the notion of Islamization of knowledge, but also encompass programmes aimed at the Islamization of the various disciplines in the social sciences (Al-Faruqi, 1982). As far as the social sciences are concerned, what is meant by the Islamization of knowledge?

According to al-Attas, the sciences that originated in the West and which have been disseminated throughout the world do not necessarily represent true knowledge due to their being infused with Western elements and key concepts (al-Attas, 1978: 131). Islamization of knowledge requires, first of all, the isolation of the elements and key concepts in the human sciences that constitute Western culture and civilization such as the dualistic vision of society, humanism, and the 'emulation of the allegedly universal reality of drama and tragedy in the spiritual or transcendental, or inner life of man, making drama and tragedy real and dominant elements in human nature and existence...' (al-Attas, 1978: 131–32, 155). Once knowledge is free of these Western elements and key concepts it is then infused with Islamic elements and key concepts, thereby making it true knowledge, that is, in harmony with the essential nature (*fitra*) of man (al-Attas, 1978: 156; 1980: 43). The Islamization of knowledge is the liberation of knowledge from interpretations based on secular ideology (al-Attas, 1980: 43).

The methodology of Islamized knowledge is to be based on the science of exegesis and commentary which employ the interpretive techniques of *tafsir* and *ta'wil*. The first refers to the interpretation of the firm (*muhkama*) verses of the Qur'an. *Tafsir* is based on the objective reading of the verses of the Qur'an and there is 'no room for interpretation based on subjective readings, or understandings based merely upon the idea of historical relativism...' (al-Attas, 1980: 4). *Ta'wil*, on the other hand, is an intensive form of *tafsir* and refers to the allegorical interpretation of the obscure and ambiguous (*mutashabiha*) verses of the Qur'an (al-Attas, 1989: 30). al-Attas was later to found and direct the International Institute of Islamic Thought and Civilization (ISTAC), established in 1987 (al-Attas, 1998: 33).

Modern science, with its rejection of the varied facets of a particular reality, reduced symbols to facts and was partly responsible for the desacralization of knowing and being that is so characteristic of the modern world (Nasr, 1981: 212). On the other hand, for Muslims, the universe was seen as an Islamic cosmos to be apprehended by Muslim minds and eyes transformed by the spirit and form of the Qur'an. All knowledge is to be integrated into a totality in accordance with the doctrine of *tauhid* (Unity of God) (ibid.: 8–9).

Also related to the sacralization of knowledge is Mahatma Gandhi's critique of education, which has had a profound impact, directly or indirectly on the thinking of many Indian and other scholars in the Third World. His critique of education is informed to a great extent by his views on Western civilization. As Gandhi once said, 'I bear no enmity towards the English, but I do towards their civilization' (Gandhi, 1995: 66). *Swaraj* (self-rule) involved not merely the expulsion of the British from India, but the eradication of the institutions of Western civilization that the British brought to India. Gandhi regarded modern civilization as evil, against morality and anti-religious. Indian civilization, on the other hand, is essentially spiritual. While modern civilization is preoccupied with the discovery and investigation of the laws of matter and strives to invent or discover the means of production and destruction, Indian civilization is more concerned with exploring spiritual laws. Gandhi's rejection of colonial education was part of his critique of Western civilization. The goal of education should be to restore India to her ancient spirituality and to found India upon *swadeshi* ideals (self-sufficiency). These required the turn to a spiritual and communal life. Noting that the introduction of cloth mills in India had destroyed hand-weaving occupations in various parts of India, Gandhi advocated the introduction of handicrafts in the school curriculum. These were to include spinning, weaving, leather work, pottery, metal work, basket weaving and book binding, traditionally occupations of the lower caste groups. Gandhi's idea of restructuring education was quite radical in that it favoured the lower castes and at the same time was directed towards making schools self-supporting. Furthermore, manual work would be elevated to a higher status and education would function to bring about a balance between body and spirit (Burke, 2005; Gandhi, 1993, 1997; Nanda, 1989).

While many of these ideas are original and interesting, a social science informed by Gandhi's critique of Western civilization and his normative views on education is yet to develop. Among those influenced by Gandhi was D.P. Mukerji (1958: 225, cited in Madan, 1994: 20) who made recommendations for the study of Gandhi's views on machines and technology before India went ahead with its large scale technological development. Nevertheless, Mukerji was aware of Gandhi's shortcomings when he said that Gandhi had not dealt with the problem of how India could absorb the new social forces released by the West (ibid.: 35).

Subaltern Studies

Subaltern Studies formally originated in India in 1982 with the publication of the first volume of a series by the same name, initially published by Oxford University Press in Delhi. The editor of *Subaltern Studies I*, Ranajit Guha (1982a: vii), in the preface defined the subaltern as the 'general attribute of subordination in South Asian society whether this is expressed in terms of class, caste, age, gender and office or in any other way'.

Subaltern Studies began as an attempt to reinterpret and rewrite the history of the Indian working class. It borrowed the notion of the 'subaltern' from Gramsci and was influenced by the growing number of works in the United States and Britain that critiqued state-centred or elitist approaches to the study of history and, instead, rewrote history 'from below'.

E.P. Thompson's *The Making of the English Working Class* (1963) is often referred to as the inspiration behind such studies (Ludden, 2002: 5).

Subaltern Studies began as a conscious rejection of colonial elitist and bourgeois-nationalist elitist approaches to the study of Indian history. It aims to show that the formation of the Indian nation and the development of nationalist consciousness were not exclusively elite achievements (Guha, 1982b: 1). There was an autonomous domain, parallel to that of elite politics—which was a domain of the indigenous or colonial elite—but not originated from or dependent on it (ibid.: 2). The task of Subaltern Studies, therefore, was to develop an 'alternative discourse based on the rejection of the spurious and unhistorical monism characteristic of its view of Indian nationalism and on the recognition of the co-existence and interaction of the elite and subaltern domains of politics' (ibid.: 7). The writings of the Subaltern Studies scholars depart from modernization discourse in that they seek to challenge elitist perspectives in historiography and replace them with subaltern ones (Prakash, 1992: 8). In doing so, the 'agency of change is located in the insurgent or "subaltern"' (Spivak, 1987: 197).

The original Subaltern Studies involved works of a highly empirical nature in the area of social, economic and political history, but in the mid-1980s the shift was more towards cultural history, critical theory and the study of subaltern subjectivity by employing postmodernist concepts and methods (Currie, 1995, cited in Ludden, 2002: 17). Subaltern Studies then tended to draw less and less for its empirical material from particular subaltern groups, turning instead to literary evidence of colonial constructions of culture and power (Ludden, 2002: 18). The logic of the postmodern turn, as it were, in Subaltern Studies as nicely summarized by Bahl (2000), is that they 'started with the idea that subalterns were autonomous in the Indian nationalist movement and actively participated in negotiating their situation. To prove their theory this school needed to find the subaltern voices which could be done only by reading the documents "against the grain" a method borrowed from the then dominating Western ideology of postmodernism and postcolonialism' (ibid.: 89).

Postcolonial Theory

The adoption of postmodernism by Subaltern Studies, then, is partly responsible for the emergence of postcolonialism as a variety of alternative discourse. The 'postcolonial' in postcolonialism can be understood in two broad senses. One concerns its claims with regard to the periodization of contemporary history and the other relates to the insights and theories that have been brought to bear upon the study of history, culture and society.

The first has to do with the declaration that we have undergone a transition from modernity to a postmodern age. These basic changes are alleged to have taken place not only in literature, and the visual and dramatic arts but also in our political economy. Emphasis has shifted from the mode of production or economic system to information technology, and the production of signification. It is claimed that history has moved beyond modernity into a post-industrial age in which the culture industry and new social movements take centre stage (Calhoun, 1993: 77-78). 'Postcolonial' here, then, is a descriptive label of the global condition following the period of colonialism (Dirlik, 1994: 332). This global condition is thematized through the focus on the condition of marginality or hybridity, the collapse of the nation-state, and the globalization of the electronic media (Ahmad, 1995: 10). The second sense in which we may understand the 'postcolonial' in postcolonialism, concerns the postmodernist theoretical position of a group of intellectuals, which stands apart from the historical claims of an epochal break. It is in this sense that postcolonialism departs from colonialism and modernism. There are techniques, principles, and theories labelled as postmodernist, which are helpful in the study of modernity and its problems in postcolonial societies. This departure has a number of aspects to it.

1. First is the departure from structuralism and this is where postmodernism has drawn from poststructuralism. This involves the critique of—the designative theory of language, the founding subject, grand or master narratives and general truth claims.
Postcolonial criticism repudiates the Eurocentric master narrative of modernization, in both its bourgeois and Marxist modes (Dirlik, 1994: 334). In bourgeois modernization the 'older project of colonial modernity was renovated and then deployed as economic development' (Prakash, 1990: 393). The Marxist narrative, on the other hand, accepts the teleological assumptions of bourgeois modernization but views the course of history as an 'incomplete narrative and unfulfilled promise, which invites completion and fulfillment' (ibid.: 396). In both cases, the Third World continues to be managed, directed and made to have aspirations in the image of the former colonial masters.

2. Second is the departure from foundationalism. Anti-foundationalism refers to an 'extension of the Nietzschean and Heideggerian critique of metaphysics into an attack on all claims of an external standpoint for judging truth' (Calhoun, 1993: 77). The will to truth is the will to look for the secret, underlying forces at work. Once underlying truths are discovered, that which does not conform is declared false. What is false is then subject to therapy and normalization (Foucault, 1980a: 68). Modern man is, therefore, subject to control by means of various policies of normalization. However, control is effected at the discursive level with the deployment of such fields of research and study as psychoanalysis, medicine, pedagogy, and others.

Postcolonialism's anti-foundationalism requires it to reject 'those modes of thinking which configure the third world in such irreducible essences as religiosity, underdevelopment, poverty, nationhood, non-Westerness; and it asks that we repudiate attempts to see third-world histories in terms of these quintessential principles' (Prakash, 1990: 384).

3. The third departure is from Marxism. Marxism is seen as useful for the analysis of economic processes but its neglect of language and culture render it an incomplete theory. Marxist philosophical anthropology assigns to labour the role of the foundation of humanity. A postmodernist position would be to assign this role to language. The logic of political economy is the cultural logic of capitalism and its analysis requires attention to the concept of the sign and the production of symbols (Baudrillard, 1975). This suggests specific ways in which language and power are linked. The analysis of power can no longer take law, prohibition, and state power as the model. Power is not to be understood in terms of prohibition, that is, in negative terms. In its positive forms, power is also wielded discursively, and this takes place not 'apart from or against power, but in the very space and as a means of its exercise' (Foucault, 1980a: 32). The understanding of power cannot be restricted to prohibition, restriction, punishment, and blockage.

Postcolonial criticism opposes the persistent continuity of colonialist knowledge in bourgeois and Marxist narratives (Prakash, 1992: 8–9) whether these operate to project the West as the centre of civilization or to legitimize modernization policies and strategies of normalization.

The Nationalization of the Social Sciences

Another frequently heard call for alternative social science is what I would refer to as, the nationalization of the social sciences. A definition of this concept can be brought out best by reference to some prominent examples from China, Taiwan, Korea,[10] India, Indonesia, and the Philippines.

In India, the nationalization of the social sciences is understood as the simultaneous advancement of universal sciences. Original and significant contributions to international social science can only arise from decolonizing the mind and learning to nationalize problems. A national school [of social science] 'can add relevance, meaning and potency to our science; continued assent to the international system cannot' (Uberoi, 1968: 123). Indian social science is to be based on the *swaraj*-ist attitude of intellectual self-reliance. This does not mean that Indian social science would possess a distinctive method, for method in the philosophical sense is universal. It is at the level of theory, where method and observation are linked, that the *swaraj*-ist attitude has to be developed (Uberoi, 1974: 136). In the case of the development of an Indian school of structuralism, this would entail establishing a dialogue between the Sanskrit tradition and Western structuralism. Sanskrit phonology, syntax and semantics have potential contributions to make in this regard, while Western structuralism is domesticated (ibid.: 149).

In Indonesia, the call for Indocentric approaches were initially made by Dutch scholars such as J.C. van Leur (1955) and G.J. Resink (1950). During the colonial period, there was a tendency to look at Indonesia from the points of view of Arabia, India and the Netherlands. A quarter of a century later, however, more regio-centric views, of which the Javacentric view was an important component, began to appear. The regio-centric view served to heighten an appreciation of the hitherto underestimated indigenous cultural influences in Indonesia and downplay the overestimated role of foreign influences (Resink, 1950: 22-23). Meanwhile, an Indocentric view began to develop among Dutch and Indonesian scholars alike, with a focus on sub-elite social groups and the consideration of Indonesia as a nation (van den Muijzenberg, 1988: 13; Resink, 1950: 23, 26). Indocentric writing tended to develop only after Indonesians began to influence their own destiny thereby creating the possibility of a national history (Kartodirdjo, 1982: 29-30; Resink, 1952-53: 374). Another example of nationalized social science is Filipinology or the study of Filipino society through the use of indigenous concepts and perspectives (Salazar, 1992: xiv).

The nationalization of the social sciences, with its particular variants such as sinicization, *swaraj*-ist social science, Filipinology, and Indocentric social science, implies the derivation of concepts and theories from the national culture and their application to the study of the nation. In the course of doing so, Western social science is not repudiated but rather domesticated. In this way, the nationalization of social science advances the universalization of social science by multiplying national voices in the social sciences.

The cases of China and Taiwan deserve attention as well. Sociology was introduced in China at the beginning of this century with the translation of Spencer's *Study of Sociology* in 1903 (Gipouloux, 1989: 52; Gransow, 1985: 140). It was abolished in 1952 with historical materialism becoming its substitute (Gipouloux, 1989: 55–56). Marxist theory was to account for all social psychological, economic and political phenomena (Lin, 1987: 127). The discipline was reestablished in 1979 as a result of the perception that rapid economic growth forecasted for the last two decades of the century, accompanied by fundamental changes in lifestyles, values and mentalities, necessitated the restoration of sociology (Gipouloux, 1989: 56). The nationalization of sociology in China took the form of sinicization.

Calls for a sinicized sociology had been heard in China since the 1930s, although the understanding of what sinicization entailed varied greatly. For some, sinicization meant social research directed towards social reform. For others it referred to comparative community research (Gransow, 1993: 101). A more theoretical approach saw sinicized sociology as rooted in a national Chinese culture (ibid.: 101–2). It is this understanding of sinicization that corresponds to the nationalization of social science because it involves the 'incorporation into sociology as a discipline the distinctive characteristics of Chinese society' (Lin, 1987: 130). This is to be distinguished from Chinese sociology which refers to the intellectual and professional activities of sociologists in China.

For Lin, the sinicization of sociology could be measured by the degree to which Chinese characteristics attained a level of generality and were introduced into sociology (Lin, 1987: 130). Lin's notion of sinicization came under attack because it equated culture with traditional Chinese culture in neo-Confucianist terms. What was needed, it was argued, was a Chinese school of sociology—a national sociology inspired by, and based on the diversity in the national culture of the People's Republic of China, which included traditional, modern, national and foreign elements (Gransow, 1993: 108). According to another line of thinking, the revival of sociology in China should be equated with the establishment of a sinicized Marxist sociology (Cheng & So, 1983: 484). The sinicization programme was seen to be legitimated by the demands of a Chinese flavoured socialism. Such a sociology was to consist of three positions (Gipouloux, 1989: 60-61; Gransow, 1985: 145). The first was the sinicization of the object and methods of sociological study, which meant the study of the laws of development of the social formation that constituted China as a nation. The second involved the unity of theory and practice on the basis of Marxism and foreign experiences.

A third position in China favoured the indigenization of sociology, but insisted on the necessity of internationalizing the discipline as well. Chinese sociology had hardly begun to equip itself with an orientation that gave it specificity and knowledge of foreign sociology and Chinese society was still far too fragmented for it to be presented in terms of a globalized social science (Gipouloux, 1989: 61).

The indigenization of the social sciences debate made its way into Taiwan by the early 1980s. It is interesting to note that at this time the terms indigenization (*bentuhua*) and sinicization (*zhongguohua*) were understood as being interchangeable by European observers. While most Taiwanese writers during this period used the term 'sinicization of social science',[11] European commentaries on these works used the term indigenization (Gransow, 1993; Schmutz, 1989) to describe the same movement.[12] In fact, the distinction is important to the Taiwanese. C.K. Hsu (1991) noted that sinicization is the recontextualization of Western theory with China as the point of reference. Taiwan, having its own history and culture is in need of its own recontextualization, properly referred to as indigenization (ibid.: 35).[13] Hsu would lay emphasis on Taiwan as the subject matter of indigenized social science. Hence, the inapplicability of the term sinicization. Symbolic of this stance was the formal change in name of the Chinese Sociological Association in Taipei to the Taiwanese Sociological Association.[14] The use of the term indigenization in all these cases is consistent with nationalization, as the reference point is the nation-state.

Delinking

Asian social science communities are dependent to the extent that their selection of problem areas and methods, and the standards of excellence that they uphold, are derived from other social science communities. The theory of delinking recognizes an imbalance in the production of social sciences across societies and the resultant division of labour between the producers and consumers of such knowledge (Oommen, 1991: 67). Thus, it is no coincidence that the great economic powers are also the great social science powers (Garreau, 1985: 64, 81, 89).

The dependence of Third World academic communities on First World social science establishments and institutions along these four dimensions constitute the vertical relations upon which global social science is founded. Therefore, the proponents of academic dependency theory advocated delinking from the main centres of social science in the West to allow for the development of autonomous or indigenized social sciences (Garreau, 1985: 114-15). Academic aid from the West is seen to distort the development of the normal process of scholarship. It would be wise, it is held, to declare a moratorium on foreign academic aid for a period to allow time for the consolidation of work in the social sciences (Kumar, 1968: 34).

Deschooling

The notion of deschooling, of course, belongs to Ivan Illich (1973) whose theory of education is well known. Illich spoke out against compulsory schooling because it inculcated in children a blind and critical acceptance of a highly rationalized and discipline-oriented social order. Schools also tend to be great levellers, reducing people to the lowest common denominator and, therefore, precluding the development of individual creativity. While Illich did not call for the abolishment of all forms of educational organization, he did suggest that education be less structured and made more available to children and adults alike, with curricula personalized to suit the individual needs of students.

Giddens (1993: 417) notes that while such proposals may seem utopian under the present structuring of economic life, the possibility of a reduction in paid work in the future would make Illich's ideas more plausible. From a leftist point of view, as the possibility for taking over the means of production diminish, the goal should be to 'free oneself from work' (Gorz, 1982, cited in Giddens, 1993: 332-33) in order to develop one's interests and talents to potential.

In the context of the Third World, deschooling in Illich's sense is less likely to be an option as the problem in many countries is the lack of education and not too much of it. Nevertheless, Illich's point with regard to the need to revamp education is well-taken. There is a need to study the hidden curricula of the educational system, to make education more widely diffused, and to strike a better balance between data acquisition on the one hand and critical and creative thinking on the other, and to introduce more indigenous content in syllabi. This would be a vital prerequisite to any programme that aims to make the social sciences more relevant to society. For example, any serious efforts at endogenous intellectual creativity or decolonization of knowledge would require the introduction of more indigenous literature in syllabi.[15]

The Marginal Status of Alternative Discourses

If alternative discourses are so numerous, this raises questions regarding the nature of the problem. The claim of this study is that alternative discourses in Asian social science remain on the margins of global social science. This begs the question of what we mean by the marginality of alternative discourses. Take for example, the social thought of Ibn Khaldun, José Rizal, Tagore or Gandhi. They get scattered attention in courses despite the fact that whole books are written on them. Yet, they rarely appear in courses or as topics of seminars or conferences on par with Marx, Weber, and Durkheim. This is because their ideas have not been developed over the centuries or decades by theorists, to make their work more systematic like sociological theory and, therefore, more accessible. As a result, they are often mentioned but not methodologically or theoretically encountered and reconstructed as sociologists or sociological theorists. A host of non-western thinkers like Ibn Khaldun, José Rizal, Tagore and Gandhi remain marginal because of the continuing Eurocentrism. Their marginal status means that their works do not receive the kind of attention that is required for an approach or perspective to become part of the canon.

The kind of attention that I am referring to has six aspects or levels: (a) metatheory this refers to the attention to, among other things, the epistemological and methodological dimensions underlying the thought of non-Western thinkers; (b) theory refers to the systematic exposition, analysis and critique of non-Western thought with reference to the main concepts utilized, the type of evidence marshalled, the assumptions about the subject matter, and empirical verification; (c) theory building refers to the abstraction from non-Western thought to generate what one might call neo-Khaldunian, neo-Rizalian, or neo-Tagorian theory and applying this to space-times other than their own; (d) critical assessment of existing scholarship that has attempted applications of these non-Western thinkers; (e) teaching these non-Western thinkers in mainstream sociology and social science courses from mainstream sociology or sociological theory textbooks; and (f) dissemination via regular panels or papers at mainstream conferences in the social sciences on these thinkers and their ideas.

It is only when all this is done that we can say that non-Western thinkers and their ideas are institutionalized in a discipline and not, therefore, neglected.

The Critique of Alternative Discourses

The enumeration of alternative discourses listed above is not meant to be exhaustive, nor are the types mutually exclusive. There are some overlaps between the different types of orientations. For example, Subaltern Studies sees itself as being engaged in the decolonization of knowledge. No attempt to develop an elaborate typology of mutually exclusive categories was attempted here. Neither have I entered into a detailed critique of each of the orientations that presents itself as an alternative discourse. These two tasks will be left to another project. What I have done in this chapter is to detail the variety that is to be found in discourses that see themselves, in one way or another, as alternatives to the dominant Eurocentric social sciences. What I do in subsequent chapters is to critically assess alternative discourses as a whole. Chapter Five looks at two varieties of alternative discourses, that is, nativist and autonomous social science. It argues that the main divide within alternative discourses is between these two types. Chapter Six raises the problem of the lack of conceptualization of relevance and irrelevance in the social sciences and offers such a conceptualization. Chapter Seven discusses the relationship between alternative discourses and power and Chapter Eight discusses the question of teaching alternative discourses.

Having covered thus far both theories of the state of the social sciences as well as responses to them in the form of the rise of alternative discourses, the next four chapters focus on a number of problems associated with alternative discourses. These are problems that in one way or another impinge on the ability of alternative discourses to develop and make their impact felt on mainstream social science. Chapter Five discusses the problem of nativism, Chapter Six the lack of the conceptualization of irrelevance, Chapter Seven the relationship between alternative discourses and power, and Chapter Eight the problem of thematizing Eurocentrism in the teaching of the social sciences.

Notes

1. For other examples see Bennagen (1980), Enriquez (1994), Kleden (1986) and Siti Hawa (1991).
2. See Kim (1996b) for examples of indigenized social science at the levels of concepts derived from the classical tradition of China and Korea and from the everyday practices of the Korean people.
3. Syed Hussein Alatas, personal communication, Manila, 29 May 1996.
4. Zeus Salazar, personal communication, Manila, 1 June 1996.
5. Kim Kyong-Dong, personal communication, Seoul, 21 June 1996.
6. For the proceedings of this conference see al-Attas (1979). See also al-Attas (1978: Chap Five) and (1980).
7. Al-Faruqi (1981).
8. See Nasr (1964, 1968, 1976, 1980, 1981, 1993).
9. Personal correspondence with Professor Seyyed Hossein Nasr, April 10, 1995.
10. The cases of China, Taiwan and Korea have been discussed in some detail in Alatas (1998a).
11. The beginning of the sinicization movement in Taiwanese social sciences was marked by the convening of a conference by the same name in 1982. See Yang & Wen (1982) and Sun (1993).
12. On sinicization see also Chan (1993, 1994).
13. I am grateful to Dr Hsu for translating some passages in his article for me.
14. This took place on 16 December 1995. I understand that beginning with issue no. 19, the *Chinese Journal of Sociology* became known as the *Taiwanese Journal of Sociology* [communication with Dr Michael Hsiao Hsin-Huang].
15. 'Educationists call for more indigenous literature in syllabuses', *Straits Times*, 22 April 1995.

5

Nativist or Autonomous Social Science: A Clash of Orientations

Among the varieties of alternative discourse presented in the social sciences are the two opposing attitudes or orientations of nativism and autonomy. What the two orientations have in common is their disdain for intellectual tutelage and mental captivity, as well as their revolt against Eurocentric and Orientalist social science. The resemblance however is soon replaced by a stark contrast in attitudes towards knowledge from the West.

Nativism

The problem of academic imperialism, mental captivity and the uncritical adoption of Western concepts and research agendas had become so pervasive in the social scientific traditions of developing societies that there were, from time to time, reactionary calls among critics of Western social science. The result is a high degree of intolerance toward the Western social sciences in terms of theories, methodologies, and the selection of problems. Consider the following viewpoint from a Muslim.

The fact that concerns us here most is that all the social sciences of the West reflect social orders and have no relationship or relevance to Muslims, and even less to Islam. If we learn and apply Western social sciences, then we are not serious about Islam (Siddiqui, n.d.).

This attitude can be captured under the notion of Orientalism in reverse or nativism. The idea of Orientalism in reverse was developed by the Syrian philosopher, Sadiq Jalal al-'Azm (1984). He quotes from the work of a fellow Syrian, Georges Saddikni, on the Arabic notion of man (*insan*) which runs thus, the philosophy of Hobbes is based on his famous saying that 'every man is a wolf unto other men', while, on the contrary, the inner philosophy implicit in the word *insan* preaches that 'every man is a brother unto other men' (Saddikni, cited in al-'Azm, 1984: 368). Al-'Azm (1984) then continues with an assessment of the above:

> I submit that this piece of so-called analysis and comparison contains, in a highly condensed form, the entire apparatus of metaphysical abstractions and ideological mystifications so characteristic of Ontological Orientalism and so deftly and justly denounced in Said's book. The only new element is the fact that the Orientalist essentialist ontology has been reversed to favour one specific people of the Orient (ibid.: 368).

Orientalism in reverse involves an essentialist approach to both the Orient and the Occident and is, therefore, a form of auto-Orientalism. This can be illustrated by the Japanese case. There is a tradition in Japanese sociology that is defined by *nihonjinron* (theories of Japanese people) which are informed by essentialized views on Japanese society, with the stress being on cultural homogeneity and historical continuity. This remains squarely in the tradition of Western scholarship on Japan with the difference that the knowing subjects are Japanese. Hence, the term auto-Orientalism (Lie, 1996: 5). In her paper, Sinha (1998) notes that Indian scholars continue to 'reproduce the image of India as an exotic "other"', and through the particular project of indigenizing anthropology, the image of India as an "exotic" self' (ibid.: 18–19), thereby continuing the Orientalist tradition in the form of auto-Orientalism. There is a hint of nativism in statements such as, 'in choosing our intellectual forebears we must look increasingly to Indian sociologists rather than to sociologists of India' (Guha, 1989: 343) or, 'one has to abandon thinking in terms of Western categories of thought in order to arrive at the threshold of an understanding of the Indian tradition' (Sharma, 1990: 253). Pertierra (1997: 25) has similar concerns when he warns that indigenized social science in the Filipino context 'risks essentializing Filipinohood by reducing its differences' because of the 'insistence on unproblematically using the nation as its referent point...' at the expense of the personal, global, local and other referents. Also, consider this statement about the Indian-ness of anthropology:

> But it does not mean that social anthropology in India should overlook what may be termed 'Indianness' of its science. Perhaps to some extent it has not done so, as it has not progressed under the spell of unthinking imitation...Then we have had our own sets of social thinkers who have given thought to the

social problems from time to time and who have also given direction to them... Also, with the series of thinkers, ancient scriptures like the *Vedas*, *Upanishads*, *Smritis*, *Puranas* and epics etc. are full of social facts and they need to be studied carefully to develop 'Indianness' in the social anthropology of India, which should be specially used in the study of cultural process and civilizational history of India (Vidyarthi, 1980: 20, cited in Sinha, 1998: 16).

This presents an interesting case for nativism if Indian-ness is understood in a way that includes some and excludes others. Pertierra's concerns expressed above applies as much to the Indian as it does in the Filipino context.

The logical consequence of Orientalism in reverse and auto-Orientalism is nativism. This refers to the trend of going 'native' among Western and local scholars alike, in which the native's point of view becomes the criterion by which descriptions and analyses are to be judged. This may entail a near total rejection of Western knowledge or an attitude of rejection, based on the national or cultural origins of ideas rather than their utility, cogency and precision. This trend is so pervasive that it effects the casual assessment of the idea of alternative discourses by those who are not very familiar with it but who nevertheless end up forming opinions based on extreme reactions in circulation among some nativists.

The type of anthropology that Evans (1997) wants to typify as indigenized but which is at odds with most definitions of indigenization of social science, is closer to the idea of nativism. This is an anthropology that is informed by a problematic notion of indigeneity, as pointed out by Evans, and which makes claims such as 'only the Chinese can really understand Chinese culture and society', and so on (1997: 13). Similarly, van Bremen warns of the danger that scholarship faces of the, 'reappearance in places of the idea that anthropological knowledge and scholarship is grounded in an ethnic membership, or even the property of a presumed race, as proclaimed by some anthropologists today' (Kuwayama & van Bremen, 1997: 64).

As Said (1995) states:

> The question is not whether we should read more black literature or less literature by white men. The issue is excellence—we need everything, as much as possible, for understanding the human adventure in its fullest, without resorting to enormous abstractions and generalizations, without replacing Euro-centrism with other varieties of ethnocentrism or, say, Islamo-centrism or Afro-centrism or gynocentrism. Is it a game of substitution? That's where intellectuals have to clarify themselves (ibid.: 318).

Apart from nativism, another question that emerges from time to time is the extent to which the indigenization of anthropology is a project in service of the state? In fact, a vast majority of the proponents of the indigenization of anthropology in particular—and the social sciences in general—would distance themselves from this political stance. This is not to say that such scholars are averse to working with the state or in engaging in policy-related research. Nevertheless, they do not associate the indigenization of anthropology to mean the realignment of the discipline with the objectives of the state.

The nationalization of the social sciences is a process that had been taking place *pari passu* with the indigenization of the social sciences. The case of the sinicization of Marxist sociology in China is associated with the project of the nationalization of the social sciences that, for example, legitimized the Chinese version of socialism and China as a nation (Alatas, 1998a: 75–76). But, because of the nationalist connotations of the term sinicization, many Taiwanese anthropologists and sociologists eventually dropped the term. They found the term indigenization more acceptable, as their subject matter was the recontextualization of their disciplines vis-à-vis Taiwan, and not China (Hsu, 1991: 35).[1] But in this case, indigenization appears to be synonymous with Taiwanization. It is not surprising, therefore, that many understand indigenization as referring to the development of a nationalized social sciences. As Pertierra (1997: 12) notes, while there may be a quest to generate an indigenous Filipino psychology, there are no demands for an Ifugao one. Indian anthropologists similarly lament that the indigenization of anthropology had failed to take into account the social and cultural diversity of the country. Instead, it posited the possibility of an 'Indian' anthropology as projecting a homogeneous Indian viewpoint or way of thinking (Sinha, 1998: 24). As noted by an Indian scholar, 'there are multiple versions of indigenization, including those popularized by the multinational foundations as well as ruling classes. The tragedy of indigenization is its failure to take account of the country's socio-cultural diversity and multiple centres of culture and history' (Pathy, 1988: 18, cited in Sinha, 1998: 18).

The danger of anthropology aligning itself too closely with the interests of the state is all the more apparent when it is realized that in many developing societies, a great deal of anthropological research is funded by governments rather than private foundations, for instance, as is evident in India (Sinha, 1998). Competition for funds often results in anthropologists seeking to demonstrate their utility in policy formulation and programmatic change (ibid.: 27). Relevant here is Shamsul's (1995) discussion of the problems faced by the social sciences in Malaysia and Indonesia referred to as the 'kratonization' of the social sciences. By this he means the fragmentation of the social sciences into 'government versus academic versus private sector types of social science' (ibid.: 108). When priorities are dictated by extra-academic considerations, then research agenda and writing tend to be dominated by 'policy-oriented matters or profit-motivated business issues' (Shamsul, 1995: 101).[2] This is an important issue that poses a challenge to the social sciences from within a nation's borders while the problems of academic dependency and academic imperialism originate from outside. To the extent that alternative discourses see themselves as liberating discourses, they may be compromised by too close an association with the state and being defined at the level of the nation by glossing over internal diversities.

Autonomous Social Science

Opposing both nativism and the nation-state as the bases of alternative discourse is the idea of autonomous social science, a conception developed by Syed Hussein Alatas (1972a).

The logical consequence of an awareness of the problem of the captive mind is the development of an autonomous social science tradition that would function to eliminate or restrict the intellectual demonstration effect of the captive mind (Alatas, 1972a: 20). An autonomous social science tradition is defined as one which independently raises problems, creates concepts and creatively applies methodologies without being intellectually dominated by another tradition (Alatas, 2002: 151). This does not mean that there are no influences from, and no learning involved from other traditions. Ideas are not to be rejected on the grounds of their national or cultural origins.

Speaking for the Asian context, Alatas (2002: 151) defines an autonomous social science tradition as one which links social science research and thinking to specifically Asian problems. Such a social science tradition would raise its own problems and develop concepts and methods that are appropriate to the treatment of those problems and it would not isolate itself from knowledge from the West and elsewhere. In this regard, Alatas (ibid.: 153) distinguishes between three types of knowledge:

1. Universally valid knowledge.
2. Knowledge on the West, which is of little interest to developing societies.

3. Knowledge on the West, which is of comparative value to developing societies.

On universal scientific knowledge, the task is to distinguish the universal from the particular. An example would be the concept of feudalism. The concept has been applied to the study of pre-colonial Malaya without dealing with the universal and particular elements of European feudalism. If we wish to apply a concept to areas outside the time and place of its origin, care must be taken to understand and retrieve its universal core (Alatas, 2002: 153). Knowledge on the West that is of little relevance to Asia is easy to isolate. What requires more effort is the identification of knowledge of Western origin, which is of comparative value to Asia. The example given by Alatas (ibid.) is of the implementation of research and policies used in the fight against corruption in America.

Translating the notion of autonomous social science into practice involves the following aspects: (*a*) restricting the development of the captive mind by encouraging a process of selective and independent assimilation of knowledge from the West; (*b*) setting higher scientific and intellectual standards by comparing local and regional social sciences with their counterparts in developed countries; (*c*) encouraging interest in comparative studies in the training of social scientists; (*d*) creating awareness in government and among the elite in the development of an autonomous social science tradition; (*e*) obtaining the support of foreign scholars sympathetic to the idea; (*f*) attacking faulty development planning and the abuse of social science thought that arises from the workings of the captive mind with reference to concrete local targets; (*g*) awakening the consciousness of social scientists regarding their intellectual servitude (Alatas, 1972a: 20–21).

The idea of autonomous social science suggests that the problem is not merely one of the domination and control of the social sciences by the West. As implied in earlier chapters, the influence of Eurocentrism and mental captivity in the Third World social sciences is not due to a conscious and concerted effort on the part of Western social science establishments to dominate. Rather, the captive mind operates with Eurocentric categories and concepts within an overall structure of academic dependency that is global in reach. The domination is structural. The global division of labour discussed in Chapter Three conditions research and teaching in the social sciences in ways that leave the scholars unaware of the nature and function of their participation. Autonomous social science, therefore, refers to that social science that is conscious of this domination and influence and seeks to break out. The goal is to be autonomous and not anti-Western in orientation. It was mentioned above that nativist social science rejects Western knowledge *in toto* and may also result in an alignment with the interests of the state, unlike autonomous social science.

Autonomous social science is neither anti-Western nor pro-state. Rather, it is autonomous from both Western social science establishments and their ideas, and as well as the state—while at the same time open to ideas from them, or working with them. The chief traits of autonomous social science are autonomy in the conceptualization and prioritization of problems, in the development of research agenda, in the building of original theory, and in the conduct of empirical research. Autonomy leads to a constructive critique of Western knowledge as well as a serious consideration of non-Western sources of knowledge. Let us consider examples of both these dimensions of autonomous social science in relation to Western knowledge.

Constructive Critiques of Western Knowledge

First, as examples to the constructive critique of Western knowledge, I would like to offer the works of D.P. Mukerji, D.D. Kosambi, André Béteille and Surendra Munshi.

D.P. Mukerji's approach to Indian history and society relied on Marxism to a great extent, but he was not a slavish follower of Marx. Although some Marxist claim that Mukerji was one of them, he himself denied it, calling himself only a 'Marxologist' (Singh, 1973: 216, cited in Madan, 1994: 14). Mukerji was against Marx's view of Indian history as a stagnant Asiatic society with 'no known history' that required British colonial intervention to revolutionize it. Not content to be passive and to allow others to determine what Indian history was, Mukerji (1945: 46, cited in Madan, 1994: 15) wrote that our sole interest is to

> write and to act Indian History. Action means making.....Making involves changing, which in turn requires (*a*) a scientific study of the tendencies which make up this specificity, and (*b*) a deep understanding of the Crisis [which marks the beginning of no less than the end of an epoch]. In all these matters, the Marxian method...is likely to be more useful than other methods. If it is not, it can be discarded.

In other words, as observed by Madan, Mukerji wanted Marxist theories and concepts to be grounded in the empirical reality or specificity of Indian history (Mukerji, 1945: 45; 1946: 162ff, cited in Madan, 1994: 15). For example, Mukerji did not accept the simplistic formula explaining the development of Indian society from slave to feudal to capitalist.

Another example of a critical approach to Marxism can be found in the works of D.D. Kosambi (1965) who differed from many Indian Marxists in his use of the concept of 'mode of production'. Although he did understand history as the 'presentation in chronological order of successive changes in the means and relations of production', he was however, opposed to a mechanical and economically deterministic scheme in which the content of Indian historical data was sacrificed due to loyalty to the abstract Marxist formula (ibid.: 10). He differed from the majority of Soviet and Indian Marxists by insisting on the need to take into account the 'logic of Indian societal developments' and 'Indian cultural elements' (ibid.: 10). As a result, Kosambi's periodization of Indian history was a departure from earlier Marxist and non-Marxist attempts. He did not make use of the formula, slavery–feudalism–capitalism, nor that of ancient–medieval–modern. Kosambi tended to think of Indian history not in terms of fixed periods but rather 'main advances', such as the following: (*a*) the Indus valley culture; (*b*) Aryanization; (*c*) the settlement of the Gangetic alluvial plain; (*d*) 'primitive' feudalism; (*e*) 'pure' feudalism and (*f*) modern capitalism (Chattopadhyaya, 2002: xxvii).

On the related question of whether there was an Asiatic mode of production in India, Kosambi's (1965) discussion is worth taking seriously. He says that the central feature of the Asiatic mode of production as defined by Marx, that is, the regulation of the water supply—was true of the Punjab, the Gangetic plain and the Mysore plateau. To this characteristic he further added caste. He viewed caste as '*class at a primitive level of production, a religious method of forming social consciousness in such a manner that the primary producer is deprived of his surplus with the minimum coercion*' [italics in the original] (ibid.: 59). These two features, the central regulation of the water supply and caste, Kosambi (2002: 59) observed, were spread over the entire subcontinent making it clear to him that an Asiatic mode of production did exist in India. What is interesting about Kosambi's work here is that it is neither a dogmatic application nor an ideological rejection of Marxism, but the reworking of a Marxist concept in the light of Indian historical data.

Another example of the critique of Western scholarship is the work of André Béteille. Béteille (2002) was critical of the tendency amongst scholars such as Dumont, to imagine a sharp contrast in values, between India and the West. An example of such a contrast is the idea that India is characterized by holism and hierarchy while the West is characterized by individualism and equality (Dumont, 1966; 1977, cited in Béteille, 2002: 45). While Béteille recognizes the value of Dumont's contributions to the study of Indian society, he is very conscious of the limitations of Dumont's work as well. Granting that there is validity in Dumont's work in so far as it applies to the study of holism and hierarchy in traditional Indian society, Béteille makes the keen observation that in the India of today, equality and the individual are central concerns in the constitutional and legal systems and that it is impossible to understand Indian society without looking at its Constitution, law and politics (Béteille, 1986: 122). The point here is not to go into the details of Béteille's critique of Dumont and the debate between them (Dumont, 1987). What is important is the critique of ideas, in this case of Western scholarship, with the aim of refining concepts that may have been uncritically applied in non-European contexts.

My last example of the critique of Western knowledge is derived from the work of Surendra Munshi (1988) on Max Weber. As noted by Munshi, Weber has not been discussed seriously in India. In fact, the same can be said of many other Third World social science communities. There were attempts by foreign scholars to ask 'Weberian' questions about social change in India. Often, these turned out to be attempts by American scholars to provide Weberian correctives to historical materialism by using India as the empirical field (ibid.: 2). Munshi suggests that the issue of the correct image of India, while important in itself, should not blind one to the task of assessing Weber's contribution to the study of Hinduism whose value cannot be considered to be self-evident (ibid.). Munshi set himself the task of assessing Weber's study of Hinduism. After considering various points, Munshi came to the conclusion that of greater relevance in Weber's study is his observation that the rise of the European city was obstructed in the Indian context (ibid.: 26). Munshi goes on to note that the identification of India as an ideal negative type in Weber's work was to distinguish India from Western civilization in order to explain the emergence of modern, rational capitalism in Europe. Munshi characterizes this approach of Weber as founded upon 'exteriority'. Exteriority according to Said (1979) is the basis of Orientalism and it refers to the 'fact that the Orientalist, poet or scholar, makes the Orient speak, describes the Orient, renders its mysteries plain for and to the West…The principal product of this exteriority is of course representation' (ibid.: 20-21). This is the Orientalism which Weber endorses, which reduces Hinduism to magic and ritualism. What Weber does not see, among other things, is the conflict between the idealism of the *Vedanta* and the this-worldly philosophy of the *Lokayata*. This was possibly because of the Orientalist denial of the conflict of ideas in Indian thought (Munshi, 1988: 30). A critical exercise such as that undertaken by Munshi is significant in that it reveals how seminal thinkers such as Weber claimed universality for what were exclusively Occidental phenomena (ibid.: 31).

Non-Western Sources of Knowledge

I now turn to some examples of non-Western sources of social science knowledge. To illustrate, let me take an example from the historical study of the Iranian political economy. In the 1970s and 80s, the dominant influences in the analyses of Iranian pre-capitalist economies were either Western or Soviet Marxism. No attempt was made among Iranian students of political economy to be autonomous by considering another tradition while still incorporating elements of Marxist political economy. I have in mind the application of Ibn Khaldun's theory of state formation to the pre-capitalist political economy of Iran. The dynamics of the Safavi and Qajar states, for example, can be explained in terms of Ibn Khaldun's theory of state formation, the role of 'asabiyyah (a type of social cohesion also known as group feeling) and tribal military support. Nevertheless, beyond the mere recognition of Ibn Khaldun as a precursor or founder of sociology, there have been practically no works that aimed towards the integration of his ideas within a modern social scientific theoretical framework (for the exceptions see Alatas, 1993a; Carre, 1988; Cheddadi, 1980; Gellner, 1981; Lacoste, 1984; Laroui, 1988; Michaud, 1981). An example would be a Khaldunian explanation of the rise and decline of the Iranian Safavid state.

Ibn Khaldun's theory furnishes us with a means to understand social change but does not conceptualize the economic system. One option is to utilize the Marxist concept of mode of production and then explain changes in Safavid history in terms of co-existing modes of production. Marxist concepts maybe combined with Khaldunian ones such as 'asabiyyah (group feeling) and *mulk* and *khilafah* (both, types of authority) to theorize the Safavid Iranian state (Alatas, 1993a). A Khaldunian approach may also help in dealing with certain problems in the study of Indian history. Traditionalist-secularist debates surrounding the question of how and why India fell to Afghan-Turk invaders in the thirteenth century, even though the latter supposedly belonged to a less powerful civilization (Handa, 1982), can be enriched by a Khaldunian perspective on the superiority of tribal military power.

The autonomy in utilizing the Khaldunian perspective lies in the effort to take a non-Western tradition of thought seriously enough so that it becomes a source of concept-formation and theory-building. At the same time, Western social science is not abandoned but selectively assimilated. The building of an autonomous social science tradition, therefore, is a creative process involving an entire social science community. It has been suggested that an autonomous social sciences tradition would draw upon the various non-western historical experiences and cultural practices for its concepts and theories. This would require a turn to local philosophies, epistemologies, and historical experiences. While there have been decades of discourse on the need for this, there has been little by way of such practice. An exemplar for an autonomous social science tradition and an alternative discourse is Ibn Khaldun. While Ibn Khaldun has, since the nineteenth century, been recognized as a precursor of many modern disciplines in the social sciences, there have been practically no attempts to develop Khaldunian or neo-Khaldunian theory. One of the very few exceptions is the work of Ernest Gellner (1981: Chapter One) who offered a model of traditional Muslim civilization based on a fusion of Ibn Khaldun's political sociology with David Hume's oscillation theory of religion. This is an example of an alternative discourse because it regards non-conventional, non-Western sources as legitimate, and attempts to develop an integrated model by bringing in Western thought as well. The inclusion of Western theory is not seen as a legitimation of the exercise of autonomous social science but is rather a recognition of all civilizations as sources of not only data but theory as well—and as part of the creative process.

Marriott (1989) understands this problem of creativity, noting that the creation of a 'theoretical social science for a culture requires somewhat more than providing a meaningful cultural account: it requires building from the culture's natural categories a general system of concepts that can be formally defined in relation to each other...' (ibid.: 4). In other words, it is not sufficient to apply interpretive methods from the social sciences to the study of cultures if the concepts of these cultures are themselves not utilized as a basis for conceptualization.

An example of such a utilization comes from the work of Batra (1980), who, in discussing the history of Iranian civilization, uses a theory of social cycle derived from Sarkar's (1967) philosophy of history. Merits aside, this theory is a fine example of an indigenous theory of social and political change because it is deeply rooted in Hindu philosophy. According to this theory, society is divided into four types of people, corresponding to the four groupings of the caste system—the *Shudras*,

Khatris, Vipras and *Vaishyas*. Each group reflects a particular type of mindset, action, and outlook toward life. Society is said to evolve over time in terms of four distinct eras, each dominated by one of these four groups (Batra, 1980). This is an example of a theory of social change that is not confined to the study of Hindu society but seeks to understand the Iranian revolution in terms of the historical evolution of Iranian society (ibid.). It is important to note that the field of application of culturally derived concepts is not restricted to the society or civilization in which it was developed. The purpose of this example is to show what is meant by the cultural-rootedness or culture-specific nature of theories.

In this regard, it would be important to itemize the sources of theories and concepts from within the domain of local historical experiences and cultural practices. Here, it is vital to make a distinction that suggests two sources of theories and concepts. The distinction is made by Kim Kyong-Dong in the context of Korean social science—between the classical tradition (Confucianism, philosophy, etc.) and the world of popular discourse.[3] Examples of utilizing the former as a resource for theorizing would involve drawing upon the *ying-yang* dialectic (Kim, 1994a) and developing a critical 'Confucian ethic' mode of analysis (Kim, 1996a, 1994b).

In this respect, Kim (1991) had made an important contribution by going beyond the use of Confucianism as a subject of study, to Confucianism as a source of conceptualization. For example, he refers to the conscious and unconscious use of Confucian elements of statecraft by the ruling elite for rationalizing central authoritarian rule. But he also uses a framework of analysis based on the idea of *yin-yang* dialectics. In this framework, democratization and liberalization are viewed in terms of a 'dialectical interaction between forces that attempt to retain the power to monopolize decision making and to influence others and forces that try to change the existing distribution of power and influence' (ibid.: 138). The challenge here would be to develop a mode of dialectical analysis that is different from existing ones.

The world of popular discourse as a resource of social scientific theories and concepts refers to common sayings and terminologies in popular discourse and everyday language that not only reflect the cultural heritage but also reflect cultural perceptions of particular social phenomenon (Kim, 1995: 173). An example of work done by Kim along these lines is the study of cultural images of the aged in Korea with reference to Korean proverbs and common sayings (ibid.). Another example is the notion of *min-joong*—a term that bears some resemblance to the Gramscian idea of the *subaltern*.

The call for original Asian social science is not to suggest that Asia is a culturally homogeneous entity that could have its own brand of social sciences. What it does suggest, however, is that the social science, like other forms of knowledge, are social and historical in nature and must be made relevant to particular historical and social realities (Lee, 1996). One way to achieve this is to draw upon the philosophical traditions and the popular discourses present in these societies for relevant and original social scientific concepts and theories. This is part of the effort to create a social science free of cultural dependency and ethnocentrism, that is, one that is truly universal (Kim, 1996b).

Another good example of an indigenous concept in the social sciences, which also gives us an idea of how an autonomous social sciences tradition may emerge is that of 'Sanskritization', as developed by M.N. Srinivas. Unlike the theory and concepts associated with Ibn Khaldun which are pre-modern and pre-date Western influence, Sanskritization as a concept is not unconnected to Indological and Orientalist discourses in that it is founded on the critique of the reduction of Indian society to certain aspects of Hinduism and caste (Sinha, forthcoming). At the same time it is a concept that emerges out of a concern with understanding peculiarly Indian aspects of social change by referring to a process in which a '"low" caste, or tribal or other group, changes its customs, ritual, ideology and way of life in the direction of a high caste' (Srinivas, 1967: 6, cited in Sinha, forthcoming). Srinivas' conceptualization was somewhat universalistic, potentially transcending its origins in essentialized notions of Indian society, in the sense that he saw it as being applicable to non-Hindu tribal groups as well (Munshi, 1979: 299). In fact, Srinivas developed the concept when he was conducting his study of the Coorgs who were originally outside the Hindu fold (ibid.: 299-300). Once a group like the Coorgs undergoes the process of Sanskritisation, it assumes the features of a caste and is gradually assimilated into Hinduism (Srinivas, 1966: 7, cited in Munshi, 1979: 300). The concept, however, has not evolved to its true potential which would make it applicable to a wider range of social phenomena both within and out of India. Although various problems associated with Srinivas' conceptualization of Sanskritisation have been noted (for example, Munshi, 1979; Sinha, forthcoming), perhaps the most serious criticism and one that would partly explain the failure of the concept in becoming universal, is the one made by Munshi (1979). According to him, Srinivas lacks a general theory of society and social change that could guide the collection and interpretation of empirical data. As a result, Srinivas' object of study is transformed into a theory that conditioned the study to begin with. Referring to the ideal model of *Varna*, Munshi suggests that Srinivas accepted the ruling ideas of society as interpretations of the empirical reality he studied. His analysis was, therefore, ideological (Munshi, 1979: 304). For example, Srinivas's uncritical acceptance of the ritual hierarchy, that is, the relative place of ritual in the conceptualization of a caste hierarchy by different castes, was conditioned by Srinivas' recognition that ritual was dominant in Brahmanical life (ibid.: 305). As long as the development of concepts such as that of Sanskritization are hindered by ideological barriers, their universalization will be delayed.

Yet, another example of drawing upon local traditions, culture and thinking comes from Nandy's (1995) discussion on orientations to history and biography. Nandy suggests that India's popular histories furnish us with an analytical framework with which to understand times and persons of the past (ibid.: 4). Nandy notes three distinct attitudes to the past that are found in India's popular histories—that of the traditional minstrels or *charans*, that of the Brahmanic *barots* (genealogists and chroniclers), and that of the court historians or *bhats*. The first attitude subordinates the individuality of historical persons and events to the process of cultural continuity and renewal. The second attitude reduces persons and events to data and statistics. The third attitude 'makes for the delightful exaggerations and absurd eulogies' in Indian biographies (ibid.: 4–7). These three attitudes are utilized by Nandy to examine the biographies of two Indian scientists, Jagadis Chandra Bose and Srinivasa Ramanujan.

Another example of the exercise of autonomous social science would be Fe Hsiao-t'ung's concept of the 'gradated network' which he developed to explain the prevalence of selfishness among peasants in pre-revolutionary China (Lee, 1992: 84).

The Korean concept of *min-joong*, referring to those who are politically oppressed, economically exploited and socially discriminated against is also another illustration of an autonomous social science (Han, 1992: 439). This group does not fall neatly within the proletariat as it includes members of the middle class who are persecuted in various ways and who come to identify with the masses (Han, 1996).

In each of the above examples, autonomy is exercised because the authors do not confine themselves to the Western tradition of social science but draw upon alternative traditions for their theories and concepts. Their thinking on the subject-matter is not dominated by current trends in Western social science establishments and there is a conscious effort to be independent in thought.

The critique of Eurocentrism and Orientalism implies that alternative traditions to Euro-American social science are possible. One aspect of this would be the generation of concepts and theories in the social sciences that are home-grown or local. Concept-formation in the social sciences is understood as a process in which ideas, information and data collected and reflected upon during various stages of the research process are recast in the form of abstractions. These abstractions are what are known as concepts. But this process does not take place in an historical and cultural vacuum. At the same time, there is a recognition that concepts should be of universal applicability. The process of concept formation in this context seems elusive to most, including the advocates of alternative discourses. For this reason, it has been felt necessary to provide illustrations of theories and concepts that attempt to transcend the problems identified in the critique of Orientalism and Eurocentrism.

Two points should be made about autonomous social science here. First, the question of autonomy is not confined to the context of Eurocentrism or mental captivity. We have been speaking here of autonomy from Eurocentric social science and the need to isolate the captive mind. We can extend the idea of autonomy to other contexts such as ethnicity, gender and the state. However, the ethnic and gender bias in the teaching of the social sciences has often been thematized in Europe and North America, while Eurocentrism and the captive mind have not. Second, autonomous social science as a corrective to Eurocentric social sciences is ultimately concerned with a social science that is relevant to its surrounding. This raises the question as to what is meant by relevance and irrelevance, an issue taken up in detail in the next chapter. Chapter Six discusses the need for an adequate conceptualization of relevance and irrelevance in order that the call for alternative and autonomous social sciences is more meaningful.

Notes

1. I wish to thank Dr Hsu for translating and explaining the meaning of some passages in his article for me.
2. For other assessments of the social sciences in Malaysia and Indonesia see Garna & Rustam (1990), Malo (1989), Rais et al (1984), and Rustam & Norani (1991).
3. Kim Kyong-Dong, personal communication, 21 June 1996. Prof. Kim had also referred to this in a paper (Kim, 1996b).

6

Towards an Adequate Conceptualization of Relevance and Irrelevance in the Social Sciences

The fact that the humanities and social sciences in developing societies generally originated in the West had raised the issue of the relevance of these disciplines to the needs and problems of Third World societies. In Chapter Two, on the varieties of meta-analysis it was seen that the various approaches took an already developed social science as their subject matter. But meta-analysis has also been defined in a way that privileges its capability to provide overarching philosophical and methodological principles to be applied in research.[1] Ritzer (1988: 189) suggests that such an understanding of meta-analysis 'puts the cart before the horse' as it suggests that philosophical and methodological issues must be resolved before theoretical analysis and substantive research can proceed. In the context of the present study however, this objection to meta-analysis is not necessarily valid. To me, the task of meta-analysis should not be confined to the study of the extant social sciences, but should also develop the criteria of relevance and irrelevance that may guide the generation of alternative and autonomous social sciences, as is attempted in what follows. The purpose of this chapter is to recognize colonial and postcolonial concerns with the problem of irrelevance of the social sciences to the Third World, as a legitimate line of inquiry within the philosophy and sociology of the social sciences. This is done by discussing two types of approaches to the claims of reliability of knowledge—the epistemological and the sociological. It is suggested that the critique of the social sciences as they are practised in the Third World cannot be adequately made on epistemological grounds alone. Sociological approaches to the question of what constitutes reliable and objective knowledge have informed a great number of theoretical works on the state of the social sciences in the Third World. This chapter seeks to extend the sociological approach to take cognizance of the fact that in addition to the question of the reliability claims to knowledge, there is now a concern with the question of the relevance of knowledge. While the problem of irrelevance had long been recognized in assessments of the theoretical and practical uses of 'Western' social science, neither irrelevance nor relevance has been adequately defined and conceptualized. This I attempt to do here through a discussion of the sociological approach, in which the definition and criteria of irrelevance and relevance are established.

The implantation of disciplines and adoption of research agendas from the West in the developing countries had brought forth reactions among Third World scholars who questioned their relevance for developing countries (Marriott, 1989; Misra, 1972; Myrdal, 1957; Uberoi, 1968). Disciplines dehumanized and far removed from contemporary realities became entrenched in Third World social science discourse. For example, even though it seemed that a less technical, humanistic political economy would be more relevant to Asia as it stressed the role of non-economic variables in development, it was modern economic science in the form of abstract models that established itself in much of the Third World (Pieris, 1969: 439-40). For Pieris as well as Myrdal (1968), the abstraction of technical terms such as markets, prices, consumption and savings from the context of advanced industrialized nations may lead to valid inferences, while a similar procedure in the Third World may not. A different set of abstractions that take into account variables such as, attitudes, institutions, culture and different standards of living, would have to be generated (Myrdal, 1968: 19-20).

In the discipline of geography, more theoretical works addressing the relevance of Western-derived development models began to appear in the 1970s and 80s (Raguraman & Huang, 1993: 285). Mabogunje (1980) noted that Western and Western-trained students of underdevelopment attempted to craft theoretical frameworks and research agendas based on the historical experiences of advanced industrialized nations which, it was held, would show the Third World its own future image (ibid.: 14, 25). It was pointed out by critics that neo-classical inspired theories of development were irrelevant because they were ahistorical, lacked class analysis, and failed to consider the significance of the spatial structure in the process of development (ibid.: 27-28).

Since the nineteenth century, there has been a strong awareness of a lack of fit between the Western social sciences and non-Western realities.

Many examples of the irrelevance of Western concepts, theories and assumptions have been noted in the literature on Third World social sciences. The fact that the social sciences emerged in the West, were initially practised in the Third World by colonialists and other European scholars, and then finally implanted among the locals during and after formal independence, had raised the question of the relevance of these bodies of knowledge to Third World societies and their problems. Some non-Western scholars in the nineteenth century and more during the post colonial period, recognized that the social sciences cannot be transplanted to a different historical and socio-economic setting without doing injustice and violence to their respective realities. In short, there was a recognition of the problem of irrelevance of Western social science and of the corresponding need to generate relevant alternatives. For the most part, those who made these observations did not regard the entire Western social science tradition as irrelevant and did not reject knowledge on the grounds of origin. The general idea was that the Western social sciences are indigenous to their own settings and that the call for relevance is meant to contribute to the universalization of the social sciences.

However, at a conceptual level the meaning of irrelevance and relevance has rarely been the subject of discussion. This does not mean that there have been no discussions on relevance. P.C. Joshi wrote an article entitled 'The Question of Relevance' (1972) and another entitled 'Perspectives in Social Science Research: The Problem of Relevance or of Value Orientation' (1982). This was published in the volume, *Relevance in Social Science* Research (Joshi, 1972, 1982). Relevance here was mainly understood in terms of the inability of the social sciences to solve social problems seen in the cultural bias of concepts. In the 1970s and 80s, there was a great deal of concern with the relevance in this sense. During this period, many workshops recognized relevance as an issue. Sociologists, economists and political scientists advocated the indigenization of basic concepts in order that their disciplines would be able to better understand reality (Singh, 1986: 16). In the mid-1980s, a periodical devoted to the issue of relevance was published. Its editor was J.S. Gandhi and chief editorial advisor, Yogendra Singh. Entitled *Relevant Sociology: A Journal of Contemporary Sociology*, it survived for only a few years, but it was symbolic of the widespread and increasing concern with the problem of relevance in India and elsewhere.

What was lacking, however, was the systematic conceptualization of relevance. This conceptualization is vital to the projects of making relevant social science. In the absence of such conceptualization, the prescriptive calls for relevance are necessarily vague. This is in no small measure due to the unsystematic way in which irrelevance is discussed. There is not much beyond the enumeration of examples and little by way of typology. It would be difficult to come by a lucid notion of relevance if there is uncertainty as to what irrelevance is. For example, are we referring to political or social irrelevance, or irrelevance at the level of culture, or at the level of theory?

As a result, the calls for more relevant social science, often reflected in moves to decolonize, indigenize, or nationalize the social sciences, are equally incoherent. If colonialism was the context in which intellectual dependency emerged, decolonization and formal independence is the backdrop against which the question of relevance can be viewed. In this respect, the experience from the discipline of geography is instructive and may be held true for other disciplines as well. In the case of the former, political decolonization was accompanied by the spread of polycentrism in world geography in which the relevance of Western or Anglo-American models has been questioned (Hooson, 1994: 5-6). In Argentina in the 1800s, for example, geography was enlisted to aid in the task of nation-building, which involved—clarifying the relationship between territory and national character, articulating a territorial identity and creating the aesthetics of the patriotic landscape (Escolar, Palacios & Reboratti, 1994: 352). It was only much later that such nationalistic discourse led to the development and legitimation of geography as a discipline. In the effort to rediscover or reconstruct national history, geography aids in creating a poetic space which defines the landscape of the nation and identifies its sacred sites and historical monuments (Smith, 1986: 182, cited in Taylor, 1989: 177). What is important here is that the roots of these developments are to be found in the quest for national identity.

Reflection on the question of the relevance and utility of the social sciences for non-Western societies is a consequence of the encounter between a largely Western-oriented social science tradition on the one hand, and specifically national/regional socio-political issues on the other. This chapter seeks to clear some ground in this area by discussing, theories of the state of the social sciences, the problem of irrelevance and the various prescriptions for the creation of relevant social science.

I begin by outlining the problem of irrelevance as it has been discussed in a broad range of social science literature spanning the nineteenth century. This literature was implicitly concerned with the problem of irrelevance but had not attempted to conceptualize it. The second section follows with an itemization of the types of irrelevance. This typology of irrelevance is rationally constructed from various theoretical perspectives on the state of the social sciences in developing societies in which the theme of irrelevance is present, but implicit and unarticulated.

The third section is devoted to a discussion of the nature of relevant social science, which are defined by a set of criteria drawn from the typology of irrelevance from section one. I list the prescriptions found in a variety of disciplines for the creation of more relevant social sciences for non-Western societies. As in the case of irrelevance, the theme of relevance is implicit but not conceptualized in these prescriptions. There is a vague conception of relevance and, for the most part, of what would constitute more relevant theory, methods and practice. The typology of relevance that I introduce allows for a construction of relevant social science at different levels such as meta-analysis, theory, empirical studies and applied social science.

Sections one and two undertake a rational reconstruction of the critique of Western social science on the one hand, and the prescriptions for alternative social science on the other. This allows for the translation of the discourse on the critiques of Western social science and the proponents of alternative discourses into a conceptual discourse relating to irrelevance and relevance. The aim of doing this is to construct the thought of such critics and proponents in such a way that would be consistent with what they themselves would have constructed had they been explicitly concerned with conceptualizing irrelevance and relevance. The result is a conceptual framework for the study of relevance and irrelevance, both of which would have otherwise remained implicit in the literature.

The Discovery of Irrelevance

The formative period of the various social sciences disciplines and the institutions in which they were taught in much of Asia and Africa, was initiated and sustained by colonial scholars and administrators since the eighteenth century, as well as by other Europeans directly and indirectly in vicariously colonized areas.

Reflection upon the question of irrelevance at the philosophical, theoretical, empirical and applied levels is a consequence of the encounter between Western theory and modelling on the one hand, and local/national/regional realities on the other. It should be noted, however, that the discourse critiquing this state of affairs was by no means unified and that it was almost always the case that the critical assessment of Western social science did not result in reflections upon the concepts of relevance and irrelevance. Recognition of the problem of the applicability of the social sciences dates back to the nineteenth century during the colonial period and we can cite numerous works in which scholars and activists from the periphery of the capitalist world-system studied the 'language of the oppressor' and often assessed its applicability, pertinence and attunement to their own political and cultural contexts. The last two centuries of critiques contain statements that adumbrate a lack of fit between Western theory and non-Western realities, but do not attempt to introduce irrelevance and relevance as concepts in the sociology and philosophy of social science and explore their nature and typology. It is precisely for this reason that the concern with relevance/irrelevance has to be read into these critiques. Let us consider a few examples of cases where irrelevance was at least implicitly seen as a problem.

(a) *Islamic socialism.* One of the most outstanding nationalist organizations of colonial Indonesia was the Sarekat Islam (Islamic Union), founded in 1912. By 1919 its membership had grown to two and a half million. The Indische Social-Democratische Vereniging (ISDV) or the Indies Social Democratic Organization was established in 1914. This was later to become the PKI (Partai Komunis Indonesia or Indonesian Communist Party) and played a crucial role in the radicalization of Sarekat Islam, especially since ISDV members had membership in Sarekat Islam branches as well. At the First National Sarekat Islam Congress held in 1916, a Sarekat Islam member, Hasan Ali Soerati, a capitalist of Arab origin, raised the issue of combining Islam and socialism. Others who thought along similar lines pressed for the establishment of labour unions (Sarekat Islam Congress, 1916). During the Fourth National Congress of Sarekat Islam, the idea of an association of labour unions to combat capitalism and foreign domination was proposed (van Niel, 1960: 152). As Marxist elements within Sarekat Islam sought to minimize the role of Islam and stress the need for a class struggle against capitalism, another group led by Agus Salim espoused an Islamic socialism (ibid.: 152–53). This was to eventually influence the thinking of the Sarekat Islam leader, H.O.S. Tjokroaminoto in the 1920s who sought to indigenize socialism in Indonesia by founding it upon Islamic principles. This required him to separate what was considered as inappropriate or irrelevant European views on religion and philosophy from the idea of socialism as an economic system (Tjokroaminoto, 1988: 30). Adolf Baars, editor of Het Vrije Woord, the organ of the ISDV, recognized that despite what he regarded as the anti-socialist position and bourgeois tendencies of Sarekat Islam, it actually signified progress in Indonesia because it encouraged people towards self-assertion and independent thinking (Baars, 1916).

(b) *Public opinion polls.* Ralph Pieris (1969) noted that while the development of sociology in the West was an outcome of the need for a new science that could discern the nature of rapid social change that eluded the older disciplines of philosophy, political economy and law—the type of social science that was introduced into the colonies 'precluded indigenous self-awareness' because these sciences defined their object of study from the outside, thereby alienating their practitioners from their fellow-men (ibid.: 433-36). An example of the lack of concordance between the assumptions of Western scholars and, say, Indian reality comes from the study of public opinion. Surveys of public opinion may undermine the goals of the research to the extent that respondents were uncertain of their own opinions until they consulted the decision makers. This was because public opinion was the result of consensus rather than individual decision (ibid.: 439-40).

(c) *Postmodernism in China.* This is a case of misreading the cultural context in which literature is produced. Contemporary studies of Chinese literature have been described as part of the postmodernist debate in the West (Liu Kang, 1993: 14). Mu Ling (1955), however, notes that this is a misrepresentation of Chinese literature and literary criticism of the 1980s because the cultural and political contexts within which Chinese writers and critics were writing differed from that of the West. They were less involved with the postmodernist debates in the West and more concerned with the political struggle within China (ibid.: 420). Mu Ling shows how Huang Ziping's rereading of Wang Anyi's novella *Xiaobao Village* appropriated postmodernist literary ideas for a different agenda, the interest in postmodernism being to undermine Maoist literary theory and practice but under the guise of an aesthetic quest which could get past government censors (ibid.: 434-35).

(d) *The Western point of reference.* Another example of irrelevance concerns the discussions on Max Weber in the context of the development of capitalism outside of Europe. Many sought to discover a Protestant prototype in religions such as Islam and Buddhism. They approached the matter from a 'Protestant' point of view, seeking to discover what was said to be missing in other religions. An alternative formulation, one of several possible viewpoints, might ask why Islam was able to avoid the breakdown of prebendal feudalism and pastoral nomadism for as long as it did, or suggest reasons for China's regression into capitalism!

(e) *Imported models.* The inapplicability of imported models in studying Third World realities is seen in the example below. The development staff of a rural development programme in Nueva Ecija, the Philippines, failed to understand the complexity of peasant behaviour by viewing peasants as self-maximizing rational individuals that conform to the tenets of micro-economic theory. Peasant defaults on bank loans were viewed by the development staff as irrational (Weeks, 1986: 18-19). The peasants, however, were quite happy to receive the first loan and utilize it for purposes other than for which it was intended, default on it, and forfeit receiving subsequent low interest loans, as it enabled them to make payments for certain items that they would otherwise not have been able to purchase (ibid.: 19). Presumably, the development staff would have liked the peasants to be more 'rational', not realizing that what is irrational from one point of view may constitute economic rationality from another because of different economic and cultural contexts.

Another example illustrating the problem of imported models comes from Iran. Reporters who have travelled to that country seem to be puzzled by what appears to be a paradox, that is, the co-existence of a lively civil society with secular and consumerist yearnings on the one hand, and a theocratic regime on the other. However, as Ehsani (1995: 48) notes, the situation seems paradoxical only if one thinks within the confines of a Western model of progress, according to which religious social movements are antithetical to modernity. Against the feminist claim that the *hijab* (veil) is a tool of state oppression and, at the same time, without denying the repressive aspects of forced veiling, Ehsani notes that it enabled many lower middle class urban women to enter the public sphere as social actors and constituted a 'powerful and culturally legitimate instrument to overcome the patriarchal control and restrictions of their male-dominated homes and families' (ibid.: 50).

(f) *Orientalist concepts.* Before the emergence of capitalism, the Ottoman social system was undergoing transformations that possibly involved a non-capitalist route. Yet, Ottoman history is constructed with concepts and themes based on Western European experiences (Aricanli & Thomas, 1994: 25). When these concepts are uncritically applied the West becomes the primary referent for the study of Ottoman history, with the standard concern being why processes of transformation in the direction of capitalism did not take place. The Orientalist perspective operates on the assumption that Ottoman, like other Islamic societies, was so different from European societies that concepts such as class, progress, revolution, and the like did not apply, at least until the time that Ottoman society attempted to reform as a result of contact with the West. When these concepts are applied, the internal logic of development of Ottoman society does not occupy centre stage. Change is largely assumed to be possible after contact with Western civilization and through the influence of modernization.

Social and political changes that did take place but did not take Ottoman history on to a capitalist path remain invisible because transformation is associated with the sphere of production (Aricanli & Thomas, 1994: 26). Aricanli and Thomas contend that through a critical application of concepts like class, property, social surplus and the state, Ottoman history can be reconstructed to reveal a dynamic but non-modern trajectory of development. An alternative framework for looking at change would be the Khaldunian theory of state formation. Ibn Khaldun's theory, which addresses itself to the reconstruction of the pattern and rhythm of historical change can be applied to Ottoman history, while the Ottoman political economy may be conceptualized in terms of modes of production (Alatas, 1990).

The above examples illustrate that many have noted various problems surrounding the irrelevance of Western knowledge in non-Western contexts. These problems range from the inappropriateness of European views on religion, to the distorting effect of survey research methods and to the inapplicability of Western models. So great have such concerns been that they had resulted in the formulation of a number of theoretical perspectives on the state of the social sciences in the postcolonial world that provide critical assessments of the Western social sciences and of their impact on the various disciplines in the Third World. These have been enumerated in Chapter Two and include theories of Orientalism, Eurocentrism, postcolonial criticism, rhetorical theories of social science, mental captivity, pedagogical theories of modernization, modern colonial critiques, and academic dependency. While these theories are aware of the phenomenon of irrelevance and they frequently critique knowledge that originates in one socio-historical context but is transferred to and applied in another, they are not, however, concerned with the conceptualization of irrelevance.

Conceptualizing Irrelevance

Weber (1949) substitutes the epistemological question of what constitutes reliable or valid knowledge with that of the value-relevance of social scientific knowledge. He made a distinction between the existential knowledge of 'what is' and the normative knowledge of 'what should be'. Values should be restricted to the times before research begins and after the analysis is done. They influence what we choose to study and how we choose to use the results of our study for social policy. In this sense the social sciences are value-relevant. They are at the same time objective to the extent that social scientists avoid making personal value judgements on social reality. The social sciences cannot derive ideals or ethical goals and are ethically neutral in that sense.

The idea of the social basis of knowledge received further treatment by Karl Mannheim (1936). The traditional problem of reason versus experience as the source of genuine knowledge receded into the background with the recognition that knowledge did not arise from an act of purely theoretical contemplation (ibid.: 28). This is not to say that the question of whether knowledge is derived from sensory experience as opposed to *a priori* categories of the mind is not important. Mannheim argued, taking his cues from Marx, that the logical categories of the mind are not *a priori* but social products, and that 'knowing is fundamentally collective knowing' (ibid.: 28). Truth, therefore, becomes relational in the sense that the subject's knowledge varies with her social location. The question of the nature of knowledge, therefore, had shifted from the concern with validity to a concern with the social basis of knowledge. This does not merely signal a shift in attention but suggests that there is no socially independent criteria of truth.

The inappropriateness of epistemological approaches to the question of the validity of knowledge is due to the fact that they do not reveal problems of the social sciences in the Third World which are peculiar to the state of postcoloniality. One such problem is that of the irrelevance in the social sciences. What is clear from the literature of the last forty years is the strong awareness of a lack of fit between Western theory and non-Western realities. Many examples of the irrelevance or non-applicability of Western concepts, theories and assumptions have been noted (see Alatas, 1972a, 1974; Alatas, 1995, 1998; Fahim, 1970; Fahim & Helmer, 1980; Parekh, 1992; Pieris, 1969; Uberoi, 1968) and will not be repeated here. Epistemological issues concerning the reliability of truth claims or the origin of knowledge are common to social sciences in both the countries of their origin as well as in postcolonial societies. The problem of irrelevance, therefore, is not an epistemological one.

On the other hand, sociological approaches concerned with the questions of objectivity or the social basis of knowledge, have generally not raised irrelevance as a problem. Objectivity and the social basis on knowledge are universal concerns while the problem of irrelevance is peculiar to the social sciences of some societies. Therefore, the sociological approach to the question of reliable knowledge must be extended to include political, phenomenological and various other sociological aspects of the cognitive process, hitherto not dealt with in the sociology of knowledge. It is necessary first to conceptualize irrelevance by presenting a preliminary typology of the phenomenon in order to show the limitations of the sociology of knowledge approach and how it may be extended.

The various theoretical problems identified on the state of the social sciences in the Third World in Chapter Two illustrate some aspect of the phenomenon of irrelevance, from which we can derive a preliminary typology of irrelevance.[2]

(a) *Lack of originality*. According to the theory of mental captivity, the captive mind is characterized by a way of thinking that is dominated by Western thought. The problem is not the appropriation of Western thought *per se* but rather the uncritical and imitative manner in which Western knowledge is assimilated. An 'uncritical demonstration effect' results in imitation at all levels of scholarly activities, including problem-setting, analysis, generalization, conceptualization, description, explanation and interpretation (Alatas, 1972a: 11-12). Therefore, from the theory of mental captivity we may derive an understanding of irrelevance as typifying social science that is defined by the inability to raise original problems and to devise original methods of problem-solving. An example of such a lack of originality would be the absence of a philosophy of social science that was derived from the particular circumstances of the social sciences outside of North America and Europe.

(b) *Disaccord between assumptions and reality*. The scholarly writings of the captive mind are also founded upon the 'unreality of basic assumptions, misplaced abstraction, ignorance or misinterpretation of data, and an erroneous conception of problems and their significance' in social science (Alatas, 1972a: 11). The theories of Orientalism and Eurocentrism that discuss the discursive construction of the Orient and of world history also suggest this aspect of irrelevance, that is, the disaccord or disparity between assumptions and reality. For example, many of the observations of Marx and Weber of non-European societies were problematic as they were not merely factually wrong but based on unfounded assumptions with regard to the basic characteristics of 'Oriental' societies.

(c) *Inapplicability*. The problem of the disaccord between assumptions and reality then results in the more practical problem of the inapplicability of theories, concepts or models. The theories of Orientalism, Eurocentrism and postcolonial criticism have tirelessly demonstrated how inapplicable theories are forced unwillingly on to data, which end up in the form of problematic constructions. A classic example is Marx's concept of the Asiatic mode of production. The inapplicability here is due to the discrepancy between theory and empirical reality to which the theory is being applied.

(d) *Alienation*. The problems of lack of originality and the disaccord between assumptions and reality suggest the alienation of the social science enterprise from its surroundings. This refers to the discrepancy between the concerns of social science and the needs of the community of which the social scientists are a part. Consider, for example, the kinds of issues raised in the sociology of education in contrast to the types of problems existing in the education systems of many developing societies. Very often, the thinking and research of social scientists in developing societies is more a reflection of what they had learnt from sociology of education texts rather than from the real and functioning systems of education in their own settings.

(e) *Redundance*. The theory of mental captivity also discusses redundance as a problem (Alatas, 1972a: 12). This refers to the propensity for scholars in developing societies to uncritically assimilate verbal inventions and tautological expressions which do not represent new ideas. These problems have been well documented (Andreski, 1972: ch 6) and have been also attributed to cultural studies (Ferguson & Golding, 1997: xiii). The uncritical imitation of redundant propositions (that are already known) provides us with yet another aspect of irrelevance in the form of unimportance or triviality. A good example of redundance is furnished by Dipankar Gupta (1996) when he says that the postmodernists are not as radical as they claim to be. The politics of deconstruction may seem to suggest something new but what it amounts to at the level of practice is local engagements, self-management and the de-legitimization of grand political schemes, all of which are old and familiar (ibid.: 180).

(f) *Mystification.* Irrelevance also connotes sophistry, perversion and mystification. Here, we speak of social science as irrelevant when it mystifies through the use of jargon and comes across as being sophisticated. Such social science is irrelevant in the sense that the use of such jargon and 'obfuscating convolutions', to borrow an expression from Andreski (1972: 82), do not add to knowledge. An example would be the work of Althusser on relative autonomy, which according to Kolakowski (1971: 120), is merely a repetition of Engel's principle of the relative autonomy of the superstructure with respect to the economic base, in 'extremely pretentious language'.

(g) *Mediocrity.* Irrelevance also implies mediocrity. Here, we refer to mediocre or shallow social science that nevertheless gains a respectability in the non-Western outbacks that, owing to its irrelevance, far outweighs its interpretive and cognitive powers.

Each of these types of irrelevance, that is, lack of originality, disaccord between assumptions and reality, inapplicability, alienation, redundance, mystification, and mediocrity are seen to plague the social sciences at different levels. These are the levels of meta-analysis, theory, empirical studies, and applied social science.

(a) Meta-analysis concerns the reflexive study of a discipline, body of work or theory. The concern is less with theoretical or substantive content and more with philosophical underpinnings, social and historical contexts, or cultural assumptions. The misreading of the cultural context of modern literature studies in China discussed earlier is an example of irrelevance (disaccord) at the meta-analysis level.

(b) The assumption that there is a functional analogue to the Protestant ethic in East Asia or the Confucian ethic, and the resulting theorization, is an example of irrelevance (disaccord) at the level of theory.

(c) Research conducted within the framework of modernization or Marxist theory, with their Orientalist assumptions is an example of irrelevance (inapplicability) at the level of empirical studies.

(d) The inability of the development staff in Nueva Ecija to understand the behaviour of peasants is due to the irrelevance (disaccord) of their assumptions on peasant rationality. This is irrelevance at the level of applied social science. The socially irrelevant, servile (alien) commitments of many social scientists to Western social science agendas, that may have little applied value in their own settings, is an example of irrelevance (alienation) at the level of applied social science.

The absence of conceptualization of irrelevance in terms of its typology and the lack of attention to the manifestations of irrelevance at the different levels of social science activities perpetuates the various problems that form the context of irrelevant social science (for example, Eurocentrism, academic dependency, and mental captivity), which in turn make it possible for irrelevance to persist. For example, mental captivity would continue in the absence of efforts to raise consciousness of the problem of irrelevance. Academic dependency, in terms of the reliance on mainly North American and British scholars and institutions for research agendas, theories and models, and the technology of research and social science education, therefore, persists.

It might be pointed out that some aspects of irrelevance, such as, disaccord, inapplicability and mystification are not specific to non-Western social science but plague research in the West itself. While this is true, it is vital to note a number of points:

(a) The social sciences are 'indigenous' to the West in the sense that they arose amidst concerns with problems relating to the emergence of modernity, i.e., the theoretical and empirical research agendas were internally generated, while this was generally not the case in Asia and elsewhere.

(b) It has to be stressed that to the extent that the social sciences, as they emerged in Western Europe and the United States, are universal, they are not to be rejected. What is being rejected are those aspects deemed irrelevant. Rejection is not based on origin but on the criteria of relevance.

(c) Problems such as disaccord, inapplicability, mystification and the like have been widely discussed and debated in the West and have become integral aspects of the philosophy of social science, while they have not in the non-West.

(d) While certain aspects of irrelevance may not be specific to the non-West, they do appear in non-Western social science in a different context, that of postcoloniality and academic dependency. Their phenomenology is therefore distinct although the categories of irrelevance may be common.

Consider a Weber inspired Confucian ethic thesis that explains the phenomenal rise of the East and Southeast Asian economies since the 1980s. According to this thesis, Confucianism instils respect for authority, frugality and hard work, which explains political stability and high growth rates. This thesis can be critiqued for being irrelevant in terms of disaccord between assumptions and reality. For example, the tenability of the assumption that the Chinese of Singapore, Malaysia and Indonesia are Confucianists or are under the influence of Confucianism to the same degree that Protestantism influenced Weber's bourgeois businessmen, can be questioned. If this untenability is to be accepted, but if it is further claimed that Weber's assumptions of the influence of Protestantism on merchants of the sixteenth and seventeenth centuries in Western Europe too are untenable, then we would be justified in saying that irrelevance characterizes both theories. But the significance of this irrelevance for the West and the non-West differs. This aspect of irrelevance, that is, disaccord, may not be specific to the non-Western world but its connotations and implications for the non-West are different, this difference being due in large part to conditions peculiar to any particular society that we may be referring to. In the case of the Confucian ethic thesis, the exposé of irrelevance is bound up with revealing; first, the context of academic dependency and mental captivity, and second, the ideological and doctrinal basis of authoritarianism in East Asia, in the sense that irrelevance had the function of empowering authoritarian governments and international funding agencies. Therefore, while social scientists everywhere may subscribe to irrelevant theories, the context and significance of irrelevance differs.

(e) Following from the preceding point, irrelevance at all these levels leads to social science, which as we understand from the theories of Orientalism, academic dependency theory and postcolonial criticism, empowers others (Western social scientists, academic institutions, funding agencies, students, etc.) and not its practitioners (Third World social scientists or those on whose behalf they speak, that is, the 'natives', subaltern groups, etc.). Those who are empowered are colonizers and neo-colonizers, transnational capital, and authoritarian states, whether this is done through the denigration of natives or the worship of capital.

(f) It is also vital to note that while irrelevance may be a problem of the social sciences in the West as well, for the most part Western scholars have not been preoccupied with advancing the conceptualization of irrelevance and relevance in the context of Third World concerns or the global spread of the social sciences.

The Categories of Irrelevance

All the types of irrelevance listed above (as well as others not yet identified) can be regrouped into four categories derived from four sociological aspects of the cognitive process, thereby extending the sociological approach towards a more exhaustive account of the problem of irrelevance:

(a) *Conceptual irrelevance.* The study of the history and logic of concept-formation in the social sciences reveals how concepts derived from one cultural language are elevated to the level of universal concepts and comparative dimensions, the application of which veils discrepancies between text and reality (Matthes, 1992). An example would be the use of concepts from the sociology of religion such as church, sect and even religion itself to talk about Islam. Durkheim was possibly guilty of this. The manner in which he treated magic, for example, was according to the self-understanding of Christianity (personal communication with Prof Joachim Matthes, Singapore, September 13, 1997). Irrelevance types (d) (Alienation) and (e) (Redundancy) are found in this category.

(b) *Value irrelevance.* As mentioned earlier, the role of values in prioritizing research according to extra- or non-academic criteria must be taken into account in understanding the establishment and perpetuation of research agendas in the social sciences. An example of this problem comes from Egypt where researchers complain of funds being spent on surveys to find out what people think of the veil, a topic deemed to be of low priority (personal communication with Dr Ezzat Hegazy, Cairo, June, 1997). Often value commitments not rooted in the immediate surroundings of the researcher prevail. Irrelevance type (d) is found in this category.

(c) *Mimetic irrelevance.* This refers to the uncritical adoption of theories, concepts and methods from external sources, which due to the uncritical and imitative treatment, results in redundancy, mystification and mediocrity. Included in this category are irrelevance types (c), (f) and (g).

(d) *Topical irrelevance.* This arises when what is deemed to be problematic does not stand out but rather remains in the midst of expected familiarity, in the 'field of the unproblematic' (Schutz 1970, 25). Irrelevance type (e) comes under this category.

Relevant Social Science and Its levels

The identification of the problem of irrelevance and the proliferation of perspectives with which to understand and gauge the state of the social sciences in the Third World, is the proper context in which to read the call for relevance.[3] These have taken the form of pleas for endogenous intellectual creativity (Alatas, 1981), an autonomous social science tradition (Smail, 1961), decolonization of knowledge (Boehmer, 1995; ben Jelloun, 1985; Khatibi, 1967; Zawiah, 1994; Zghlal & Karoui, 1973), the globalization of social science (Bell, 1994; Hudson, 1977; Taylor, 1993), the sacralization of knowledge,[4] the indigenization of social sciences (Atal, 1981; Bennagen, 1980; Fahim, 1970; Fahim & Helmer, 1980; Sinha, 1998), deschooling (Illich, 1973), postcolonial theory,[5] the nationalization of social science (Agbowuro, 1976; Chan, 1993, 1994), and delinking from the structures of academic dependency.[6] Just as the theories on the state of the social sciences in the Third World recognize the problem of irrelevance but do not conceptualize irrelevance, so do these prescriptions just listed recognize the need for relevance without advancing the concept of relevance. The recognition of the need for relevance arose from the reading of irrelevance in social scientific works in the theoretical, empirical and applied areas. Therefore, it is suggested that an adequate conceptualization of relevance can be derived from a prior conceptualization of irrelevance.

It follows that what must be regarded as relevance is the reversal of all that has been presented above as constituting irrelevance. Relevant social science would then refer to originality, accordance (between assumptions and reality), applicability, affinity (between the social science enterprise and its surroundings, that is, non-alienated social science), succinctness (non-redundance), demystification, and rigour, which can be seen to exist at all levels of social science. To be sure, these aspects of relevance are not to be understood in any absolute sense. While it is true that all, including First World social science, would aspire to be more relevant, how a particular discipline or community of scholars define rigour, demystification, accordance, etc., may be dependent upon extra-scientific criteria. The location of Third World or postcolonial scholars helps to define these extra-scientific criteria. For example, whatever aspect of relevance may be under consideration, what is ultimately deemed relevant is that social science which empowers postcolonial social scientists and those on whose behalf, or with whom they speak (for example, the 'natives', subaltern groups, etc.). At least, this is how many who have been critical of irrelevance in the relationship between the West and the non-West in the social sciences would envision relevant social science.

As part of our effort to not only present examples of relevant social science but also theorize relevance by way of establishing its sociological criteria, we put into reverse the four categories of irrelevance which can be worked out as follows:

(a) *Conceptual relevance*. This requires rethinking the universality of concepts and comparative dimensions, by first of all, establishing non-dominant cultural languages as sources, and then working to develop truly universal or canopy-like categories. What would a sociology of religion look like if its concepts were derived from Islam rather than Christianity? The classification of religion may not include Catholicism and Protestantism under the same category of Christianity, because their doctrines and rituals differ too greatly to warrant their inclusion under one religion. Such a sociology of religion would be equally ethnocentric as the Eurocentric sociology of religion that it sets out to correct. The task would be to move beyond such one-sided constructions.

(b) *Value relevance*. This refers to the selection of values that we establish as a criterion or standard for the selection of research topics, the drawing up of research agenda, and for policy-making.

(c) *Mimetic relevance*. Mimesis can be turned into a virtue in the context of endogenous intellectual creativity which requires self-consciousness of the problem of irrelevance at both the individual and institutional levels.

(d) *Topical relevance*. This requires the ability to discover problems, unfamiliarities, in the midst of the familiar or the 'field of the unproblematic' (Schutz, 1970: 25, cited in Cox, 1978: 79). An example would be a Khaldunian theory of the stability of the Syrian state, or a Khaldunian theory of elite circulation in nineteenth century Sudan.

The result of grappling with questions such as irrelevance, imitation, and academic dependency allows us to begin to reconstruct a relevant social science. Relevance here is understood in terms of its various types at different levels of social science, that is, meta-analysis, theory, empirical studies and applied social science.

Meta-analysis

As stated earlier, meta-analysis concerns the reflexive study of a discipline, body of work or theory in which the concern is with philosophical assumptions, or social and historical contexts that underlie these works. At the level of meta-analysis, the creation of relevant social science first of all refers to the unmasking of all the types of irrelevance. Second, it refers to the production of meta-analytical work that restores relevance, that is, originality, accordance (between assumptions and reality), applicability, affinity (between the social science enterprize and its surroundings, that is, non-alienated social science), succinctness (non-redundance), demystification, and rigour.

The theories of social science referred to above are examples of relevant social science at the level of meta-analysis in the sense that they seek to expose irrelevance, as would be the meta-analysis of works on relevance themselves (Chan, 1993, 1994). Other examples of relevant social science at the meta-analytical level can be categorized as follows:

(i) Revisionary history.
(ii) Political economy of social science.
(iii) Sociology of intellectuals.

Revisionary history is what Edward Said (1993) refers to as works that reject dominant discourses and go 'beyond the reified polarities of East versus West, and in an intelligent and concrete way attempt to understand the heterogeneous and often odd developments that used to elude the so-called world historians as well as the colonial Orientalists...' (ibid.: 48)[7]

The political economy of social science involves the study of the relationship between power and knowledge. There are at least two aspects of this. One is the study of the link between academic discourses and colonial and neo-colonial practice (Driver, 1992; McKay, 1943; McWilliams, 1995; Pels, 1994). An example would be the role of the discipline of geography in enabling territorial acquisition and resource exploitation (Driver, 1992: 27). Another is Western feminist textual production of the 'Third World Woman' as a homogeneous, powerless group of victims (Mohanty, 1984). The other dimension of the political economy of social science is its academic politics seen in the 'set of institutionalized practices and relations of power that influence the production of knowledge from within academe: academic filiations, the mechanisms of institutionalization, the organization of power within and across departments, the market value of publish-or-perish prestige...' (Trouillot, 1991: 18).

The sociology of the intelligentsia and of intellectuals is a vital field to be cultivated in the context of relevant social science. Mannheim (1993: 72, 74) noted that the proletariat was the first social group which became conscious of its social identity while the intelligentsia is the last group that attempts to comprehend the sociological significance of its existence. The emergence of such consciousness among intellectuals is greatly impaired by the pre-existence of an elaborate proletarian framework of class analysis which does not acknowledge the possibility of intellectuals being anything other than a class (ibid.: 74–75). The sociology of intellectuals is required to appreciate and account for the position of intellectuals in society. The task of such a sociology, in the context of Third World societies, would be to understand the social identity of the intelligentsia and their potential role in civil society. This is all the more important in those countries where intellectuals are, in a manner of speaking, fugitives, lacking liberty, and self-perceived as irrelevant.

Theory

At the level of theory, relevant work also entails the unmasking of all the types of irrelevance as well as the production of theoretical work that restores relevance in terms of originality, accordance (between assumptions and reality), applicability, affinity (between the social science enterprise and its surroundings, that is, non-alienated social science), succinctness (non-redundance), demystification, and rigour.

This would require a critical study of received theories and concepts as well as the generation of concepts and theories from indigenous historical experiences and cultural practices. Indigenous theories and concepts are not merely local terms that substitute for Western ones. For example, the Filipino concept of *kapwa* cannot be understood in terms of 'others'. 'Others' is used in opposition to the 'self' whereas *kapwa* 'is a recognition of shared identity, an inner self shared with others' (Enriquez, 1994a: 3).

There are few cases of theory that are self-conscious of relevance, even if relevance is not conceptualized, and they have to be seriously investigated. Examples are Fe Hsiao-t'ung's concept of the 'gradated network' which he developed to explain the prevalence of selfishness among peasants in pre-revolutionary China (Lee, 1992: 84) and the neo-Khaldunian theory of state formation.

In this regard, it would be important to itemize the sources of theories and concepts from within the domain of local historical experiences and cultural practices. This will not be done here but mention can be made of a distinction that suggests two sources. This is a distinction made by Kim Kyong-Dong in the context of Korean social science between the classical tradition (Confucianism, philosophy, etc.) and the world of popular discourse. Examples have been furnished by Kim. He draws upon the *ying-yang* dialectic, that is, from the Confucian philosophical tradition, in order to develop the notion of a 'Confucian ethic' (Kim, 1994a, 1994b, 1996). He also draws upon popular discourse such as, the common sayings and terminologies of everyday language. In this way, both the high and folk traditions of a culture are regarded as sources of concepts and ideas in the social sciences.

Empirical Studies and Data Collection

At the empirical level, the creation of relevant social science would refer to the identification of irrelevance as well as the production of empirical work that restores relevance in terms of originality, accordance (between assumptions and reality), applicability, affinity (between the social science enterprise and its surroundings, that is, non-alienated social science), succinctness (non-redundancy), demystification, and rigour. Above all, this would require a focus on problems more relevant to local settings that have hitherto been neglected. Relevant social science at this level may either consist of the application of imported theories and concepts to the local situation according to criteria of relevance or the collection of data that would not have been motivated by an allegiance to Western models due to their differing concerns and priorities.

Applied Social Science

At the level of applied social science, relevant social science entails, first of all, the unmasking of irrelevant decision-making, planning and policies. Second, it refers to working with voluntary organizations, non-governmental organizations, and government, in implementation with a view to restoring relevance, that is, originality, accordance (between assumptions and reality), applicability, affinity (between the social science enterprise and its surroundings, that is, non-alienated social science), succinctness (non-redundancy), demystification and rigour.

Let us consider the case of relevant social science at the level of applied social science in terms of demystification of political and public discourse. Let me give an example of what needs to be demystified. This concerns the question of the so-called East Asian miracle, as it has been discussed in some countries of the region. There are two points among many that are worth noting.

First, Asia itself is a myth, an Orientalist construct, appropriated by Asians for a variety of reasons, including the idea that '"Asian" is a kind of sales gimmick, used for political and commercial public relations' (Buruma, 1995: 67). Apart from the fact that many local cultural practices are disappearing in Asia, what is often presented as Asian values either suspiciously promotes an authoritarian style of government or is universal in practice so as to make them indistinguishable from, say, American values. The task of demystification is not simply to expose the gimmick and place oneself in the liberal camp necessarily, but to present a third position or an alternative discourse on democracy or development that is authentic and liberating.

Another area that needs demystifying concerns the question of Southeast Asian development and pertains to the misuse of the works of Max Weber. In reply to the post hoc claim that development has taken place due to Islam/Confucianism a case can be made to the effect that (*a*) capitalist forms of development took place notwithstanding Islam/Confucianism, (*b*) Islamic and Confucianist movements may actually reject current styles of development, and (*c*) the state and media seem to domin-ate a discussion which has the potential to make sound claims about the possibility of indigenous forms of genuine democracy, not necessarily official communitarian democracy, but which, as yet, have no opportunity to do so.

Proponents of demystification do not claim monopoly over the truth. It is precisely for this reason that demystification is necessary. For the human sciences to be relevant, no one voice should dominate public discourse. This, then, leads to the question of the access that the social science community has to policy-makers and the influence they have in decision-making and policy implementation. While it is generally agreed that development is meaningful only when it involves the full participation of citizens in public affairs, whether this refers to NGOs, professional associations, the mass media, trade unions, and others, the extent to which social scientists impact upon interest and pressure groups as well as government is limited. However, if NGOs are to be effective, they must combine sophisticated research, with insightful policy analysis, and vocal advocacy of change. For this, there has to be a close working relationship among NGOs, academics and professionals, and government agencies if applied social science is to be relevant.

This is more of a problem in some countries than others. For example, in Malaysia, since the formation of the National Advisory Council for the Integration of Women in Development (NACIWD) in 1976 and the establishment of the Women's Secretariat (HAWA)[8] in 1983, several NGOs had been set up. These NGOs are all concerned with improving the status of women in Malaysia but express this concern in different ways. Some are involved in the exchange and dissemination of information and research materials on various problems such as health, reproductive rights, and domestic violence. Others are more active in raising public awareness of issues concerning women. Yet others are more practice-oriented and provide counselling, training and shelter for women. The problem is that the growing space for NGOs is not complemented by increasing participation of academics in NGO-related research and activism. Therefore, the success of applied social science depends not only on the ability to absorb indigenous and traditional knowledge into modern planning and policy implementation, and not only on the political constraints under which social scientists work, but also the crippling inertia that sometimes affects us.

Even in the relative absence of such extra-academic problems, relevant social science at the level of applied science must tackle the problem of translating theory into practice. An example is the use of traditional resource management systems based on communal property concepts (Clarke, 1990). In this case, a dilemma arose from the application of traditional systems because of the clash between communal property concepts and a capitalist logic of development.

Chapter Seven raises another set of problems that alternative discourses encounter. This has to do with the relationship between discourse and power.

Notes

1. This is how Furfey (1953, cited in Ritzer, 1988) defines metasociology.
2. This list of types of irrelevance is not meant to be exhaustive but represents what can be reconstructed from existing critiques of Western social science.
3. These various prescriptions have been enumerated in Alatas (1995a: 128–33).

4. For a critical discussion on this see Alatas (1995b).
5. For critical discussions see Ahmad (1995), Chakrabarty (1992), Dirlik (1994) and Prakash (1990, 1992, 1996).
6. For an account see Garreau (1986).
7. Examples of such works cited by Said are Alatas (1977), Batatu (1978), Gran (1979) and Tucker (1987). See also Said (1990).
8. Jabatan Hal Ehwal Wanita (HAWA), Department of Women's Affairs, Malaysia.

7

Alternative Discourses and Power*

The institutional and theoretical dependence of Third World scholars on Western social science has been noted in earlier chapters. This state of affairs had led to calls for alternative discourses among intellectuals in developing societies. However, the call for alternative discourses itself is fraught with difficulties. In the following section, the problem of imitation in the social sciences is discussed with the example of development studies. Then, I proceed with Foucault's discussion on the relationship between discourse and power. An understanding of the relationship between discourse and power is then brought to bear upon both the problems of the imitation of Western social science in developing societies as well as the problem faced in the call for alternative social science discourses in these societies. The aim here is to present an understanding of the problem of imitation as well as an insight into the obstacles faced by efforts to create alternative discourses in terms of the relationship between discourse and power.

Development Studies, Imitation and the Need for Alternative Discourses

More than thirty years ago in Cairo, Gunnar Myrdal (1957) warned against the uncritical adoption of Western theories and methodologies in developing countries. He emphasized on the need to remould economic theory to comply with the problems and interests of developing countries. At a more practical level, S.H. Alatas (1956) referred to the

---

* Revised from, 'On the Indigenization of Academic Discourse', Alternatives. Social Transformation and Human Governance, vol. 18(3), 1993. Copyright © 1993 by Alternatives. Used with permission of Lynne Reiner Publishers.

fact that Western economic systems, methods of government, law, ideas of democracy, procedures of election, and conceptions of welfare have, among other things, been uncritically adopted and advocated by the elites of developing societies. The Indian scholar, J.P.S. Uberoi (1968) had the following to say about the problem of Western social science in Asia in general and in India in particular:

> The aim and method of science are no doubt uniform throughout the world but the problem of science in relation to society is not. The problem or problems of science in a rich, technologically satiated society are different, even opposed to, its problems in a society of poverty lately liberated from colonial bondage. The two sets of problems and situations cannot, without serious falsification, be placed upon a single continuum. It is scientism and not science which conceives of them being along the single line of unilinear evolutionism. Our understanding of the prior content of science, its problems and its priorities in relation to a specific society will depend on our attitude towards this question.

Uberoi was concerned with the lack of an indigenous approach in the social sciences. This is a problem that plagues the social sciences in much of the developing world where they are either uncritically adopted or blindly imitated.[1]

This is not to deny that there are structures of academic dependency that link core and peripheral social scientists. Mental captivity exists within this context of dependency. Academicians in the periphery are dependent on their counterparts from the core for research and development funds. Scholarly journals are also controlled mainly by academic institutions in core countries. The various aspects of academic dependency have been discussed by others (Altbach, 1977; Weeks, 1990: 236–44) and in Chapter Three. My purpose in this chapter is to discuss the issues of imitation and the call for alternative discourses in the context of power, which although related to academic dependency are nevertheless, distinct problems.

The call for alternative discourses or autonomous social science traditions does not simply mean approaching specifically indigenous problems in a social scientific manner with a view to develop suitable concepts and methods, and modifying that which has been developed in Western settings. It goes beyond this to refer to the idea that social scientific theories, concepts and methodologies can also be derived from the histories and cultures of the various non-Western civilizations

(Fahim Helmer, 1980: 644-50). Such social sciences are not confined to the study of the civilizations of their origin but are extended to explain and interpret the whole world from various non-Western vantage points. The lack of alternative discourses and autonomous social science traditions in the non-Western world is a result of factors both internal and external to these societies as is evident in the other problems of underdevelopment. This lack does not allow for the transcendence of the inadequacies faced by current theories in the social sciences, especially those of development. To elucidate further, a few words must be said about these theories of development.

Modernization theory, which flourished during the 1950s and 60s, had two main components to it—the structural and the psychological. As a structural theory, modernization theory has an evolutionary vision of social, political and economic development. The roots of this vision are to be found in classical theory with its belief in progress and increasing complexities in the social, economic and political spheres (Portes, 1976: 55). Modernization theory was pioneered by Rostow (1960). From his observations of the industrialized nations, Rostow suggested that there are five stages a society must go through in order to industrialize. The application of Rostow's stages of economic growth to underdeveloped countries is questionable in the light that these five stages were derived from the experiences of Industrialized nations.

The psychological version of modernization theory claimed that Western society possessed those psychological traits that were conducive to economic success. Such traits include the concepts of achievement and economic rationality. The main proponents of this view are Hagen (1962), Inkeles & Smith (1974) and McClelland (1967). According to Inkeles & Smith, the introduction of modern institutions leads to the development of modern attitudes amongst people. Among the attitudes discussed by them is the increasing secularization of society. An event such as the Iranian revolution, on the other hand, is testimony to the fact that secularization may work against the rationale of 'development'. For this reason the Iranian revolution has been referred to as the ultimate blow to modernization theory (Pipes, 1983: 7). It represented the manifestation of dissatisfaction towards Western models of development throughout underdeveloped societies.

For a long time it was understood that the path of development experienced by industrialized countries, whether in structural or psychological terms, is not necessarily the path that can or will be followed by underdeveloped countries. Marxist and Marxist-inspired theories offer a critique of modernization theory on similar lines. Underdeveloped countries are unable to follow the same path as that of the developed countries because of the existence of a highly unequal system of relations between rich and poor countries which is the result of the historical evolution of capitalism. Unequal power relationships between the core (industrialized) countries and the periphery (underdeveloped) countries do not allow the latter to experience independent, self-sustaining development. To a great extent, underdevelopment is attributed to the policies of industrialized countries and their extensions in the form of elite groups in the periphery. Furthermore, world-system theory sees the world as constituting a single, hierarchical division of labour. These approaches are correct to criticize modernization theory for its lack of attention to the structure of the world economy and its hierarchical relationships. Nevertheless, their inadequacies are not to be denied, particularly those they share with modernization theory, of which one is neatly summed up by Walker (1981):

> They appeal to certain basic underlying forces at work:—the pursuit of power in equilibrium systems or the dynamics of economic structures. Thus, quite apart from the adequacy of each on its own terms, it is possible to question the narrow assumptions about human action on which they all depend. One may particularly question the lack of concern about those aspects of human action usually subsumed under the term 'culture'—values, aspirations, creativity, language and ideology (ibid.: 210).

What is referred to here is the notion of cultural specificity that entails variations in, or rejections of current theories that explain development as well as the creation of new theories that are nourished by the historical conditions and cultural practice of developing societies. To the extent that social science is a corrective to economic development and is concerned with social issues often ignored by economists, and charts the possibilities for social reconstruction, it should be obvious that development planning cannot but involve the social scientist (Dang, 1982: 35). The culture-specific situation of a society determines, at least in part, the concepts, theories, and methodologies that arise from tackling specifically indigenous problems. An example is the conceptualization of unemployment. Aggregate unemployment in many countries is not presented with separate figures for men and women. Thus, the unemployment problem may be overstated because in many countries male unemployment presents a more serious problem than female unemployment, because there is more absorptive capacity for females in household work than there is for males. Consequently, more males than females roam the streets (Alatas, 1974: 693).

Social scientific theories, concepts and methodologies that claim to be autonomously generated need to go beyond simply tackling indigenous problems with the appropriate modification of Western concepts and theories along the way. Systematized bodies of knowledge are needed that are based on indigenous cultures in the same way that Western social science is based on Western historical experiences and cultural practices. For example, the organic image of society that is central to functional evolutionism, which in turn informs a wide variety of theories of development, is traced back to Plato. The organic image of society is deeply rooted in Western consciousness. In a similar fashion, non-Western societies, without discarding Western social science, need to base their social sciences on indigenous philosophies, epistemologies, histories, and so on. For example, how would Ibn Khaldun's thought define a theory of development? What is needed in the Third World, then, is an indigenous social science tradition that transcends Marxist and other critiques of modernization theory and serves as a corrective to imitative social scientific work in the Third World.

In the following section, I will discuss Foucault on the relationship between discourse and power. In later sections, this will be applied to both the problem of the captive mind and the question of alternative discourses in the social sciences.

Foucault on Discourse and Power

In this section I discuss the ideas of Michel Foucault on the relationship between discourse and power because he made a connection between power and knowledge. This connection had earlier been made in the field of the sociology of knowledge. The sociology of knowledge, however, is more concerned with the external imposition of power on knowledge, whereas Foucault (1980b) is concerned with the circulation of power among scientific statements and the constitution of their internal regime of power (ibid.: 112–13). Drawing the connection between power and social scientific knowledge will be useful in placing the issue of the captive mind and alternative discourses in perspective.

In Western civilization, more than any other, language has occupied a central area of concern in the twentieth century. And this is not to be understood simply in terms of linguistics. Rather, we speak of the 'partial hegemony' of linguistics vis-à-vis other fields in the human sciences. The varieties of approaches to structuralism that have emerged from Saussure's pioneering work include, Levi-Strauss Barthes and Lacan who seeked to explain things such as kinship systems, fashion and the unconscious—thereby, placing linguistic concepts in new domains of application (Taylor, 1985a: 216). Various systems of philosophy revolve around language. Such is true of Heidegger and the post-structuralism of Derrida and Lacan. Here, our concern with language is specifically in relation to discourse.

What Foucault (1977) had in mind by discourse often refers to the 'delimitation of a field of objects, the definition of a legitimate perspective for the agent of knowledge, and the fixing of norms for the elaboration of concepts and theories' (ibid.: 199). What Foucault had to say about discourses in general turns out to be insightful when applied to the discourses on development in the Third World, as we shall see later. Here, I shall deal briefly with Foucault's understanding of how truth is imposed and power wielded through various procedures of the control and limitation of discourses, by other discourses.

Foucault shied away from language that was grounded in subjectivity and sought one that was ungrounded. This required an understanding of the two dimensions of meaningful objects—namely, designative and expressive. A sign is said to have meaning insofar as it expresses thought, perception, or belief regarding the object. The sign is related to the thought that it expresses. The dispute in history is regarding the importance of each dimension in the order of explanation. Is expressive meaning determined by designative meaning or does the reverse hold true?

For the ancient Greeks, reality was the idea of which empirical things were copies. But language was not important, words were not important; they were merely external clothings of thought. The later Augustinian view posited that the thought of God was clothed externally in creation, meaning that everything was a sign. God's creation was then understood expressively. This view set the stage for the semiological ontologies, which looked at the world as a meaningful order or text. But even here language had a marginal purpose because it was God and not man who was the expresser (Taylor, 1985a: 223).

Medieval nominalism rejected the idea of semiological ontologies. There are no such things as ideas, forms, or essences of things. All things exist as particulars. The universal is simply an effect of language. This view rejects the expressive theory of meaning. It refuses to see things as manifestations of the idea. Furthermore, words have meaning only insofar as they are words for things and not signs. The philosophic trend of nominalism rejected the view of the world as a meaningful order. In the seventeenth century, during the scientific revolution the conception of the world as consisting of objective processes naturally found an ally in the designative theory of language. The role of language was simply to designate these objective processes (Taylor, 1985a: 224, 226).

Language, as the designativists see it, is 'an instrument of control in gaining knowledge of the world as objective processes' (Taylor, 1985a: 226). In order to have control over objective processes, words that designate these processes must themselves be transparent. To posit that language is shaped independent of the thought of the subject and in turn shapes individual thought is to lose control (ibid). Modern modes of thought agree with Locke that 'every man has so inviolable a liberty to make words stand for what idea he pleases.' (Cited in Taylor, 1985a: 226–27). It is in this sense that the subject is the ground of knowledge—as a founding subject.

Foucault (1981), recognizing this, was against the designative theory of language, noting that 'Western thought has taken care to ensure that discourse should occupy the smallest possible space between thought and speech' and that it should be 'no more than a certain bridging between thinking and speaking' (ibid.: 65). The founding subject 'founds horizons of meaning' without needing to 'pass via the singular instance of discourse' (ibid.).

Although, it is clear that Foucault believed that a designative philosophy of language is inadequate for discussing the relationship between words and things, nevertheless, for him this was only one of the ways of eliding the reality of discourse—of the limitation, exclusion, and control of discourse. The designative theory of language is simply one procedure that serves to control, limit, and elide the reality of discourse. There are several other procedures.

First, there are the external procedures of exclusion that include prohibition, division and rejection, and the opposition between true and false (Foucault, 1981: 52–54). There are also the internal procedures of control that function as 'principles of classification, of ordering, of distribution' (ibid.: 56). Here, through principles such as the commentary, the author, and the discipline, discourses exercise their own control and limitation. There are also procedures of control that are neither external nor internal. These are the procedures that determine the 'condition of their [discourses] application, of imposing a certain number of rules on the individuals who hold them, and thus of not permitting everyone to have access to them' (ibid.: 61). The control, limitation and 'rarefaction' this time is of the speaking subject. No one participates in the order of discourse without being qualified or without satisfying certain requirements. Such procedures are the ritual, societies of discourse, and the doctrines (ibid.: 62-63). The designative theory of language and the idea of the founding subject are just two themes in philosophy that have come to 'correspond to these activities of limitation and exclusion, and perhaps also to reinforce them' (ibid.: 64).

Let us take a closer look at the link between discourses and the exercise of power. We need to state the tasks that Foucault sets for us in 'The Order of Discourse'. These are the four methodological requirements that must be fulfilled if the analysis of the conditions and effects of the control, limitation, and rarefaction of discourses is to be carried out (1981: 66-67). First of all, there is the principle of reversal, requiring us to look at the 'negative action of a cutting up and a rarefaction of discourses' (rather than at the positive action of creation) by such figures and systems as the author, the discipline, and the will to truth (ibid.: 67). Putting the principle of reversal into practice constitutes what Foucault called the critical set of analysis (ibid.: 70). The critical set has the task of analyzing the instances of discursive control and the procedures involved. As we have seen, Foucault rejected the designative theory of language and criticized the control and limitations that it brings about. But he offered more by way of the analysis of several procedures of the exclusion, limitation and the control of discourses referred to above.

Now we consider the other three methodological requirements that constitute the genealogical set of analysis. This set of analysis is concerned with the formation of discourses within and without the limits of discursive control as analyzed by the critical set. The genealogical set puts into practice the three principles of discontinuity, specificity, and exteriority.

In the principle of discontinuity, Foucault called upon us not to:

> Imagine that there is a great unsaid or a great unthought which runs throughout the world and intertwines with all its forms and all its events, and which we would have to articulate to think at last. Discourses must be treated as discontinuous practices, which cross each other, are sometimes juxtaposed with one another, but can just as well exclude or be unaware of each other (1981: 67).

Foucault's idea of unthought, as understood by me, refers to the unarticulated preconceptions that are necessary to and nourish thought, but are nevertheless unavailable for articulation.

For Foucault, interpretation led to the normalization and disciplinary control of man. Discovering the groundlessness of texts Foucault realized the arbitrariness of interpretation and its imposition by people. This leads us to relate the organization of discourses to the exercise of power. In modern society power is exercised at many sites. In Foucault's (1980a) words, 'It seems to me that power must be understood in the first instance as the multiplicity of force relations immanent in the sphere in which they operate and which constitute their own organization' (ibid.: 92). We must not assume at the outset the overall unity of domination couched in terms of the sovereign state or law. Rather we need to conceive of the operations of power as extending beyond the state and its apparatus (ibid.: 89). Foucault's focus was on the site of knowledge. He wished to look at power as it was wielded in the relations of knowledge rather than in the relations of production. But he was not merely looking at another arena of power. He also wanted to look at another way of exercising power, a way that requires our privileging discourse in the scheme of things rather than subordinating it to structural factors.

In the theory of the old power, Foucault maintained that power was 'centered primarily around deduction and death, [and] it is utterly incongruous with the new methods of power whose operation is not ensured by right but by technique, not by law but by normalization, not by punishment but by control' (1980a: 89). Any analysis of power and domination need not be confined to taking law, prohibition, and state power as the model, for it is not only through prohibition and blockage that power is wielded. Power not only has its negative forms through prohibitions, limitations, controls, and punishments, but has positive forms as well. Positive power is also wielded through the strategies that arise from discourses. The multiplication of discourses takes place not 'apart from or against power, but in the very space and as a means of its exercise' (ibid.: 32). In the theory of the new power, power is not vested in the subject. Power cannot be restricted to the subservience of citizens to the state or the domination of one group by another. It refers to more than just repression (ibid.: 92).

Let us try to understand the new power in terms of sexuality. In the nineteenth century there was a proliferation of the discourses on sex that set out to formulate the truth of sex, for it is sex that underlies conduct and existence, being a 'universal secret, an omnipresent cause, a fear that never ends' (Foucault, 1980b: 69). This being the case, the psychoanalyst has the hermeneutic function of verifying this obscure truth. It is this verification of truth, the will to truth, to which Foucault wanted to alert us.

Referring to the principle of specificity, Foucault (1981a) said:

> We must not imagine that the world turns to us a legible face, which we would only have to decipher; the world is not the accomplice of our knowledge; there is no prediscursive providence, which predisposes the world in our favour. We must conceive discourse as a violence, which we do to things, or, in any case as a practice, which we impose on them (ibid.: 68).

What this means is that once a domain susceptible to pathological processes is identified there arises the will to look for the secret, underlying forces at work. Once the truth of sex is discovered, for example, whatever does not conform is declared false, hence the institutions that engage in therapy and normalization (Foucault, 1980a: 68). This is domination, because once we are told the truth about sex we have to adjust our lives accordingly with the help of psychoanalysis. The modern man is, therefore, an object of control and the target of policies of normalization. The processes of normalization that seek to transform the behaviour of individuals and populations are constituted by the disciplinary control of individuals effected at the discursive level by fields such as psychoanalysis, medicine, pedagogy, and a host of other technical and scientific fields.

In the principle of exteriority, Foucault (1981) said that 'we must not go from discourse towards its interior hidden nucleus, towards the heart of a thought,' as if there were a truth or a hidden essence to be discovered (ibid.: 67). The faith in the truth or hidden essence nourishes the will to truth that brings about normalization and control.

To recapitulate, Foucault went beyond the critique of positivism that is implied in the critique of the designative theory of language. There are other procedures (external, internal, and the control of the speaking subject) by which discourses exercise control and limitation. The analyses of the procedures, together with putting into practice the principle of reversal, constitute the critical or archaeological set. The genealogical set of analysis, involving the principles of discontinuity, specificity, and exteriority, looks at the formation of discourses and their role in the normalization and the disciplinary control of man, that is, the wielding of discursive power.

It now remains to assess the value of Foucault's understanding of the relationship between discourse and power in the context of the social sciences in developing societies, especially in relation to the issue of the captive mind and the problems faced by attempts at building alternative discourses.

The Captive Mind, Power and the Discourses on Development

The problem of imitation has led to the call for alternative discourses among scholars in many developing societies. But there are several obstacles to alternative discourses that must be analyzed, and imitation is not the least important of these.

Earlier, I had referred to some inadequacies of development theories. I had also referred to the problem of the uncritical adoption or imitation of Western theories of development and the need for indigenous social sciences in the various non-Western societies. But there is a need to go beyond this. We need to go beyond mere recognition of the problem of and call into question the concept of imitation itself. Previous conceptualizations of this problem have not adequately dealt with the notion of power and domination as they come into play with the global spread of the Western social sciences.

The problem, however, can not only be restricted to imitation. It is not sufficient to say that in the periphery the imitation of Western social science does not allow for the comprehension of indigenous problems, or that it does not create a liberating discourse, or even that it maintains the 'mechanism of imperial domination' by legitimating core/periphery exploitation (Szymanski, 1981). In the cultural sphere, imitation alone cannot sustain core/periphery exploitation. Without linking imitation to power in the world system any statement on imitation would tend to be a weak and untenable thesis.

Furthermore, it should be clear that we are dealing with the cultural sphere, with the realm of ideas; the objective is to analyze a form of knowledge, Western social science, in terms of power and not merely in terms of how it legitimates the status quo. Structural causes do not take precedence over cultural/subjective ones. Western social science that is often disguised as universal social science is not a superstructure upon the world economy or the inter-state system. Rather, it intermeshes and intertwines with these structural processes. This is not to say that ideas do not legitimate ways of doing things. Specifically, I want to move away from the monotonous concept of imitation and instead look at the state of social sciences in non-Western societies in terms of reification and power, as it is wielded through the discourses on development.

Reification, a term associated with Lukacs (1968), refers to the idea that man's products are believed to have a separate existence, and are coercive over and control man. 'Man in capitalist society confronts a reality "made" by himself (as a class) which appears to him to be a natural phenomenon alien to himself, he is wholly at the mercy of its "laws"' (ibid.: 135). In Marx (1967, 1974), the concept of reification comes across very clearly in the idea of the fetishism of commodities. Labourers 'forget' that it is they themselves who impart to commodities their value. Instead they believe that value is inherent in the commodities they produce, or that the market-place produces this value (1967: 72; 1974: 157). There is also such a thing as the fetishism of ideas or the reification of ideas. Here it is believed that there are certain objective truths to be found 'out there' and that they have been discovered in Western social science. It is 'forgotten' that knowledge is a reality that is socially constructed. If we consider the body of knowledge that we call Western social science (including knowledge produced by non-Western scholars) as consisting of reified ideas, then we say that it is Western social science that dominates the various civilizational expressions in the non-Western world. Just as the capitalist controls and has access to the reified structures of capitalism, so the Western scholar controls and has access to these reified ideas. But this is not enough. We need to work out the techniques by which reified knowledge realizes power.

For this we turn to the works of Foucault and his notion of power. As previously discussed, Foucault was interested in those practices that lead to the normalization and disciplinary control of man. We are, therefore, called to relate the organization of the discourses on development to the exercise of power. The concern here is with the site of knowledge seen in terms of the discourses on development. We wish to look at power as it is wielded in the relations of knowledge rather than in the relations of production. But, like Foucault, we are not merely looking at another arena of the exercise of power. We also want to look at another way of exercising power that requires our privileging the discourses on development in the scheme of things rather than subordinating it to the structural factors of the political economy.

What this amounts to is recognizing that the Third World citizen is, therefore, an 'objective of control... [to be] examined, measured, categorized, made the target of policies of normalization' (Taylor, 1985b: 158). In order to make the link between the uncritical adoption of development theories in the Third World and normalization, it is necessary to view the problems associated with this uncritical adoption of Western development theories, which is acute in the following problematic areas.

Factorgenic versus Actorgenic Analysis

Analysis in development studies can be factorgenic or actorgenic in orientation. Factorgenic refers to results of human action; they are, however, external to man and survive longer than the individual or group. Development studies tend to stress factorgenic at the expense of actorgenic analysis (Alatas 1972a: 22). For example, in the statement 'In many developing countries, ineffective exchange rates and monetary and fiscal policies and excessive borrowing in the 1970s resulted in inflation and unsustainable balance of payments positions' (International Bank for Reconstruction and Development, 1983: 44), there is a lack of attention to actors. Why were monetary and fiscal policies ineffective? Were they misused by politicians for political ends? What part does corruption play in excessive borrowing? Are all funds used for the designated purposes? Answers to such questions require the study of concrete historical individuals and groups rather than anonymous forces.

Another example of factorgenic analysis comes from the two-gap model of Chenery and Strout (1966), according to which a country is constrained from achieving self-sustained growth by (a) the skill limitation; (b) the savings limitation, measured by the gap between the domestic investment required to achieve a certain rate of growth and domestic savings; and (c) the foreign exchange inflation, measured by the gap between foreign exchange requirements needed to maintain a certain level of domestic investment and foreign exchange earnings (ibid.: 679–733). Again, what is missing is the inclusion of historical or contemporary data surrounding actors in the various relationships that are causes and effects of these gaps.

We can say of economists of underdevelopment and of development planners that they have been, to a great extent, factorgenic in orientation. When they discuss problems the picture, which emerges, is that of anonymous forces bringing about or obstructing certain changes. They discuss the absence or presence of natural resources, the size of the market, the terms of trade, institutional impediments, labour productivity per capita and a host of other data relevant to descriptive and introductory explanations (Alatas, 1972a: 23).

Such descriptive and introductory explanations refer to pathologies of development that no doubt need to be identified. But there is more to underdevelopment than the factorgenic aspects referred to above. The normalizing procedures requiring injections of foreign aid, direct investment, and the like generally do not address the problems at hand although they serve other purposes. Alternative theories of development should, therefore, correct the imbalance between factorgenic and actorgenic analysis.

The Redundance of Development Studies

There is a tendency for development studies to be redundant due to their extremely general nature. An example of this is from an article on socialist developing countries, in which several fundamental laws and constraints on development are given (Morawetz, 1980). A country that invests too little shall not enjoy economic growth; a socialist country should attempt to strike a balance between individual and collective incentives, material and moral inducements, and so on. According to Morawetz, the bad performance of socialist developing countries is due to their not paying heed to these fundamental laws and constraints. But, the problem with this is that the analysis is too general to mean much. It is too general to enable us to understand the precise reasons for which socialist developing countries performed badly. On the other hand, such an analysis would call forth normalizing techniques of a very general nature that would be applicable across the board and, perhaps, easier to justify.

As another example, consider Alavi's (1972) theory of the postcolonial state. His account on the origins and bases of the postcolonial state is presented at too general a level to account for the differences between democratic and authoritarian postcolonial states. In his discussion on the relative autonomy of the postcolonial state—the state has the need and ability to mediate between contending interests of the mercantile bourgeoisie, indigenous bourgeoisie, and the landed classes. It is then possible for the most part to substitute any postcolonial state for Pakistan and Bangladesh in Alavi's work without invalidating the account. Even after all this, the question of why certain postcolonial states are authoritarian and why others are democratic, remains unanswered. This stems from the level of generality at which Alavi presents his theory.

The Presence of Erroneous Theories and Concepts

Here, we are concerned with the relevance of theories and concepts even in their original Western setting. Let us consider an example from economic theory. In general terms, modernization theory is based on the assumption that every man has rational, economic ends to pursue. Such a model of society depends on the idea of self-interest-seeking individuals devoid of culture and ideology. This recalls Kirzner's (1976) Martian doctoral student who, for his dissertation research, focused his telescope on a certain location on Earth. He observed a set of boxes that were lined up in a row. Every morning at 7:30 smaller boxes moved past these boxes, coming to stop at one of them along the way. The smaller moving boxes swallowed bodies that emerged from the stationary larger boxes that were lined up in a row. The Martian then postulated a law based on these discoveries, the law of moving boxes and bodies. In such a law, the fact that these moving boxes and bodies represent people trying to catch buses is obscured. The danger of imitating theories based on unrealistic assumptions such as that of economic man is quite clear. The result is normalization in the form of dehumanizing policies that seek to redress material problems while neglecting or even obstructing cultural and spiritual expression.

The Irrelevance of Western Theories and Concepts in the Non-Western Context

Here, I am referring to the idea that there are theories and concepts that may be relevant in Western societies but are not so in non-Western societies.[2] This would require looking into the possibility of indigenous alternatives. For example, concepts of authority derived from the works of Ibn Khaldun may be more relevant than those of Weber. Another example from the field of developmental studies concerns the concept of unemployment to which I have already referred.

The Inability to Differentiate the Universal from the Particular

There is much confusion regarding the status of concepts as universal and as particular. What is particular is held as universal (Alatas, 1974: 695). Consider the concept of urbanization. In the West, the city is held to be a civilizing influence and necessary for economic development. The sociological and psychological traits required for the functioning of a modern economy are bred in the city (Qadeer, 1974: 266). However, in many non-Western countries the rural-urban dichotomy suggested in Western theories is not valid as cities in such countries exhibit more similarities to rural areas than Western cities. The emphasis on urbanization in the theory of modernization amounts to a pro-urban position in the age-old debate concerning rural-urban differences. There is an assumption regarding the superiority of urban social organization, including Western urbanism, over the rural life-style (ibid.: 267).

What is assumed is that development as embodied in urbanization is the transition from rural traditional culture to urban modern culture. Urbanization is thus understood as Westernization, the taking on of modern Western values as opposed to traditional values. Urbanization in this sense is seen as a universal phenomenon, one that is both beneficial and necessary. Other phenomena that are often taken to be universal when in fact they are not are, secularization, the weakening of family ties, and indeed, that of development itself. It would seem to be clear that any policies of normalization arising from the confusion of the universal with the particular would be tantamount to Westernization.

'Negative' Imitation

Not only are the theories and concepts uncritically adopted in non-Western societies, but there is also the tendency to imitate what is not being done. A very good example of this comes from India. The former Indian food minister, C. Subramaniam, discussed the problem of protein deficiency in India. In the state of Madras, it was estimated that up to 40 per cent of children had suffered from permanent brain damage due to protein deficiency by the time they were of the school-going age. Thus, expensive and new school facilities were, to a large extent, wasted (Alatas, 1976b: 2). It is quite possible that because protein deficiency is not regarded as a problem in Western countries, it was similarly not seen as a problem in India. Similar examples exist on the educational side. There are no courses on the sociology of corruption or on the sociology of imitation in the non-Western universities. I am inclined to think that at least one reason for the absence of such courses in Western universities is a reflection of the ignorance or indifference toward these problems. In this case, the uncritical adoption of development theory results in the failure to identify the real as opposed to the discursively created pathologies of development.

The Lack of Attention to Issues Due to Methodology

Weber (1949) referred to the importance of values in shaping scholars' interests. 'To be sure, without the investigators' evaluative ideas, there would be no principle of selection of subject matter and no meaningful knowledge of the concrete reality' (ibid.: 82). It is also true to say that in some areas of development studies, apart from values, methodology also plays a role in shaping scholars' interests. In other words, methodology is one of the factors that influences the selection of the object of inquiry. An example is the problem of corruption in underdeveloped countries. In spite of the fact that such corruption is generally perceived to be a problem, it has never been the object of inquiry among development students to the extent that other problems have. This is in part due to the fact that generally applied methods such as survey research and multivariate analysis cannot be readily applied to this problem. One cannot interview corrupt people and obtain accurate data nor can one come up easily with adequate indicators of corruption. Although some studies have been done (Alatas, 1968, 1990, 1998; Carino, 1986; Gellespie & Okruhlik, 1988: 59–82; Kameir & Kursany, 1985; Scott, 1972), the problem of corruption has not become the object of a well defined field in which various theoretical perspectives have been developed and backed by empirical work. Here, too, there is a failure to identify and specify the real pathologies of development.

The discourses on development and the problems associated with their uncritical adoption in the developing world, place their subjects under procedures of normalization. Imitation, or the uncritical adoption of Western theories of development, serves as the receptacle of normalization. Imitation results in studies in the Third World that continue to be burdened by the problems that beset development studies, some of which were listed above. Imitation perpetuates works in development studies that tend to be factorgenic, redundant, based on erroneous assumptions about the nature of man, culturally innocent, and that universalize what are specifically Western traits. Each of the problems that beset development studies discussed above and that are retained in works by Third

World scholars on development prepare the Third World to undergo procedures of normalization in a number of different ways.

The Simplification of Development

The problems of factorgenic analyses and redundance in development studies serve to reduce the problems of underdevelopment to general, anonymous forces such as market size, terms of trade, direct foreign investment penetration, and so forth, thereby making out the problem to be less complex than it really is. This serves to simplify the problems of underdevelopment to prepare the Third World for the procedures of normalization. To the extent that the problems or abnormalities are presented as simple, universal and existing across the board, so are the solutions or normalizing practices such as loans, foreign aid, direct investment, technology transfer, professional training, scholarships, population control, and so on.

The Misspecification of Pathologies of Development

The problems of erroneous theories and concepts as well as irrelevant ones when transposed to non-Western settings result in the implementation of inadequate policies of normalization. Even where there may be real as opposed to discursively created abnormalities, inadequate policies are implemented. For example, the erroneous assumption of economic man is associated with dehumanizing economic policies that neglect spiritual and cultural concerns.

The Neglect of Real Pathologies of Development

Negative imitation results in the neglect of problems that are not considered as problems in the setting of advanced industrialized nations. Previously, the example of corruption was given.

Normalization as Westernization

The various practices of normalization are couched in terms of the processes of modernization. But because of the confusion between the universal and the particular, traits particular to Western civilization are taken to be universal. The procedures of normalization, therefore, take place under the aegis of Westernization, that is, in the context of Western images of man, religion, social organization, and statehood. The uncritical adoption or imitation of the social sciences in the developing world is therefore translated into the superimposition of alien forms to the extent that social scientists, state elites, and policy-makers work hand-in-hand.

This deployment of development operates through three major strategies.[3] One refers to the incorporation of problems into the domain of development. What this requires is the creation of 'abnormalities' that are to result in a field of intervention of power (Escobar 1984-85: 387). Once a domain subject to pathological processes is discovered, various techniques designed to normalize this domain can be applied. The next strategy is the professionalization of development by way of the mushrooming of fields and subfields in development studies. The goal here is a type of knowledge that seeks to identify the nature of developing societies, with a view to formulating policies and steering them in the right direction, 'to produce, in short, a regime of truth and norms about development' (ibid.: 387-88). Finally, there is the strategy of the institutionalization of development. This refers to the establishment of international organizations, national planning bodies, and local development agencies that serve as the agents of the deployment of development (ibid.: 388). Although these three strategies of the deployment of development have brought many benefits to the Third World in terms of the identification of problem areas and the implementation of policies and programmes, they have also enabled their practitioners to maintain some degree of control and vigilance over the Third World to the extent that underdevelopment is perpetuated by the policies and actions of the industrialized nations and their allies in the Third World.

The discourses on development have to be analyzed not only in terms of oppression, law, or exploitation but also in terms of the power they bring about through normalization. The discourses on development manage development, inserting it into 'systems of utility'. It is not only sex but also whole societies that are defined as domains susceptible to the pathological processes and, therefore, as objects to be normalized. These pathological processes are identified in the developing world, and an agenda of normalization is set up whether its composers are liberals or neo-Marxists. The processes of normalization that derive from the discourses on development are manifested in policy formulation and planning and provide the context within which the problem of the imitation of Western social science should be seen. The various disciplines dealing with development and their consolidation into the field of development studies are designed to speak the truth of development so that developing societies can be normalized (for example, the infusion of Western values, or how to silence tradition/religion to facilitate development).

The goals of normalization are ostensibly to raise the standard of living, increase productivity, improve the distribution of income, raise educational levels, and so on. Some of these aims are fulfilled in some areas, but the processes of normalization and disciplinary control can still be discerned. The process of normalization in the Third World affects scholars too as they undergo training in the various metropolitan establishments, thus perpetuating and reinforcing the normalization of developing societies, because rather than uncovering the discursive creation of pathologies of development, they aid in the creation of such pathologies. It is therefore crucial that the uncritical imitation of Western social science be seen in the context of such normalization.

The problems associated with the imitation of Western development theories that have been discussed above are to be seen within the context of normalization,[4] for only then can they be related to power and domination in the world economy through the social sciences.

Some Obstacles to the Emergence of Alternative Discourses

The efforts to create alternative social sciences face a number of obstacles as a result of the colonial encounter and the continuing dominance of Western social sciences in the Third World. The Western social sciences are well entrenched in much of the developing world. Western standards of scholarship, cogency, precision, and the like are the criteria by which these alternative social sciences in their embryonic form are judged. My interest here is to apply Foucauldian theory to the understanding of the problems that beset the attempts by the developing world to create alternative social sciences in their encounter with the Western social sciences.

As stated earlier, in the designative theory of meaning language becomes an instrument of control to obtain knowledge of an objective world. The world is seen to consist of objective processes. As such, the language that is used to describe such processes must itself be transparent. Language:

> cannot itself be the locus of mystery, that is, of everything, which might be irreducible to objectivity. The meaning of words can only consist in the ideas

(or things) they designate. ... The alternative is to lose control, to slip into a kind of slavery, where it is no longer I who make my lexicon, by definitional flat, but rather it takes shape independently and in doing this shapes my thought (Taylor, 1985a: 226).

If the world consists of objective processes and if language simply designates these processes, then language can be said to be neutral in the sense that it does not reflect the values, interests, or the cultural context of the speaker. By extension, then, the language of Western social science is also neutral, which is the same thing as saying that social science is universal. Discourse and the practitioners of discourse do not mediate between the subject and the object. They only report what is objectively out there. This is a Western social science disguised as universal. It has its own theories, concepts, and categories. Practitioners of the social science in the positivist and empiricist traditions, including those in the Third World, are deluded into thinking that their categories are universal. They ignore the differences in meanings between Western and non-Western settings and persist in using Western categories. This analysis is helpful because it enables us to see how, say, Arabic, Chinese, or Indian categories would have less legitimacy in the presence of Western 'objective' ones. And all this occurs because we have all become followers of the designative view. We see how holding on to a designative view aids in the elision of the reality of indigenous discourse. From Foucault, however, we learn of several other procedures of exclusion, limitation, and control by applying the critical set of analysis. For example, in discussing division and rejection as part of the procedure of exclusion Foucault (1981) refers to the opposition between reason and madness.

> Since the depths of the Middle Ages, the madman has been one whose discourses cannot have the same currency as others. His word may be considered null and void, having neither truth nor importance. ... it was through his words that his madness was recognised; they were the place where the division between reason and madness were exercised, but they were never recorded or listened to. No doctor before the end of the eighteenth century had ever thought of finding out what was said, or how and why it was said, in this speech, which nonetheless determined the difference (ibid.: 53).

Foucault goes on to say that although today the doctor does listen, it is within the context of the same division referred to above. This is similar to the exclusion of another voice, that of the indigenous writers in the Third World. For example, the plight of the traditional Muslim scholars (*'alim*, pl. *ulama*), rooted in the Islamic tradition, can be paralleled to that of the madman. Although the *alim*'s words are not considered null and void, his point of view is not considered scientific and, as a result, does not have the same currency as the one who is trained in the Western social sciences. A point of view is held to be more relevant because it is modern and speaks the 'truth'. For example, the views of the *ulama* on— Westernization, the social consequences of the unveiling of women and of premarital sex, and the problem of secularization were never looked at as sources of insight into an alien reality. Instead of looking at reality with the aid of the views of the *ulama* it was the *ulama*'s views themselves that became the object of meta-analyses.

More importantly, Muslim points of view are cordoned off in a separate area, the area studies. Thus, universities even in Muslim countries have departments of Islamic studies in which Islam is treated as an object of study, instead of being studied as projecting a particular point of view. Such scholars are not regarded as qualified to contribute to the discourses on man and society, as these lie within the domain of the sociologist, political scientist, and historian. As Foucault said, 'There is a rarefaction, this time, of the speaking subject; none shall enter the order of discourse if he does not satisfy certain requirements or if he is not, from the outset, qualified to do so' (1981: 61). The same can be said of the scholarly traditions emanating from other religions.

When Islam or any other religious traditions of knowledge are relegated to an area of study and not considered as a point of view, then its practitioner is restricted to the role of an area specialist and thereby, excluded from other areas of discourse. Instead of viewing the world from a Muslim stance, he views only Islam, for his object of study is not the world through the mask of Islam, but only the mask.

An internal procedure for the exclusion of discourses is the organization of disciplines. Those among the indigenous social scientists who aspire for their craft, to attain the level of disciplines, are up against numerous obstacles, for there is more to a discipline than 'the possibility of formulating new propositions ad infinitum' (Foucault, 1981: 59). A set of propositions that is presented as constituting Chinese sociology, for instance, needs to fulfil seemingly insurmountable requirements to be able to belong to the discipline of sociology. Such requirements include an experimental-statistical methodology over which Western social science has a comparative advantage.[5] Works that seek to indigenize the social sciences in their respective societies would not generally be accepted as part of the various social science disciplines. For these works to qualify for membership, they must deal with a determinate range of objects that should be reducible to variables. Statements about these variables are true only if there is a one-to-one correspondence with objectively verified situations. In a world in which positivist social science dominates, Third World social scientists, whose epistemological validity is being denied, cannot hope to have their voices heard.

Yet another means by which discourse exerts control is by way of 'fellowships of discourse'. These function to reproduce discourse within a closed community, according to strict rules. The 'fellowships of discourse' in the social sciences are diffuse, yet constraining (Foucault, 1981: 63-64). An example of the workings of such fellowships would be the proliferation of terms, concepts, theories, techniques and methods that may as well be trade secrets as far as Third World scholars are concerned, in view of the costs and other difficulties involved in keeping up with the latest journals, monographs, and computer software and hardware.

In our final example, we discuss the opposition between true and false as a way to exclude and control discourses. In the opposition or division between true and false, the will to truth 'tends to exert a sort of pressure and something like a power of constraint... on other discourses' (Foucault, 1981: 55). Foucault gave the example of how Western literature for centuries tried to ground itself on science, that is, on 'true' discourses (1981: 55). The will to truth operates through the form that discourses deploy, the plane of objects that they address and the techniques they use.

For example, expression in the social sciences of the Muslim world are governed by the will to truth (as synonymous with Western social sciences) in two ways that correspond to two main trends in the Muslim social sciences. In the first trend, the aspiration is to return to a past logic discovery, a rationality that was prudential rather than instrumental. The goal of such a rationality was to show man the way to ascent from the perceptions of a physical world to that of the spiritual. This type of rationality comes up against a technical-economic or instrumental rationality that excludes the non-technical as unreason. The modern positivist conception of instrumental rationality, therefore, denies legitimacy to Muslim forms of thought and action.

The second trend in the Muslim social sciences is a 'scientific' one as it attempts to ground itself on positivist science as it is conceived in the West. I have in mind attempts at 'Islamic economics' that have sought to base the discourse on a theory of wealth and distribution just like the Western economic sciences. Such economics is unable to solve the problems that it addresses because it amounts to being neo-classical economics dressed and made up in Islamic terminology. Like neo-classical economics, it extends a technical-economic rationality to explain a wide range of problems, which presupposes a view of different ends as comparable outcomes, which in turn entails the elimination of cultural hindrances to the comparability of outcomes. The main problem with this state of affairs is that under the guise of 'Islamic economics' the policies generated in industrialized capitalist centres are implemented and given legitimacy in the Muslim world.

Foucault criticizes the designative theory of language, and proceeds to show us in more colourful ways the control and limitation of discourses as we have seen from the application of the critical or archaeological set. Most of the means of control and limitation of alternative discourses, referred to above, had to do with the positivist and empiricist traditions in the Western social sciences, including the prominence of experimental-statistical methods. But Western social science cannot be reduced to positivist epistemologies. There are alternative interpretive traditions in the social sciences. But attempts at alternative discourses in the social science do not necessarily find allies in interpretive social science. The encounter between autonomous and interpretive social science is no less limiting to the former if it encourages nativism.

Foucault's genealogical set of analysis is concerned with the formation of discourses both within and without the limits of discursive control analyzed by the critical set. What is important in connection with nativism is the principle of exteriority from the genealogical set of analysis in which Foucault cautions us against proceeding toward essences, or the 'hidden nucleus, towards the heart of a thought' (1981: 67).

In interpretive social science the native's point of view becomes the criterion by which scholars' descriptions and analyses are judged. Nativism, however, refers to the search for 'essences' of the cultures of the Other and the highlighting of differences and absolute oppositions between Western and non-Western cultures (Abaza & Stauth, 1990; Moghadam 1989: 87–88).

The potential dangers of nativism to efforts to create alternative discourses are of two types. First, nativist social science falls into the very same trap that it wishes to oppose, that is, the tendency to uphold and perpetuate the superiority of Western cultural and political systems. For example, let us assume that there is a situation in which the experience of the Western self is incongruous with articulations that are offered in an Islamic setting. The goal of interpretation would be to study the intersubjective and common meanings embedded in Muslim social reality. These meanings would be for Muslim society and are partly constituted by self-definitions, which can in turn be re-expressed. But there are those who may not understand a particular self-definition that is said to underlie a Muslim society. In order for them to do so they would have to change their orientation to become socialized into the Muslim way.

Although such interpretive methods represent improvements, objective social science is not entirely free of its problems. We cannot assume that the Muslims are more in touch with their reality than an outsider. For example, a Western intellectual historian studying the phenomenon of 'Islamic social science' cannot take for granted that Muslim social scientists themselves are aware of the processes of normalization that are going on in their own society. All he can be sure of is that Muslim social scientists are calling into question the universality of the Western social sciences and are attempting to contest the accompanying control and normalization processes. Beyond that, it is conceivable that the 'Islamic social sciences', stimulated by processes of normalization in Western culture, are themselves a victim of these said processes. And in fact, this is the case to some extent.

For example, when the uninitiated attempt to study the burgeoning literature in Islamic economics, they do so by trying to identify some hidden essence of Islam that underlies this economics. This attempt to understand Islamic economics in terms of the self-understanding of the Islamic economists leads them to the same lack of awareness as the Islamic economists have about the true conditions in their society. After all, Islamic economics is merely a branch of neo-classical economics, serving the interests of capitalist expansion by supposedly opposing it. In attempting to ground itself on a theory of rational man and a hypothetico-deductive methodology it has merely substituted Islamic terms for neo-classical ones, retaining the same assumptions, procedures, and valuations. As such, it has failed to engage in the analysis and critique of a highly unequal capitalist world-system in which the gaps are ever widening. What this shows is that the intellectual historian attempting to share the author's point of view—in this case, that of the Islamic economist—may not necessarily understand what Islamic economics means and may miss how this supposedly anti-Western economics was co-opted and made to serve those very trends that it claims to oppose.

Second, in nativist social science, the celebration of the opposition between Western and Eastern culture, often results in a wholesale rejection of Western thought, which is to be substituted with indigenous thought. For example, consider Arab social science, which in the 1980s tended to substitute the concept of *'umran* (the Khaldunian concept of civilization) for Western notions of society (Abaza & Stauth, 1990: 220).

The critique of Western social science in terms of the control and limitation it exerts over indigenous attempts at social science is not only to be confined to the critique of positivist epistemology, but should be extended to nativist tendencies in interpretive social science.

Conclusion

It is clear that the call to indigenization is simultaneously the call for a liberating discourse that is able to break through the regimes of power and the techniques of control and normalization. Whereas positivist social science contributes to the normalization of developing societies, interpretive methods are not necessarily able to uncover the same processes of normalization that are propagated by indigenous actors (the problem of nativism). The situation of academic dependency in which Third World scholars find themselves, leaves them susceptible to the imitation and wholesale adoption of Western ideas and techniques, which in turn perpetuates this normalization. The idea, then, is to break out of this cycle with a liberating discourse. The quest for alternative of discourses is simultaneously the quest for a liberating discourse because of the specific historical circumstances in which the Third World finds itself. What would alternative social science projects involve at the conceptual and empirical levels?

First, they would call for studies on imitation or the uncritical adoption of Western social science in the developing world. This would require a classification of the various forms of imitation in the areas of metatheory, methodology, theory building, empirical research, and policy formulation. It would be necessary to establish a set of criteria of relevance in order to distinguish between the uncritically adopted and the creatively applied or indigenized. Furthermore, the mechanisms and ways in which this uncritical adoption hinders or merely does not facilitate development must be mapped. For example, what are the implications of positivist social science for development theory and policy? To what extent is current empirical research in developing societies irrelevant to the needs of these societies? In what ways are policies simply transplanted from advanced indistrialized nations without taking into account local conditions?

Second, the call for alternative discourses would involve the study of the strategies and techniques of normalization that have arisen from the uncritical adoption and application of development theory in the Third World. What are the development policies and programmes engaged in this process of normalization? Here it would be necessary in the research to draw a distinction between genuine problems of development, on the one hand, and the creations of 'abnormalities,' on the other. For example, poverty is a genuine problem but the lack of a 'beautiful body' is a discursively created abnormality. A related question regards the forms of institutionalization of normalization. Advertising would be one of them. Yet another question concerns the classification of normalization. Are there different forms and manifestations of normalization, and how can they be identified?

Third, alternative social scientific activity means the study of the various ways in which indigenous voices are elided and controlled. Some of the procedures and principles involved in this have been discussed in the previous sections with reference to Foucault. To be sure, there are other principles as well as techniques. A possible example would be journal refereeing. How and to what extent is indigenous creativity stifled by the standards, prerequisites, and valuations involved in international journal refereeing?

Fourth, there must be conscious attempts to engage in social scientific activity with a view to taking into account the world views, socio-historical contexts, and cultural practices of Asian societies so that alternative concepts and theories can be generated. Some examples of this have been presented in previous chapters.

Fifth, it is imperative that such attempts at alternative social science have their own implications for political practice, social work, policy formulation, and programme implementation. But just how alternative theories of development influence practice must be articulated. For example, how does having an indigenous concept of unemployment affect macroeconomic policies designed to curb unemployment?

Some would argue, as Taylor does, that Foucault blocks out 'the possibility of a change of life-form which can be understood as a move towards... greater freedom' (Taylor, 1985b: 158). Taylor accused Foucault of adopting a 'Nietzschean-derived stance of neutrality between different historical systems of power, and thus seems to neutralize the evaluations which arise out of his analysis' (ibid.: 163). An example is Foucault's discussion on the classical and modern ideas on punishment. In the classical epoch punishment is a liturgy. Some crimes are looked upon as violations against the political order, which is a part of the cosmic order. And so punishment is not a matter of deterrence or reparation but rather one of restoring the order (Taylor, 1985b: 154). Although most tend to see the modern philosophies of punishment as improvements over the classical and less barbaric, for Foucault modernity was just another system of power, a 'bio-power' that normalizes and disciplines to maintain a 'bio-mass'. This raises the issue of how an autonomous social science tradition in the various developing societies can at the same time be a liberating discourse. Insofar as alternative social science yields research that is relevant to the problems of developing societies, it would be a liberating discourse. But here the reference is to liberation from the hegemony of Western discourses on development. This does not mean to say that autonomous or alternative discourses themselves do not wield power through the processes of normalization and disciplinary control. But this would be a different regime of knowledge/power requiring separate treatment.

Apart from the problem discussed in Chapters Five, Six and Seven, alternative discourses or autonomous social sciences are also faced with difficulties in the teaching arena. Chapter Eight argues that as long as Eurocentrism is not thematized in the teaching of the social sciences, alternative discourses will remain on the margins of both Asian as well as global social science.

Notes

1. For a detailed discussion of these problems, refer back to Chapters One, Two and Three.
2. For more on this, see Edwards (1989).
3. Escobar (1984-85). For further illustrations of normalization, see Du Bois (1991: 1-30). It is not my purpose in this paper to describe and analyze the processes and procedures of normalization. The various policies formulated and implemented as outcomes of the strategies of normalization serve to advance the ideal and material

interests of advanced industrialized nations in the Third World. These policies and the interests behind them have been studied by neo-Marxist, dependency, and world system theorists. My aim here is to make the link between normalization and the uncritical adoption or imitation of the social sciences in the Third World.

4. These normalization tendencies are going on everywhere. Presumably, an indigenous social science would not be free of the processes of normalization. But the relevant distinction here is normalization effected by an alien social science tradition versus that undeveloped indigenously. In this article I am concerned with the former. The distinction is important because the procedures and principles of the control and limitation of discourses would be different in each case.

5. Western orientations in methodology are entrenched in many Third World societies even when inappropriate. For example, experimental-statistical methods are regarded as 'correct' methods even where basic and reliable data are unavailable. See Altbach (1977: 197). Admittedly, this generally applies to expensive research technologies, which favour the rich. This principle of exclusion does not necessarily apply to the fields of history, philosophy, ethnography, social theory, and so forth, to which other principles of exclusion may apply. Nevertheless, to the extent that positivist and experimental-statistical methods dominate the social sciences, this principle of exclusion is important.

8

Rethinking the Teaching of the Social Sciences

While the critique of Eurocentrism in the social sciences is well known, this has yet to be reflected in the teaching of basic and mainstream social science courses in most universities around the world. Basic introductory course in the social sciences is generally biased in favour of American or British theoretical perspectives, illustrations and reading materials. On the other hand, the logical consequence of the critique of Eurocentrism, Orientalism, academic dependency and other problems in the social sciences (identified in earlier chapters of this book) is the development of alternative concepts and theories that are not dependent on the West as the sole source of knowledge. This chapter focuses on how Eurocentrism is encountered as a problem in the teaching of the social sciences. I suggest that in order for alternative discourses to attain greater currency in teaching and research, these critiques of Eurocentrism must become an essential part of the social science syllabi. However, it is the very domination of Eurocentrism that obstructs its thematization in teaching. This chapter discusses Eurocentrism in social science curricula, using the example of the teaching of sociological theory, and suggests how it can be counteracted.

Eurocentrism in the Social Science Curricula

The impact of Eurocentrism is evident in the syllabi for the history of sociological theory as well in sociological theory itself. Here, a number of characteristics of Eurocentrism are to be found. These are the perpetuation of the subject-object dichotomy, the projection of Europeans in the foreground, as originators, and the dominance of European categories and concepts.

The Subject-Object Dichotomy

In most textbooks of sociological theory or writings on the history of social theory, the subject-object dichotomy is a dominant, albeit unarticulated principle of organization. Europeans are the social theorists who do the thinking and writing, and are therefore, the knowing subject. Non-Europeans appear in texts, if at all, as the objects of study of the European theorists rather than as knowing subjects, that is, as the sources of sociological theories and ideas. The nineteenth century for example, is seen as the period when most theories regarding the nature of society and its development were developed by European thinkers like Marx, Weber and Durkheim while no similar contributions came from Asian and African thinkers. The only non-Europeans that appeared in these works were anonymous objects, mentioned or referred to by the European thinkers whose ideas are being discussed.

The absence of non-European thinkers is particularly glaring in accounts where they had actually influenced the development of social thought. Typically, a course on the history of social thought and theory would cover thinkers such as Montesquieu, Vico, Comte, Spencer, Marx, Weber, Durkheim, Simmel, Toennies, Sombart, Mannheim, Pareto, Sumner, Ward, Small, and others. Though, generally non-Western thinkers are excluded, if included they are cited out of historical interest rather than as sources of ideas. For example, Ibn Khaldun is occasionally referred to in histories of social thought as a precursor or proto-sociologist, but is rarely seen as a source of relevant sociological theories and concepts.

Europeans in the Foreground

The subject-object dichotomy places Europeans and later, North American scholars in the foreground in the social sciences. One interesting exception in sociology would be the work of Becker and Barnes called *Social Thought from Lore to Science*. First published in 1938, this book discusses the ideas of Ibn Khaldun in great detail (Becker & Barnes, 1961, vol I: 266–79). According to the authors the first writer after Polybius to apply modern-like ideas in historical sociology was not a European but Ibn Khaldun (ibid.: 266). A few scholars like Becker and Barnes, in the nineteenth and early twentieth century were responsible for the recognition that Ibn Khaldun got in the West by discussing the influence of his ideas on some European thinkers. Although these influences have been recognized in some early works, today they are hardly discussed in mainstream sociological theory textbooks and courses.

Europeans as Originators

The West, particularly the Americans, British, French and Germans, are seen as the sole originators of ideas in the social sciences. The question of the multicultural origins of the social sciences is not raised. Many social thinkers from India, China, Japan, and Southeast Asia who during the nineteenth and early twentieth century were contemporaries of Marx, Weber and Durkheim, are either only briefly mentioned in works on the history of sociology or totally ignored. Examples of such thinkers are José Rizal (Philippines, 1861-1896), Benoy Kumar Sarkar (India, 1887-1949), and Yanagita Kunio (Japan, 1875-1962).

The Dominance of European Categories and Concepts

A serious consequence of this is that the social sciences are dominated by theories, concepts and categories that were developed in Europe and North America. In fact, it is 'impossible to *think* of anywhere in the world without invoking certain categories and concepts, the genealogies of which go deep into the intellectual and even theological traditions of Europe' (Chakrabarty, 2001: 4). This domination has been at the expense of non-European ideas and concepts. I had mentioned earlier that the interest in Ibn Khaldun was primarily historical. There has never been much interest in studying his concepts with a view to developing a theoretical perspective for sociological studies. While there may be exceptions seen in attempts to develop a neo-Khaldunian sociology, they remain marginal to mainstream social science teaching and research. Another example, comes from the study of religion where I find it astonishing that the social scientific study of religion does not take into account the conceptual vocabulary of the various religions in its presentation of concepts. Rather it draws its concepts almost exclusively from the Christian Western tradition with the belief that these concepts are of universal value. While that may be true, it is equally true that the concepts of Islam, Buddhism and Hinduism have the same potential to be universalized.

Reversing Eurocentrism via Teaching in the Social Sciences

Clearly, the task for those concerned with the problem of the neglect of ideas emanating from non-Western societies and with the development of a more universalistic approach to knowledge, is to counteract Eurocentrism in the social sciences by reversing the subject-object dichotomy, bringing in non-Europeans into the foreground, recognizing them as originators, and turning attention to non-European concepts and categories.

As far as teaching is concerned, the most serious reversal necessary is in the area of non-European concepts, and theories. To demonstrate the magnitude of the problem, I would like to provide an illustration of the lingering problem of Eurocentrism with recourse to the example of the concept of religion for which I draw from the work of Joachim Matthes (2000). This concerns the translation of cultural terms such as religion into scientific concepts, something that has already been referred to in the introduction. Social scientific concepts originate from cultural terms in everyday language. As such these concepts present problems when brought into scientific discourse to talk about areas and periods outside of those of their origins. The result is a distortion of the phenomena that they are applied to.

The Latin *religio*, from which the English term religion is derived, was a collective term referring to diverse practices and cults in and around Rome, prior to the emergence of Christianity. When Rome became Christian, Christianity became the dominant belief and all other beliefs were absorbed or eliminated. But *religio* was not applied to Christianity for as the only legitimate belief it was just known as the Church. With Luther and the Protestant Reformation, *religio* came to be associated with Christian beliefs and a way of life separate from the Catholic Church. Protestantism was opposed to the clergy and was therefore, seen more as the layman's religion. In 1593, the French philosopher, Jean Bodin published his *Colloquium Heptaplomeres* (Colloquium of the Seven about the Secrets of the Sublime), which put forth a generalized understanding of religion including non-Christian faiths as well. By the eighteenth century 'religion' came to be used as a scientific concept, referring to belief systems other than Christianity. But while 'religion' meant all beliefs, when European scholars wrote about religion critically, they had in mind Protestantism (as in Marx's reference to religion as the opium of the intellectuals) or the institutional religion (Catholicism) as opposed to the religion of the believers (Protestants) (Matthes, 2000).

When 'religion' is applied to beliefs other than Christianity, for example, Islam or Hinduism, there is an implicit or explicit comparison with Christianity, which results in an elision of reality. According to Matthes (2000), the logic of comparison is such that the two things to be compared are subsumed under a third unit which is at a higher unit of abstraction. For example, apples and pears are subsumed under fruits. 'Fruits' becomes the *tertium comparationis* (the third part of the comparison). Similarly, a comparison between Christianity and Islam is subsumed under religion. The problem with this is that the characteristics of religion are derived from Christianity to begin with. Therefore, the supposedly general scientific concept 'religion' is culturally defined by Christianity and Islam is not compared to it in terms of a *tertium comparationis*, or a general concept of 'religion'—but rather in terms of the Christian idea of religion. (Matthes, 2000).

What kind of reality is lost in the distortion done to Islam? Religion as it is understood in the West is a private matter. Dualities such as, sacred versus profane, religious versus non-religious and so on emerge from such a separation. Also, religion in the West refers to the beliefs and private lives of the followers. The danger of such an approach is when Islam is also seen in these terms, whereas, in fact, no such dualities exist in Islam. For example, there is no distinction between secular and religious education. All knowledge and education in Islam is either about God or the creations of God. Another example of this problem from a previous section, was in relation to Hinduism when seen in terms of the concept of religion.

The example of religion is presented here to highlight the fact that European categories and concepts continue to dominate any analysis in the human sciences. While the implications of this problem seem to be clear enough, yet, the field of the sociology of religion as well as other disciplines concerned with the study of religion have not gone through the kind of fundamental changes that one would expect if the issue of the appropriate *tertium comparationis* and the attendant conceptual problems were to be taken seriously. It should be noted that the study of religion, especially where Buddhism, Hinduism and Islam are concerned, is rather backward in this regard. A proper approach would be to develop the *tertium comparationis* from a comparative study of concepts as found in all these belief systems. The development of what we may term as alternatives to Eurocentric discourses, therefore, requires familiarity with the local or indigenous tradition, which is understood by Kim Kyong-Dong to mean both the classical tradition as well as the world of popular discourse.[1]

The need for alternative discourses in the human sciences should go beyond the critique of Eurocentrism to include the development of new concepts and categories, new interpretations of history, and the establishment of the concern with Eurocentrism within the field of the philosophy of the social sciences. Across Asia, in spite of the exceptions noted above, the human sciences have not gone beyond the critique of Eurocentrism and in fact continue to be informed largely by European categories and concepts.

This task should be undertaken not with the idea of displacing modern social science but to truly universalize it. The attempt should not be to develop a social scientific tradition that is equally parochial as the one being critiqued here. I proposed that Eurocentrism can be counteracted at a number of levels of social science activities, as discussed in Chapter Six. I would further like to suggest how this can be done.

One level is that of metatheory. By metatheory is meant the reflexive study of theory, that is, the study of the underlying structure of theory or the social context within which theory emerges. Metatheory would include an examination of its methodological and logical underpinnings. Such studies are necessary if the contributions of a particular scholar are to be kept alive and regarded as relevant. For example, Ibn Khaldun's theory of state formation must continuously be discussed in terms of its method, its logical underpinnings, and the social context in which it emerged.

Apart from that, more theoretical work has to be undertaken. These works have to be more than descriptive and should involve theoretical applications and extensions of Ibn Khaldun's ideas. There are many works that describe Ibn Khaldun's theory, but there has been a negligible amount of theory-building that would result in what we may call neo-Khaldunian social theory. Works that should go beyond the mere comparison of some of Ibn Khaldun's ideas and concepts with those of Western theorists, towards a more theoretical integration of his theory into a framework that employs some of the tools of modern social science (Alatas, 1993a; Carre, 1988; Cheddadi, 1980; Gellner, 1981; Lacoste, 1984; Michaud, 1981). The stress here should be on drawing upon hitherto marginalized and untapped sources of knowledge.

There also has to be critical assessment of existing attempts to generate alternatives or counter-Eurocentric discourse. For example, Gellner's (1981) attempts to take non-European ideas at the level of building a theory of Muslim reform based on a fusion of the ideas of Ibn Khaldun and David Hume was not taken up and discussed seriously by others.

Essential to counteracting Eurocentric discourse is the introduction of non-European ideas into the teaching of mainstream social science courses and in social science textbooks. Due to the relatively greater autonomy that university teachers enjoy as compared to teachers in schools, it is easier to inject more non-European content into the courses that we teach. There is no reason why social thinkers such as José Rizal, Benoy Kumar Sarkar and Yanagita Kunio cannot be introduced into a course on social thought and theory, for example. This is something that a colleague, Vineeta Sinha and I have been doing for some years at the National University of Singapore. We departed from the conventional classical sociological theory course, confined to the teaching of Comte, Marx, Weber, Durkheim, de Tocqueville and other Europeans of the nineteenth and early twentieth century and systematically introduced the ideas of non-Western social thinkers like, Ibn Khaldun, José Rizal, Sarkar and others. At the same time, we do not neglect Western thinkers. Still, when it comes to Western thinkers such as Marx and Weber, the focus is on those topics generally neglected in similar courses taught in Europe and North America, such as Marx's concept of the Asiatic mode of production, his views on colonialism in India or Weber's work on Islam and Confucianism. The details on the revamping of the course was reported in the journal, *Teaching Sociology* (Alatas and Sinha, 2001).

Teaching in the Spirit of Alternative Discourses

It is this critical tradition of alternative discourses that a colleague and I at the National University of Singapore, have tried to bring into our teaching. I am not suggesting that other colleagues in Singapore do not draw from Indian works or experiences but I can also say with confidence that these cases are extremely rare.

Turning to a more personal account, let me illustrate our concerns with Indian scholarship in the social sciences with an example from our teaching of sociological theory at the National University of Singapore.

Why read or teach the works of Marx, Weber and Durkheim or other European authors, long since departed, to a class of Singaporean or Southeast Asian students? What have the ideas of three European theorists born in the last century in a different cultural milieu to do with the non-European regions of the world today? While the various calls for alternative discourses have in theory questioned the existing paradigms in the social sciences, they have so far been unable to displace the fundamental assumptions of specific disciplines in practice. The pragmatic need to reproduce disciplines such as sociology and anthropology demands that certain continuities with the past be maintained. Hence, it is not insignificant that the critique of the social sciences are confined to the professional arena (eg. journals, conferences and other academic forums) with the participants being established scholars and not students.

The critique of the social sciences that emanated from academic institutions in Asia, Africa and Latin America tended to remain at an abstract and reflexive level. There had been several thoughtful pieces on the state of the various disciplines, raising the issue of the lack of connectedness between the social sciences and the societies in which they were taught. But the calls to decolonize the social sciences were generally not followed by successful attempts to build 'indigenous' theories and autonomous social science traditions, delinked from the academic core of Western Europe and North America.

Neither have these calls manifested themselves at the level of teaching in the social sciences. As far as courses on sociological theory are concerned, throughout the world there is a tendency to restrict themselves to the discussion and exposition of the works of Marx, Weber and Durkheim in addition to those of other nineteenth century Western scholars.

Given this scenario, we have attempted to deal with the issue of teaching sociological theory by way of a more universalistic approach to the study of sociological theory. This includes raising the question of whether sociological theorizing had been done outside of the bounds of European modernity. The example of Ibn Khaldun comes to mind. This would imply changes in the curricula for sociological theory. We have been experimenting with various approaches entailing changes in the way sociological theory is taught. Some interesting results came out of such changes which we discussed in *Teaching Sociology* (2001).

These changes involved, among other things, introducing Indian thinkers who were faced with problems of emerging modernity similar to nineteenth century European scholars. For example, the works of Rammohun Roy and Benoy Kumar Sarkar were taught in addition to those of Marx, Weber and Durkheim.

I followed a similar logic in another course I taught called, 'Development and Social Change'. The aim of this course was to understand the different reasons for which people's lives in so many parts of the world are affected in one way or another by poverty, income inequality, low levels of education, corruption, political oppression, and other features of underdevelopment. The complexity of the development process can be grasped from the multitude of explanations that have emerged since the nineteenth century including those from India such as D. Naoroji who wrote at the turn of the last century (1962 [1901]) and the Indian Marxist M. N. Roy (1971 [1922]).

The purpose behind making changes in the curriculum lies in the need to educate people about the multicultural origins of modern civilization, about the contributions of Muslims, Indians and Chinese to modern Europe, about the positive aspects of all these civilizations, and about the common values and problems that humanity shares. A course on World Religions should be introduced in schools so that children can learn not only about their own religions but about all other religions. Apart from having such a subject, the theme of inter-religious experience and inter-civilizational relations should be a part of other subjects such as social studies, literature, geography and history. All this would require a serious re-examination of school and university curricula.

For university professors it is easier to make changes in the courses that we teach, even if the entire curricula cannot be revamped along these lines. In addition to the two courses mentioned above, I have attempted to put into practice some themes that I believe should inform the dialogue among civilization in a course entitled 'Islam and Contemporary Muslim Civilizations'.[2]

As an introductory course in Muslim civilization, the emphasis is on the historical, cultural and social context within which Islam emerged and developed and the great diversity that is found in the Muslim world, right from Morocco in the west to Indonesia in the east. The course is divided into five sections. The first, consisting of two lectures, provides an introduction to the study of civilizations in general, defines Islam as belief and practice, creed and civilization, and briefly discusses the origins of Islam. The next set of lectures discusses the spread of Islam and the encounter between Islam and the West in the past. This part of the course introduces the major cultural areas within Muslim civilization, that is, the Arab, Persian, Ottoman, Moghul, and Malay, and covers topics such as the Muslim conquest of Spain and Sicily, the Crusades, and the Islamization of Southeast Asia. The third part of the course examines the cultural dimension of Muslim civilization, with particular emphasis on the religious and rational sciences that developed among the Arabs and Persians, their contact with the Greek heritage, and the impact that Islam had on medieval European philosophy and science. Also discussed in this part of the course are the literary and artistic dimensions of Muslim civilization. The fourth part of the course focuses on current issues in the contemporary period (post World War II). Particular emphasis is given to the emergence of Orientalism in Europe and the Islamic response to it. This section also provides an overview of the political economy of the Muslim world, setting the stage for discussions on a number of contemporary problems and issues such as gender, underdevelopment, Islamic revivalism, and imperialism.

All this seems to be a lot to cover in one course. It would be if the objective of the course was to impart knowledge of the facts and events concerning Islam as a civilization. But this is not the dominant aim of the course. The main objective is to bring students to an understanding of what I see as the three central themes of the study of civilizations.

1. *Inter-civilizational encounters.* The study of Islam is one case of the study of the encounter between civilizations. As Islam was the only civilization to have conquered the West and to be in continuous conflict with it, the idea is not to view such civilizational encounters as always negative. The Crusades, for example, resulted in much scientific and cultural borrowings between the Muslims and the Europeans.
2. *Multicultural origins of modernity.* Modern civilization is usually defined in Western terms. But many aspects of modern civilization come from Islam and other civilizations, including the sciences, the arts, cuisine, commercial techniques, and so on. The university is a fine example. The notion of a degree granting institution of learning was developed and put into practice by the Muslims by the tenth century and adopted by the Europeans in the thirteenth century. This includes the idea of the hierarchy of teachers and scholars and the idea of the degree. When we add the examination system developed by the Chinese to this, we get the modern university.
3. *The variety of points of view.* The study of Islam provides us with an opportunity to experience the multiplicity of perspectives from which any one fact or event can be viewed. For example, most works on the Crusades provide accounts from the point of view of the European crusaders. The perspective of the Muslims who fought against the European crusaders and then lived amongst them when the latter settled in and around the Holy Land between Crusades,

is instructive as it helps complete the picture of an otherwise fragmented reality. Another example of this concerns the *hijab* or head covering worn by many Muslim women. While in some settings it co-exists with the oppression of women, in others it is a symbol of liberation. It is important to expose students to the experiences of Muslim women who took to the *hijab* in order to escape the critical gaze of the fashion and beauty industry.

Counteracting Eurocentrism in the social sciences also requires our being active in terms of popularizing non-European ideas by regularly and continuously organizing panels or presenting papers on these ideas or their founders at mainstream social science conferences. This is a matter of organization and funding but also requires a lot of will on our part.

Finally, I would like to suggest that we ought to spread awareness of the need for alternative, counter-Eurocentric discourses in the social sciences by simply making it a point to cite the works of like-minded scholars around the world. This would increase the visibility of the more universal perspectives in the social sciences.

Having discussed numerous problems and obstacles faced by what has been defined as a marginal set of discourses that see themselves as alternatives to Eurocentric and Orientalist social sciences, what are the prospects and future of alternative discourses in Asia. Some thoughts on this are offered in the concluding Chapter Nine.

Notes

1. See Chapter 5, p. 13.
2. This is ucv 2201, a course I regularly teach at the University Scholars Programme, National University of Singapore.

9

The Prospects and Future of Alternative Discourses in Asia

To set the stage for the concluding discussion on the problem of the irrelevance of knowledge and the necessity for alternative discourses, consider *the following quote from the author's introduction to al-Wabar's*[1] *classic, The Shi'ite Ethic and the Spirit of Capitalism:*

> Early attempts by the Arabs to make inroads into Europe were relatively unsuccessful. After the subjugation of the North African coast and the conquest of the Iberian Peninsular in the early years of the 8th century AD, further incursions into Europe by Arab-Berber armies appeared to have been checked between Tours and Poitiers by Charles Martel. By the 16th century, the Ottoman Turks had overrun most of Eastern Europe and their empire extended from northwestern Iran in the east to Budapest in the West. *However, both Arab and Ottoman territories throughout Central Asia, the Mediterranean and Eastern Europe came under the threat of Shi'ite heresy* which traces its origin to the 14th century.
> Contemporaneous with the emergence of the Ottoman Empire in the 14th century was the founding of the Safavid Sufi movement by Sheikh Safi al-Din. His descendant, Ismail (905-930 AH/1499-1524 AD), a Turkoman from Azarbaijan, was the founder of the Safavid dynasty. In the mid-tenth century, during Ottoman attempts to centralize their control in Eastern Anatolia, Ismail took advantage of the turmoil and attempted to make inroads there. His tribal support came from a number of Turkoman tribes, the *Ustajlu, Shamlu, Taqalu, Baharlu, Zulqadar, Qajar* and *Afshar*, collectively known as the *qizilbash* (Turk. red head). What held these tribes together was an *'asabiyyah* (Arabic. *espirit du corps*) based on the Safavid mystical order to which the *qizilbash* owed allegiance.
> *So successful were Ismail and his followers in Anatolia, that by the eve of his death the Shi'ites had captured most of Ottoman territories in Europe and controlled Azerbaijan, western Iran, and the Tigris-Euphrates basin. By the reign of Shah Tahmasb I (930-984 AH), the Turkic Shi'ite conquerers had extended the rule of*

Islam to as far as north as the nahr al-rayn (Arabic. the river Rhine²). Only the lands to the east of the nahr al-rayn and stretching all the way south into Central Asia and Iran remained under Turkic Shi'ite rule while the regions to the west and south-west of the nahr al-rayn cotinued to be under Arab Sunni control as in Iberia or were ruled as various Catholic, Lutheran, Orthodox and Jewish principalities as was the case in France, Italy, the Netherlands, and Western Germany. The Turkish Shi'ite domains came to be known as Eastern Eurasia. We now come to the question that is being posed in this book: Why had modern rational capitalism and the industrial organization of life originated in Eastern Eurasia and not in other parts of Europe or Asia? In other words, why was the spirit of capitalism, the foundation of the capitalistic organization of life, able to fight its way to supremacy against various hostile forces here in Eurasia beginning in the sixteenth century and nowhere else? The answer undoubtedly has much to do with a certain elective affinity between the spirit of modern capitalism and the Shi'ite ethic. By the fifteenth century, the Shi'ite ethic had presented itself as constituting an ascetic compulsion to be economically successful while at the same time rejecting indulgence in the material world. The wordly asceticism of a number of puritan Shi'ite sects must be contrasted to the warrior ethic of Sunni Islam on the one hand and and the retreatist monasticism of the nahraynian sects on the other, characterising Western Eurasia by an economic traditionalism so inimical to rational capitalist order.

These circumstances present to us the possibility of a sociological theory of the origins of modern rational capitalism. Such a theory requires not only the delineation of the features of the Shi'ite ethic to reveal the affinity with the spirit of capitalism but also an excursus into Nahraynianism and Sunni Islam in order to confirm the absence of such an affinity. Let us begin with Nahraynianism.

The term nahr al-rayn, from which Nahraynianism was derived, denoting the Catholic, Lutheran, Orthodox and Jewish sects of Western Eurasia, was first applied by the Arabs to the Rhine river in northern Eurasia. Those who lived on either side of the Rhine were referred to as Nahraynians (Ar. nahrayni). It was only after the arrival of the Turks in the 16th century AD onwards that the term Nahraynianism gained currency in assigning the peoples of Western Eurasia, who did not convert to shi'ism, their religious identity. Nahraynianism, therefore, was understood by the Turkic Shi'ites to refer to the unconverted natives of Eurasia. This is not to suggest, however, that there is no naturally occuring entitiy that can be designated by the term Nahraynianism. This religion consists of Catholic, Lutheran, Orthodox and Jewish sects which all trace their origins to a Europeanised rendition of the faith of Abraham. They profess one God, a personal God, immanent but yet transcendant. They believe in a common set of scriptures, variously known as the Torah, Talmud and Bible. Furthermore, all the sects of Nahraynianism are characterised by their monastic, other-wordly and traditionalistic ethos. This made it impossible for an attitude based on frugality, discipline and systematic work centred on wordly affairs to take root.³

Who would accept such an account on the religion of Nahraynianism? Who would even accept that there is such an entitity called Nahraynianism?

What is clear from the above is a number of problems that can be said to beset Eurasian Turkic Shi'ite sociology:

1. The mix of fact and fiction. For example, there is a recognition of the existence of Catholicism, Orthodoxy, Lutheranism and Judaism as well as the Torah, Talmud and Bible but these are not understood according to the self-understanding of these religions.
2. The imposition of a category, Nahraynianism, from the outside, that is, by Arab and Turkic Shi'ite scholars. This is an imposition which does not match with the self-description of the Catholics, Lutherans, the Orthodox Church and the Jews.
3. There is an attempt to homogenize societies and communities, thereby hiding complexities. Simply stating the commonalities of the Catholics, Lutherans, the Orthodox church and the Jews, veils not only the contrary self-understandings but also the variety and heterogeneity of religion in Western Europe.
4. The approach is guilty of textualism in that it attempts to understand the reality of religion in Western Europe in terms of religious texts such as the Torah, Talmud and Bible, assuming that reality corresponds to the text.
5. Stereotyping is rife as the approach essentializes and reduces Western European society of the sixteenth century to characteristics such as traditionalism, monasticism and other-wordly asceticism, when it was quite likely that these characterized only a section of society.

We would generally be critical of such social science by pointing to its irrelevant aspects, while at the same times being conscious of its positive and useful aspects. It would be held to be irrelevant because it (a) mixes fact and fiction, (b) imposes categories and concepts from the outside that clash with the culture's self-understandings, (c) homogenizes heterogeneous entities, (d) adopts a textualist approach, and (e) essentializes and stereotypes whole societies.

Such social science, as that found in *The Shi'ite Ethic and the Spirit of Capitalism* seems simple enough to refute and one may wonder whether such bad and irrelevant social science does exist in the first place to warrant our attention to the problem of irrelevance. As ridiculous as the above account on Nahraynianism may seem, in fact, such irrelevance exists even in Western European and North American accounts of various parts of Asia and Africa. A case in point is the study of the 'religion' of

Hinduism, a name which bears a relation with the Indus river in the Indian sub-continent, that was imposed from the outside to encompass a wide variety of beliefs over a vast area of land. The adherents of such beliefs did not always consider themselves as belonging to a single entity called Hinduism. Yet, many textualist and essentialist studies of Hinduism, such as that of Max Weber,[4] subscribe to such constructed myths.

Irrelevance in various forms continues to plague the social sciences. Euro-American categories and concepts still dominate at the expense of other approaches. While these problems have been recognized for decades, they have made little impact in teaching and research in the social sciences as this book has tried to show.

Prospects for Alternative Discourses and Autonomous Social Science Traditions in Global Social Science

Obstacles to the emergence and institutionalization of alternative discourses in the social sciences are varied and have been discussed in previous chapters. There are at least two which are universal. One concerns the structure of academic dependency and the other is the cultural environment of academic discourse.

Academic Dependency

Academic dependency is perpetuated by the relative abundance of American and European funding for research and training, the high levels of prestige attached to publishing in American and British scholarly journals, the greater value attached to a Western university education, as well as other factors. The intellectual dependency on ideas exists within this context. For example, the social sciences in former British colonies are likely to be dominated by Anglo-Saxon theoretical traditions. Such a context that is presented by the structure of academic dependency is not conducive to the emergence of an autonomous social science tradition. But what are the possibilities of reversing academic dependency?

One practice that would augur well for the emergence of alternative discourses is to rely less on European or American standards that may not be appropriate, and at the same time work towards the upgrading of local publication capabilities. Emphasis on the development of local publications such as journals, working paper and monograph series must have high priority. This would also free academics from being tied to themes and research agenda that are determined by the contents of American and European publications. But this can only work if credit at the same level is given for locally published works by evaluators and promotion and tenure committees, as it is for international publications. Producing local journals and other publication series is not a problem. What is more difficult is to attach sufficient value and rewards to these publications such that they would attract higher quality works, tasks that require a great deal of will.

Eades' (1997) account of where Japanese academics publish furnishes us with an example of a line of action. Most scholarly publications in the social sciences and humanities in Japan appear in in-house university journals, working paper series, monograph series, and other occasional publications. What is revealing about the Japanese case is that there does not appear to be any discrimination against these in-house publications when it comes to the evaluation of academic staff for promotion (Eades, 1997: 22). This would be a very positive move in the development of alternative and autonomous social sciences in Asia as it would serve to increase self-reliance and also facilitate efforts to improve the academic standards of local and regional publications. More importantly, it would encourage academics to generate themes and research agendas in an independent fashion.

The Cultural Environment of Academic Discourse

Another obstacle is connected to the cultural environment of intellectual discourse. Even if inroads are made towards dismantling the structure of academic dependency, in the final analysis what must change is the intellectual culture in Asia. This means a consciousness of the problem of mental captivity and the irrelevance of an uncritically applied social science. Conscientiousness amongst people can only take place through the various media of intellectual socialization, including schools, universities and other institutions of higher learning. For example, a more universalistic approach to the teaching of sociological theory would raise the question of whether sociological theory was found in pre-modern, non-European areas. Also, the teaching of the context within which sociological theory arose can not only be defined by the series of political revolutions in Europe since the seventeenth century or the industrial revolution, but also by colonization and the emergence of Eurocentrism. This in turn would imply changes in the way sociological theory is taught. For example, there would be more emphasis on the Orientalist and Eurocentric dimensions of Marx and Weber's work.

The Aesthetic Appeal for Alternative Discourses

The project for greater relevance and universality in the social sciences can be further justified on grounds other than the already stated advantages of relevance.

Consider the appeal to aesthetics. The contemporary social sciences consist of many cultural voids. The practice of relevant social science at all levels involves filling these voids by looking at the various non-Western philosophies, cultures and historical experiences as sources of inspiration, insights, concepts and theories for the social sciences. The Western social sciences are truly indigenous in the sense that they arose as a result of responses to European social and political revolutions and are rooted, at least partially, in European medieval absorption of Greek philosophy whether directly or via the Muslims. The implicit assumption here is that there is a pluralistic and rhetorical dimension to knowledge and that, therefore, the source of knowledge should not be restricted to one civilization.

All knowledge is constructed from a particular point of view and is, therefore, metaphoric (Brown, 1977: 77). A root metaphor is a fundamental image of reality from which models can be derived. The five great root metaphors in sociology are that of the organism, machine, language, drama, and game (ibid.: 78). Insofar as metaphors are rooted in definite historical philosophic traditions, it would be rather appealing to widen our civilizational horizons, to engage in the search for new metaphors and entertain the possibilities of resultant models and theories. Apart from an aesthetic criterion of progress in the human sciences, it would be more astute, theoretically speaking, to be open to other civilizational sources of ideas as indicated by the example of Ibn Khaldun.

At a more down-to-earth level, there is a need to problematize irrelevance because of the practical implications of social research. An interesting comment on the matter was made on the Progressive Sociologists Network in connection with the comparison between Andre Gunder Frank and Fernando Henrique Cardoso (Karim, 1995). Karim was responding to a view that Frank is intellectually isolated for failing to connect social critique to action while Cardoso has been successful in filling the highest political position in his country. For Karim, while both are to be respected as scholars, Cardoso's record for resisting neo-liberal privatization, ensuring worker's rights, and stopping ecological destruction 'actually makes Bill Clinton look pretty good'. Karim's contrary view is that 'a lonely Frank is infinitely preferable to a Cardoso surrounded by the wrong crowd'.

Social science has an important role to play in public discourse to the extent that social scientific discussions precede, parallel and follow policy decisions (Wingens & Weymann, 1988). Social science knowledge often sets the standards, directly or indirectly, according to which policy decisions and implementation are evaluated and justified. Often, this is unrelated to whether social science tells policy-makers something they do not already know. The ideas of Marx, Weber, Durkheim, and Freud do find their way into public discourse, often in a distorted fashion (ibid.: 94). The social sciences may, therefore, either enchant or disenchant, mystify or demystify. For Marx and Engels, the task of scientific socialism was to 'impart to the proletariat a full knowledge of the conditions and the meanings of the momentous act it is called upon to accomplish...' (Marx & Engels, 1968), that is, to raise consciousness. If for 'proletariat' we read all those people subordinated by class, caste, age, ethnicity, gender and office (Sen, 1987: 203), the practical task of the social sciences becomes enormous.

The Need for Universality in the Social Sciences and the Levels of Relevance

At best, the problem is that the social sciences in the Third World are divorced from the realities that they claim to study or that they generate erroneous theories. At worst, they are detrimental to their own communities as a result of their direct or indirect complicity in the coercion, discipline and control of entire peoples. I have in mind, for example, works that seek to identify a functional analogue of the Protestant ethic in Islam or Confucianism for a psycho-cultural theory of capitalist development. Such social science, whether in the service of boundary maintenance and conflict, ethnocide and genocide (Basu & Biswas, 1980: 3), or soft authoritarian practices, operates to the benefit of the ruling classes, their clients and their transnational allies, and to the detriment of others.

The more systematic, cogent and precise we are with respect to the notions of irrelevance and relevance, the more likely the relevance-seeking project is to crystallize into an intellectual movement, no doubt pluralistic in outlook, but systematic and thorough in its aims and approaches. Nevertheless, there are other problems in this effort that must also be addressed.

In line with the view that the call for alternative discourses (understood as a call for autonomous social science traditions and not nativist social sciences) and universalization are one and the same thing, autonomous social science does not wish to discard Western social science, but instead open up the possibilities for local, national and regional philosophies, epistemologies, and histories to become bases of knowledge. Without the project for autonomous social sciences, it is just one set of indigenous (Western) discourse that dominates.

Evans suggests that what is needed in Asia is not an indigenous or indigenized anthropology 'but an anthropology that is more self-consciously and sensitively internationalized' (1997: 18). This is in fact what has been proposed by the vast majority of proponents of alternative discourses. They conceive of the call for alternative discourses as the selective adaptation of Western social science to local needs. The acceptance, rejection or extension of knowledge from the West is not based on the grounds of origin but rather on the criteria of relevance that are established as a result of the consciousness of the problems of academic imperialism, mental captivity and uncritical imitation. The call for alternative discourses is simultaneously a call for the universalization of the social sciences. This call generally accepts the notion of social science as a universal discourse which is constituted by various civilizational or cultural expressions all contributing to the understanding of the human condition. To the extent that the internationalization of the social sciences requires a plurality of philosophical and cultural expressions, then the call for alternative discourses around Asia and the rest of the world must be seen as adding to the hitherto dominant Euro-American voice.

On the other hand, the extent to which the search for relevance in the social sciences, in their attempts to 'correct' Eurocentric discourses, becomes a form of nativism or Orientalism in reverse[5], is a matter that must be taken seriously. 'Going native' among both Western and indigenous scholars, constitutes the elevation of the native's point of view to the status of the criterion by which descriptions and analyses are to be judged, to the extent that the social sciences from the West are held to be irrelevant (Abaza & Stauth, 1990; Amin, 1989; Moghadam, 1989). It cannot be emphasized enough that projects such as indigenization, postcolonialism, decolonization and others, stand for the universalization of the social sciences. This they do in varying degrees of universality. At the simplest level, relevant social science would insist on a cautious application of Western theory to the local situation. At a higher level of universality, both indigenous and Western theory are applied to the local context.

At yet another level of universality, local, Western and other indigenous theories and concepts (that is, indigenous to other non-Western societies) are applied to the local setting. I have in mind as an example, the application of the neo-Khaldunian theory of state formation to the Mongol conquest of China. The highest level of universality refers to the application of indigenous theory from within and without one's own society to areas outside of one's own area. Whatever the level of universality, for most critics of the Western social sciences, there is in principle a commitment to the universal source of theories, concepts and ideas in general, although the extent to which ideas from without the locality are brought in and domesticated varies from one level and locale to another, and is dependent upon adherence to the criteria of relevance.

It is necessary that there be an active minority of social scientists in each of the major universities in Asia who are concerned with some of the problems that have been raised above, who are interested in revisiting the diagnostic and prescriptive literature of the past, and who have the interest and will to generate new concepts, categories, methods and techniques, and research agenda.

The quest for relevant social science is a potentially liberating project. It is a historically located, contra-colonial and neo-colonial discourse. Its critical and emancipatory tone is a very strong reason to maintain an allegiance to the project.

Notes

1. *Muhammad ibn al-Wabar (1864–1920 AD), the Andalusian sociologist, who continued the Khaldunian tradition in theoretical history in Eurasia.*
2. *Named so after the Arabic as it was largely Arabic geographical studies which provided detailed systematic accounts of Eurasian climate, ecosystems and natural resources.*
3. *The preceding sections in italics are fictitious parts of this account of what may have happened had the Turkic Shi'ite tribes actually succeeded in their quest to conquer Ottoman territory.*
4. Max Weber, *The Religion of India: The Sociology of Hinduism and Buddhism*, Hans Gerth & Don Martindale, trans. & eds., New York: The Free Press, 1958.
5. Orientalism in reverse is a notion originated by al-'Azm (1984: 368). See Chapter Five.

Bibliography

Abaza, Mona & Georg Stauth, 1990, 'Occidental Reason, Orientalism, Islamic Fundamentalism: A Critique,' in Martin Albrow and Elizabeth King (eds), *Globalization, Knowledge and Society: Readings from International Sociology*, pp. 209-30, London: Sage Publications.
Abdalla, Ismail-Sabri, 1978, 'Heterogeneity and Differentiation—The End for the Third World?', *Development Dialogue*, 2(2): 3-21.
Abdel-Malek, A., 1963, 'Orientalism in Crisis', *Diogenes*, 44: 103-40.
Abdel-Malek, A. & A.N. Pandeya (eds), 1981, *Intellectual Creativity in Endogenous Culture*, Tokyo: The United Nations University.
bin Abdul Kadir, Munshi Abdullah, 1965, *Kesah Pelayaran Abdullah*, Singapore: Malaysian Publications.
Abdul Samad Hadi, 1983, 'Mengkonsepsi Mobiliti Penduduk Semasa Urbanisasi di Semenanjung Malaysia: Satu Perbincangan Berasaskan Pengalaman di beberapa buah Kampung di Negeri Sembilan', *Akademika*, 22, 63-81.
Agbowuro, Joseph, 1976, 'Nigerianization and the Nigerian Universities', *Comparative Education*, 12(3): 243-54.
Ahmad, Aijaz, 1995, 'The Politics of Literary Postcoloniality', *Race and Class*, 36(3): 1-20.
Akiwowo, A.A., 1990, 'Contributions to the Sociology of Knowledge from an African Oral Poetry', in Martin Albrow and Elizabeth King (eds), *Globalization, Knowledge and Society: Readings from International Sociology*, pp. 103-17, London: Sage Publications.
Al-Attas, Sharifah Shifa, 1998, *ISTAC Illuminated: A Pictorial Tour of the International Institute of Islamic Thought and Civilization (ISTAC) Kuala Lumpur*, Drawings and calligraphy by Syed Muhammad Naquib al-Attas, Kuala Lumpur: The International Institute of Islamic Thought and Civilization (ISTAC).
Al-Attas, Syed Muhammad Naquib, 1968, *The Origin of the Malay Sha'ir*, Kuala Lumpur: Dewan Bahasa and Pustaka.
——, 1969, *Preliminary Statement on a General Theory of the Islamization of the Malay-Indonesian Archipelago*, Kuala Lumpur: Dewan Bahasa and Pustaka.
——, 1970, *The Correct Date of the Trengganu Inscription*, Kuala Lumpur: Museums Department, States of Malaya.
——, 1971, *Concluding Postscript to The Origin of the Malay Sha'ir*, Kuala Lumpur: Dewan Bahasa and Pustaka.
——, 1972, *Islam dalam Sejarah dan Kebudayaan Melayu*, Kuala Lumpur: Penerbit Universiti Kebangsaan Malaysia.
——, 1975, *Comments on The Re-examination of Al-Rānīrī's Hujjatu'l-Siddiq: A Refutation*, Kuala Lumpur: Museum Negara.

Al-'Azm, Sadiq Jalal, 1984, 'Orientalism and Orientalism in Reverse', in John Rothschild (ed.), *Forbidden Agendas: Intolerance and Defiance in the Middle East*, pp. 349–76, London: Al Saqi Books.
Al-e Ahmad, Jalal (nd) *Gharbzadegi (Weststruckness)*, Tehran: Ravaq Press.
Alatas, Syed Farid, 1990, 'Ibn Khaldun and the Ottoman Modes of Production', *Arab Historical Review for Ottoman Studies*, January: 45–64.
——, 1993a, 'A Khaldunian Perspective on the Dynamics of Asiatic Societies', *Comparative Civilizations Review*, (29): 29–51.
——, 1993b, 'On the Indigenization of Academic Discourse', *Alternatives*, 18(3): 307–38.
——, 1995a, 'The Theme of "Relevance" in Third World Human Sciences', *Singapore Journal of Tropical Geography*, 16(2): 123–40.
——, 1995b, 'Dependency, Rhetorics and the Transnational Flow of Ideas in the Social Sciences', *Paper presented at the Goethe-Institute International Seminar on Cultural and Social Dimensions of Market Expansion*, 16–17 October, Labuan.
——, 1996, 'Western Theory and Asian Realities: A Critical Appraisal of the Indigenization Theme', Paper presented at the Asia Pacific Regional Conference of Sociology (APRCS), 28–31 May, Quezon City.
——, 1998a, Western Theories, East Asian Realities and the Social Sciences, in Su-Hoon Lee (ed.), *Sociology in East Asia and Its Struggle for Creativity*, ISA Pre-Congress Volumes, Social Knowledge: Heritage, Challenges, Perspectives, Montreal.
——, 1998b, 'The Rhetorics of Social Science in Developing Societies', *CAS Research Papers, Series No. 1*, Singapore: Centre for Advanced Studies, National University of Singapore.
——, 1999, Colonization of the Social Sciences and the Structure of Academic Dependency, *Replika* (Budapest) 38: 163–79. <In Hungarian>.
——, 2000a, 'Academic Dependency in the Social Sciences: Reflections on India and Malaysia', *American Studies International*, 38(2): 80–96.
——, 2000b, 'An Introduction to the Idea of Alternative Discourses', *Southeast Asian Journal of Social Science*, 28(1): 1–12.
——, 2001, 'The Study of the Social Sciences in Developing Societies: Towards an Adequate Conceptualization of Relevance', *Current Sociology*, 49(2): 1–19.
——, 2003, 'Academic Dependency and the Global Division of Labour in the Social Sciences', *Current Sociology*, 51(6): 599–613.
Alatas, Syed Farid & Vineeta Sinha, 2001, 'Teaching Classical Sociological Theory in Singapore: The Context of Eurocentrism', *Teaching Sociology*, 29(3): 316–31.
Alatas, Syed Hussein, 1956, 'Some Fundamental Problems of Colonialism', *Eastern World*, November.
——, 1962, 'Reconstruction of Malaysian History', *Revue du Sud-est Asiatique*, 3: 219–45.
——, 1964, 'Theoretical Aspects of Southeast Asian History', *Asian Studies*, 11(2): 247–60.
——, 1969, 'Academic Imperialism', Lecture delivered to the History Society, University of Singapore, 26th September.
——, 1971, *Thomas Stamford Raffles 1781–1826: Schemer or Reformer*, Sydney: Angus and Robertson.

Alatas, Syed Hussein, 1972a, 'The Captive Mind in Development Studies', *International Social Science Journal*, 34(1): 9–25.

———, 1972b, 'India and the Intellectual Awakening of Southeast Asia', in Syed Hussein Alatas, *Modernization and Social Change: Studies in Social Change in Southeast Asia*, pp. 151–63, Sydney: Angus & Robertson [Reproduced from 'India and the Intellectual Awakening of Asia', in B. Sarkar, ed., *India and Southeast Asia*, New Delhi: Indian Council for Cultural Relations, 1968].

———, 1974, 'The Captive Mind and Creative Development', *International Social Science Journal*, 36(4): 691–99.

———, 1976a, 'Erring Modernization: The Dilemma of Developing Societies', in Yogesh Atal and Ralph Pieris (eds), *Asian Rethinking on Development: A Symposium*, pp. 25–66, New Delhi: Abhinav Publications.

———, 1976b, 'Intellectual Captivity and the Developing Societies', Paper presented at the 30th International Congress of Human Sciences in Asia and North Africa, 3–8 August, Mexico.

———, 1977, *The Myth of the Lazy Native: A Study of the Image of the Malays, Filipinos, and Javanese from the Sixteenth to the Twentieth Century and its Functions in the Ideology of Colonial Capitalism*, London: Frank Cass.

———, 1978, 'Social Aspects of Endogenous Intellectual Creativity: The Problem of Obstacles—Guidelines for Research', Working Paper for Project on Socio-Cultural Development Alternatives in a Changing World, United Nations University, pp. 1–9.

———, 1979, 'Towards an Asian Social Science Tradition', *New Quest*, 17: 265–69.

———, 1981, 'Social Aspects of Endogenous Intellectual Creativity: The Problem of Obstacles—Guidelines for Research', in A. Abdel-Malek and A.N. Pandeya, (eds) *Intellectual Creativity in Endogenous Culture*, Tokyo: United Nations University.

———, 1990, *Corruption: Its Nature, Causes, and Functions*. Aldershot: Gower.

———, 2000, 'Intellectual Imperialism: Definition, Traits and Problems', *Southeast Asian Journal of Social Science*, 28(1): 23–45.

———, 2002, 'The Development of an Autonomous Social Science Tradition in Asia: Problems and Prospects', *Asian Journal of Social Science*, 30(1): 150–57.

Alavi, Hamza, 1972, 'The State in Post-Colonial Societies: Pakistan and Bangladesh', *New Left Review*, 74(1): 59–81.

Altbach, Philip G, 1975, 'Literary Colonialism: Books in the Third World', *Harvard Educational Review*, 45: 226–36.

———, 1977, 'Servitude of the Mind? Education, Dependency, and Neocolonialism,' *Teachers College Record*, 79(2): 187–204.

Altbach, Philip G. and Viswanathan Selvaratnam, (eds), 1989, *From Dependence to Autonomy: The Development of Asian Universities*, Dordrecht, the Netherlands: Kluwer Academic Publishers.

Amin, Samir, 1974, *Accumulation on a World Scale* Vols 1 & 2, New York: Monthly Review Press.

———, 1975, *Unequal Development*, New York: Monthly Review Press.

———, 1989, *Eurocentrism*, London: Zed Books.

———, 1989, *Eurocentrism*, New York: Monthly Review Press.

Amravati, G. Tamaskar, 1956, 'Geographical Knowledge in the Upanishads', *National Geographical Journal of India*, 2(2): 106–14.

Anderson, K.J., 1991, *Vancouver's Chinatown: Racial Discourse in Canada, 1857–1980*. Montreal & Buffalo: McGill-Queen's University Press.

Andreski, Stanislav, 1972, *Social Sciences as Sorcery*, London: Andre Deutsch.
Aricanli, Tosun & Mara Thomas, 1994, 'Sidestepping Capitalism: On the Ottoman Road to Elsewhere', *Journal of Historical Sociology*, 7(1): 25-48.
Ashraf, Ahmad, 1976, 'The Social Scientists and the Challenges of Development', in Yogesh Atal and Ralph Pieris (eds), *Asian Rethinking on Development: A Symposium*, pp. 103-30, New Delhi: Abhinav Publications.
Atal, Yogesh, 1981, 'The Call For Indigenization', *International Social Science Journal*, 33(1): 189-97.
Baali, Fuad & J. Brian Price, 1982, 'Ibn Khaldun and Karl Marx: On Socio-Historic Change', *Iqbal Review*, 23(1): 17-36.
Baars, Adolf, 1916, 'Het S.I-Congres te Bandung', *Het Vrije Woord*, 25th June, 1916.
Bachtiar, Harsja, 1984, 'Indonesia', in *Social Sciences in Asia and the Pacific*, pp. 249-80, Paris: UNESCO.
Baehr, Peter & Mike O'Brien, 1994, 'The Utility, Rhetoric and Interpretation of Classic Texts', in *Founders, Classics and the Concept of a Cannon*, Trend Report, Current Sociology, 42(1).
Baharuddin, Shamsul Amri, 1995, 'Malaysia: The Kratonization of Social Science', in Nico Schulte Nordholt and Leontine Visser (eds), *Social Science in Southeast Asia: From Particularism to Universalism*, pp. 87-109, Amsterdam: VU University Press.
―――, 1999, 'Colonial Knowledge and the Construction of Malay and Malayness: Exploring the Literary Component', *SARI: Journal of the Malay World and Civilization*, 17: 3-17.
Bahl, Vinay, 2000, 'Situating and Rethinking Subaltern Studies for Writing Working Class History', in Arif Dirlik, Vinay Bahl and Peter Gran (eds), *History after the Three Worlds: Post-Eurocentric Historiographies*, pp. 85-113, Maryland: Rowman and Littlefield Publishers.
Bailey, F.G., 1959, 'For a Sociology of India', *Contributions to Indian Sociology*, 3: 88-101.
Barnes, H.E., 1917, 'Sociology before Comte', *American Journal of Sociology*, 23(2): 197-98.
Bastin, John, 1959, 'The Study of Modern Southeast Asian History', An Inaugural Lecture Delivered at the University of Malaya, 14 December, Kuala Lumpur:
Basu, Amitabha & Suhas K. Biswas, 1980, 'Is Indian Anthropology Dead/Dying?', *Journal of the Indian Anthropological Society*, 15, 1-14.
Batatu, Hana, 1978, *The Old Social Classes and the Revolutionary Movements of Iraq*, Princeton: Princeton University Press.
Batra, R. 1980, *Muslim Civilization and the Crisis in Iran*, Dallas: Venus Books.
Baudrillard, Jean, 1975, *The Mirror of Production*, St Louis: Telos Press.
Becker, Howard & Harry Elmer Barnes, 1961, *Social Thought from Lore to Science*, 3 Vols., New York: Dover Publications.
Bell, Morag, 1994, 'Images, Myths and Alternative Geographies of the Third World', in Derek Gregory, Ron Martin and G. Smith (eds), *Human Geography: Society, Space and Social Science*, pp. 174-99, London: Macmillan.
Benjamin, Curtis, 1964, *Books as Forces in National Development and International Relations*, New York: National Foreign Trade Council.
Benjamin, Geoffrey, 1995, 'The Sociology of Indigeny', Paper presented at the Second ASEAN Inter-University Seminar on Social Development, 28-30 November, Cebu City, The Philippines.
Bennagen, P.L., 1980, 'The Asianization of Anthropology', *Asian Studies*, 18: 1-26.

Béteille, André, 1986, 'Individualism and Equality', *Current Anthropology*, 27(2): 121-34.

———, 2002, *Sociology: Essays on Approach and Method*, Delhi: Oxford University Press.

Blake, Myrna L., 1991, 'The Portability of Family Therapy to Different Cultural and Socio-Economic Contexts', *Asia-Pacific Journal of Social Work*, 1(2): 32-60.

Blaut, James M., 1970, 'Geographic Models of Imperialism', *Antipodes*, 2(1): 65-85.

———, 1973, 'The Theory of Development', *Antipode* 5(2) 22-26.

———, 1977. 'Two Views of Diffusion', *Annals of the Association of American Geographers*, 67: 343-49.

———, 1994, 'Diffusionism: A Uniformitarian Critique', in Kenneth E. Foote (ed.), *Re-Reading Cultural Geography*, pp. 173-90, Austin: University of Texas Press.

Bodin, Jean, 1593/1857/1976, *Colloquium of the Seven about Secrets of the Sublime (Colloquium Heptalomeres de Rerum Sublimium Arcanis Abditis)*, Translated with an Introduction by Mavion Leathers Daniels Kuntz, Princeton University Press.

Boehmer, Elleke, 1995, *Colonial and Postcolonial Literature*, Oxford: Oxford University Press.

Boff, L., 1985, *Church, Charisma and Power*, London: SCM Press.

Brookfield, H.C., 1972, 'On One Geography and a Third World', *Transactions of the Institute of British Geographers*, 58, 1-20.

———, 1975, *Interdependent Development*, Pittsburgh: University of Pittsburgh Press.

Brown, Richard H., 1977, *A Poetic for Sociology: Toward a Logic of Discovery for the Human Sciences*, Cambridge: Cambridge University Press.

———, 1985, 'Historical Science as Linguistic Figuration', *Theory and Society*, 14(5): 677-703.

Burke, Barry, 2005, 'Mahatma Gandhi on Education', http://www.infed.org/thinkers/et-gand.htm

Burn, C., 1981, 'The Third World in the 80s', *Area* 13(3): 216-17.

Buruma, Ian, 1995, 'The Singapore Way', *The New York Review of Books*, October 19: 66-71.

Calhoun, Craig, 1993, 'Postmodernism as Pseudohistory', *Theory, Culture & Society*, 10: 75-96.

Carino, Ledivina V. (ed.), 1986, *Bureaucratic Corruption in Asia: Causes, Consequences and Controls*, Quezon City: JMC Press and Manila: College of Public Administration, University of the Phillippines.

Carre, Olivier, 1988, 'A Propos de Vues Neo-Khalduniennnes sur Quelques Systemes Politiques Arabes Actuels', *Arabica*, 35(3): 368-87.

Catapusan, B., 1957, 'Development of Sociology in the Philippines', *Philippine Sociological Review*, 4: 53-57.

Césaire, Aimé, 1955, *Discours sur le colonialisme*. Editions Présence Africaine.

———, 1972, *Discourse on Colonialism*, New York: Monthly Review.

Chakrabarti, Dilip K., (1997) *Colonial Indology: Sociopolitics of the Ancient Indian Past*, New Delhi: Munshiram Manoharlal Publishers.

Chakrabarty, Dipesh, 1992, 'Postcoloniality and the Artifice of History: Who Speaks for "Indian" Pasts?', *Representations*, 37: 1-26.

———, 2001, *Provincializing Europe: Postcolonial Thought and Historical Difference*, New Delhi: Oxford University Press.

Chan, Hoiman, (1993), 'Some Metasociological Notes on the Sinicisation of Sociology', *International Sociology* 8(1), 113-19.

Chan, Hoiman, 1994, 'Thoughts on the Building of a Chinese Sociological Tradition: Metasociological Notes II', *Hong Kong Journal of Social Science*, 3: 36-78. <in Chinese>.

Chase-Dunn, C., 1989, *Global Formation: Structures of the World-Economy*, Cambridge, MA: Basil Blackwell.

Chattopadhyaya, Brajadulal, 2002, 'Introduction', in D.D. Kosambi, *Combined Methods in Indology and Other Writings*, pp. xiii-xxxvii, Compiled, edited and introduced by Brajadulal Chattopadhyaya, New Delhi: Oxford University Press.

Cheddadi, Abdesselam, 1980, 'Le Systeme du Pouvoir en Islam d' apres Ibn Khaldun,' *Annales, Eco., So., Civ.* 3-4: 534-50.

Chee, Stephen, 1984, 'Malaysia', in *Social Sciences in Asia and the Pacific*, pp. 296-323, Paris: UNESCO.

Chekki, D.A., 1987, *American Sociological Hegemony: Transnational Explorations*, Lanham: University Press of America.

Chenery, H.B. & A.M. Strout, 1966, 'Foreign Assistance and Economic Development', *American Economic Review*, 56(4): 679-733.

Cheng, L. & A. So, 1983, 'The Reestablishment of Sociology in the PRC: Toward the Sinification of Marxian Sociology', *Annual Review of Sociology* 9, 471-98.

Chung Yuen Kay, 1989, 'Gender, Work and Ethinicity: An Ethnography of Female Factory Workers in Singapore', Unpublished Ph.D. thesis, Department of Sociology, National University of Singapore.

Clarke, William C., 1990, 'Learning from the Past: Traditional Knowledge and Sustainable Development' *The Contemporary Pacific*, 2(2): 233-53.

Cummings, William K., 1995, 'The Asian Human Resource Approach in Global Perspective', *Oxford Review of Education*, 21(1): 67-81.

Currie, Kate, 1995, 'The Challenge to Orientalist, Elitist and Western Historiography: Notes on the "Subaltern Project", 1982-9', *Dialectical Anthropology*, 20(2): 217-46.

Dahrendorf, R., 1968, 'Sociology and the Sociologist: On the Problem of Theory and Practice', in Dahrendorf, *Essays in the Theory of Society*, pp. 256-78, Stanford: Stanford University Press.

Dang, B.S., 1982, 'Future of Applied Anthropology in India', *Indian Anthropology*, 2: 31-36.

Davis, Murray S., 1986, '"That's Classic!" The Phenomenology and Rhetoric of Successful Social Theories', *Philosophy of the Social Sciences*, 16: 285-301.

Dei, George J.S., 1993, 'Indigenous African Knowledge Systems: Local Traditions of Sustainable Forestry', *Singapore Journal of Tropical Geography*, 14(1): 28-41.

Dicken, P., 1986, *Global Shift: Industrial Change in a Turbulent World*, London: Paul Chapman.

Van Dijk, T.A., 1994, 'Academic Nationalism', *Discourse and Society*, 5(3): 275-76.

Dirlik, Arif, 1994, 'The Postcolonial Aura: Third World Criticism in the Age of Global Capitalism', *Critical Inquiry*, 20: 328-56.

Driver, F., 1992, 'Geography's Empire: Histories of Geographical Knowledge', *Environment and Planning: Society and Space*, 10(1): 23-40.

Du Bois, Marc, 1991, 'The Governance of the Third World', *Alternatives*, 16(1): 1-30.

Dube, S.C., 1984, 'India', in *Social Sciences in Asia and the Pacific*, pp. 229-48, Paris: UNESCO.

Duesenberry, J.S., 1949, *Income, Saving and the Theory of Consumer Behavior*, Cambridge: Harvard University Press.

Dumont, Louis, 1966, *Homo Hierarchicus*, Paris: Gallimard.

Dumont, Louis, 1977, *From Mandeville to Marx*, Chicago: University of Chicago Press.
———, 1987, 'On Individualism and Equality' *Current Anthropology*, 28(5): 669-72.
Dumont, L. & D.F. Pocock, 1957, 'For a Sociology of India', *Contributions to Indian Sociology*, 1: 7-22
———, 1960, 'For a Sociology of India: A Rejoinder to Dr. Bailey', *Contributions to Indian Sociology*, 4: 82-89.
Eades, Jerry, 1997, 'Anthropological Work on China in Japan in Comparative Perspective', Paper presented at the International Workshop on Indigenous and Indigenized Anthropology in Asia, 1-3 May, Leiden.
Edwards, Michel, 1989, 'The Irrelevance of Development Studies', *Third World Quarterly*, 11(1): 116-35.
Ehsani, Kaveh, 1995, 'Islam, Modernity and National Identity', *Middle East Insight*, 11(5).
Emmanuel, A., 1972, *Unequal Exchange: A Study of the Imperialism of Trade*, New York: Monthly Review Press.
Enriquez, Virgilio G., 1994a, 'Kapwa and the Struggle for Justice, Freedom and Dignity', in Teresita B. Obusan & Angelina R. Enriquez (eds), *Pamamaraan: Indigenous Knowledge and Evolving Research Paradigms*, pp. 1-18, Quezon City: Asian Center, University of the Philippines.
———, 1994b, 'Towards Cross-Cultural Knowledge through Cross-Indigenous Methods and Perspective', in Teresita B. Obusan and Angelina R. Enriquez (eds), *Pamamaraan: Indigenous Knowledge and Evolving Research Paradigms*, pp. 19-31, Quezon City: Asian Center, University of the Philippines.
Escobar, Arturo, 1984-85, 'Discourse and Power in Development: Michel Foucault and the Relevance of His Work to the Third World', *Alternatives*, 10(3): 377-400.
———, 1995, *Encountering Development: The Making and Unmaking of the Third World*, Princeton: Princeton University Press.
Escolar, M., Palacios, Silvina Quintero & Carlos Reboratti, 1994, 'Geographical Identity and Patriotic Representation in Argentina', in David Hooson, (ed.), *Geography and National Identity*, pp. 346-66, Oxford: Blackwell.
Evans, Grant, 1997, 'Indigenous and Indigenised Anthropology in Asia', Paper presented at the International Workshop on Indigenous and Indigenized Anthropology in Asia, 1-3 May, Leiden.
Faghirzadeh, Saleh, 1982, *Sociology of Sociology: In Search of Ibn-Khaldun's Sociology Then and Now*, Tehran: Soroush Press.
Fahim, Hussein, 1970, 'Indigenous Anthropology in Non-Western Countries', *Current Anthropology*, 20(2): 397.
Fahim, Hussein & Katherine Helmer, 1980, 'Indigenous Anthropology in Non-Western Countries: A Further Elaboration', *Current Anthropology*, 21(5): 644-63.
Fanon, Frantz, 1961, *Les damnés de la terre*, Paris : François Maspero Éditeur.
———, 1968, *The Wretched of the Earth*, New York: Grove Press.
Fei Hsiao-t'ung [Fei Xiaotong] (1947/1979) 'The Growth of Chinese Sociology', in Fei, *Fei Hsiao-t'ung: The Dilemma of a Chinese Intellectual*, James P. McGough, select. & trans., White Plains, New York: M.E. Sharpe.
Feliciano, Gloria D., 1984, 'Philippines', in *Social Sciences in Asia and the Pacific*, pp. 468-501, Paris: UNESCO.
Ferguson, Marjorie & Peter Golding, 1997, 'Cultural Studies and Changing Times: An Introduction', in Marjorie Ferguson and Peter Golding (eds), *Cultural Studies in Question*, pp. xiii-xxvii, London: Sage.

Forbers, Dean, 1981, 'Beyond the Geography of Development', *Singapore Journal of Tropical Geography*, 2(2): 68–80.
Foucault, Michel, 1977, 'History of Systems of Thought', in *Michel Foucault, Language, Counter Memory, Practice: Selected Essays and Interviews*, Donald E. Bouchard and Sherry Simon (eds), trans. Ithaca, N.Y.: Cornell University Press.
———, 1980a, *History of Sexuality, Vol. 1: An Introduction*, New York: Vintage Books.
———, 1980b, *Power/Knowledge: Selected Interviews and Other Writings*. New York: Pantheon Books.
———, 1981, 'The Order of Discourse', in R. Young (ed.), *Untying the Text: A Post-Structuralist Reader*, Boston: Routledge & Kegan Paul.
Freire, Paulo, 1970, *Pedagogy of the Oppressed*, New York: Seabury Press.
Furfey, Paul Hanly, 1953, *The Scope and Method of Sociology: A Metasociological Treatise*, New York: Copper Square Publishers.
Gandhi, Mahatma, 1993, *An Autobiography: The story of My Experiments with Truth*, Boston: Beacon Press.
———, 1995, *The Penguin Gandhi Reader*, Rudrangshu Mukherjee (ed.), New York: Penguin Books.
———, 1997, *Hind Swaraj and Other Writings*, Cambridge: Cambridge University Press.
Garreau, Frederick H., 1985, 'The Multinational Version of Social Science with Emphasis upon the Discipline of Sociology', *Current Sociology*, 33(3): 1–169.
———, 1986, 'The Third World Revolt against First World Social Science: An Explication suggested by the Revolutionary Pedagogy of Paulo Freire', *International Journal of Comparative Sociology*, 27(3–4): 172–89.
———, 1988, 'Another Type of Third World Dependency: The Social Sciences', *International Sociology*, 3(2): 171–78.
———, 1991, *The Political Economy of the Social Sciences*, New York: Garland Publishing.
Garna, Judistira K. & Rustam A. Sani (eds), 1990, *Antropologi Sosiologi di Indonesia dan Malaysia: Teori Pengembangan dan Penerapan*, Bangi: Penerbit Universiti Kebangsaan Malaysia.
Gellespie, Kate & Gwen Okruhlik, 1988, 'Cleaning Up Corruption in the Middle-East' *Middle East Journal*, 42(1): 59–82.
Gellner, Ernest, 1981, *Muslim Society*, Cambridge: Cambridge University Press.
Giddens, Anthony, 1993, *Sociology*, 2nd edition, Cambridge: Polity Press.
———, 1997, *Sociology*, 3rd edition, Cambridge: Polity Press.
———, 2001, *Sociology*, 4th edition, Cambridge: Polity Press.
Gipouloux, Francois, 1989, 'Sociologie et Reforme: La Renaissance de la Sociologie en Republique Populaire de Chine', *Revue Europeenne des Sciences Sociales*, 84, 51–68.
Von Gizycki, Rainald, 1973, 'Centre and Periphery in the International Scientific Community: Germany, France and Great Britain in the 19th Century', *Minerva*, 11(4): 474–94.
Godelier, M., 1974, 'On the Definition of a Social Formation: The Example of the Incas', *Critique of Anthropology*, 1, 63–73.
Gonzales Casanova, Pablo, 1965, *La Democracia en Mexico*, Mexico City: Singlo XXI.
Gorz, Andre, 1982, *Farewell to the Working Class*, London: Pluto.
el Gowhary, Yousry, 1964, 'Geographical Ideas of Ibn Haukal', *Geografia*, 3(2): 5–10.
Gran, Peter, 1979, *The Islamic Roots of Capitalism: Egypt, 1760–1840*, Austin: University of Texas Press.

Gransow, Bettina, 1985, 'Soziologie in China oder Chinesische Sozilogie? Einige Bemerkungen zum gegenwartigen Entwicklungsstand der Soziologie in der VR China', *Zeitschrift fur Soziologie*, 14(2): 140–51.

———, 1993, 'Chinese Sociology: Sinicisation and Globalisation', *International Sociology*, 8(1): 101–12.

Grigg, D., 1985, *The World Food Problem, 1950–1980*, Oxford: Basil Blackwell.

Grossman, Lionel, 1978, 'History and Literature: Reproduction or Significance', in Robert H. Canary and Henry Kozicki (eds), *The Writing of History: Literary Form and Historical Understanding*, pp. 3–40, Madison: University of Wisconsin Press.

Guha, Ramachandra, 1989, 'Sociology in India: Some Elective Affinities', *Contributions to Indian Sociology*, 23(2): 339–46.

Guha, Ranajit, 1982a, 'Preface', in Ranajit Guha (ed.), *Subaltern Studies I: Writings on South Asian History and Society*, pp. vii–viii, Delhi: Oxford University Press.

———, 1982b, 'On Some Aspects of the Historiography of Colonial India', in Ranajit Guha (ed.), *Subaltern Studies I: Writings on South Asian History and Society*, pp. 1–8, Delhi: Oxford University Press.

Gumplowicz, Ludwig, 1899, *The Outlines of Sociology*, trans. by Frederick W. Moore, Philadelphia: American Academy of Political and Social Science.

Gupta, Dipankar, 1996, *The Context of Ethnicity: Sikh Identity in a Comparative Perspective*, New Delhi: Oxford University Press.

Guttierez, G., 1983, *A Theology of Liberation: History, Politics and Salvation*, London: SCM Press.

Hadiz, Vedi R. & Daniel Dhakidae, 2005, 'Introduction', in Vedi R. Hadiz and Daniel Dhakidae (eds), *Social Science and Power in Indonesia*, pp. 1–29, Jakarta: Equinox Publishing; Singapore: Institute of Southeast Asian Studies.

Hagen E.E., 1962, *On the Theory of Social Change: How Economic Growth Begins*, Homewood, Ill.: Dorsey.

Hall, D.G.E., 1959, *'East Asian History Today'*, Lecture delivered at the University of Hong Kong 20th May, Hong Kong University Press, Oxford University Press.

Han Sang-Jin, 1996, 'Modernization Deficits and the Quest for a Reflexive Sociology of East Asia', Paper presented to Korean Sociological Association-International Sociological Association East Asian Regional Colloquium on 'The Future of Sociology in East Asia', 22–23 November, Seoul.

Han Wan-Seng, 1992, *Korean Reality, Korean Sociology*, Seoul: Bum-Woo-Sa <in Korean>.

Handa, M.L., 1982, 'Indian Historiography: Writing and Rewriting Indian History', *Journal of Asian and African Studies*, 17(3–4): 218–34.

Herbertson, A.J., 1910, 'Geography and Some of Its Present Needs', *Geographical Journal*, 36, 468–79.

Hettne, Björn, 1991, *The Voice of the Third World: Currents in Development Thinking*, Studies on Developing Countries No. 134, Budapest: Institute for World Economics of the Hungarian Academy of Sciences.

Higgot, R.A., 1980, '"Radical" Development Theory: An Historiographical Essay' (unpublished paper, Australian Political Studies Association, 22nd Annual Conference).

Hooson, David, 1994, 'Introduction', in David Hooson (ed.), *Geography and National Identity*, pp. 1–11, Oxford: Blackwell.

Horowitz, I.L., 1965, 'The Life and Death of Project Camelot', *Trans-Action*, 3(4): ??

——— (ed.), 1967, *The Rise and Fall of Project Camelot: Studies in the Relationship Between Social Science and Practical Politics*, Cambridge: The M.I.T. Press.

Hsu, C.K., 1991, 'The Formation and Transformation of a Research Paradigm: A Revisit of Prof. Chen Shao-Hsing's Article', *Chinese Journal of Sociology*, 15: 29-40. <in Chinese>.
Hsu, Leonard Shih-Lien, 1931, 'The Sociological Movement in China', *Pacific Affairs*, 4(4): 283-307.
Huang, Lucy Jen, 1987, 'The Status of Sociology in People's Republic of China', *International Review of Modern Sociology*, 17: 111-36.
Hudson, B., 1977, 'The New Geography and the New Imperialism, 1870-1918', *Antipode*, 9: 12-19.
IDA, 1968, *Annual Report for 1968*.
IDA, 1969, *Annual Report for 1969*.
Illich, Ivan D., 1973, *Deschooling Society*, Harmondsworth: Penguin.
Inkeles, A. & D. Smith, 1974, *Becoming Modern: Individual Change in Six Developing Countries*, Cambridge, Mass.: Harvard University Press.
International Bank for Reconstruction and Development. 1983. *World Development Report*. New York: Oxford University Press, p. 44.
James, Preston E. & Geoffrey J. Martin, 1972, *All Possible Worlds*, New York: John Wiley and Sons.
Ben Jelloun, Taher, 1974, 'Décolonisation de la Sociologie au Maghreb: Utilité et Risques d'une Fonction Critique', *Le Monde Diplomatique*, August.
———, 1985, 'Decolonizing Sociology in the Maghreb: Usefulness and Risks of a Critical Function', in Saad Eddin Ibrahim and Nicholas S. Hopkins (eds), *Arab Society: Social Science Perspectives*, pp. 70-75, Cairo: American University in Cairo Press.
Jen, Huang Lucy, 1987, 'The Status of Sociology in People's Republic of China', *International Review of Modern Sociology*, 17: 111-36.
Johnston, Ron, 1985, 'To the Ends of the Earth', in Ron Johnston (ed.), *The Future of Geography*, pp. 326-38, London: Methuen.
Joshi, P.C., 1972, 'The Question of Relevance', *Seminar*, 157: 24-29.
———, 1982, 'Perspectives in Social Science Research: The Problem of Relevance or of Value Orientation', in Institute of Economic Growth, *Relevance in Social Science Research: A Colloquium*, pp. 69-93, New Delhi: Vikas Publishing House.
Kakar, Sudhir, 1982, *Shamans, Mystics and Doctors: A Psychological Inquiry into India and its Healing Traditions*, New York: Alfred Knopf.
Kameir, El-Watheig & Ibrahim Kursany, 1985, 'Corruption as the 'Fifth' Factor of Production in Sudan', *Scandinavian Institute of African Studies Research Report*, 72, Uppsala.
Kantowsky, Detlef, 1969, 'A Critical Note on the Sociology of Developing Societies', *Contributions to Indian Sociology*, 3, (ns): 128-31.
Karim, A.K. Nazmul, 1984, 'Bangladesh', in *Social Sciences in Space Asia and the Pacific*, pp. 79-92, Paris: UNESCO.
Karim, Manjur, 1995, 'Cardoso, Frank, and Achievement', *Progressive Sociologists Network* <psn@csf.colorado.edu>.
Kartodirdjo, Sartono, 1982, *Pemikiran dan Perkembangan Historiografi Indonesia: Suatu Alternatif*, Jakarta: Gramedia.
Kazmi, Yedullah, 1993, 'Panoptican: A World Order through Education or Education's Encounter with the Other/Difference', *Philosophy and Social Criticism*, 2, 195-213.
Ibn Khaldun, 'Abd al-Rahman, 1377/1981, *Muqaddimat Ibn Khaldun (The Prolegomena of Ibn Khaldun)*, Beirut: Dar al-Qalam.

Ibn Khaldun, 'Abd al-Rahman, 1958, *The Muqaddimah*, vol.3. New York: Pantheon Books.
Khatibi, M, 1967, *Bilan de la Sociologie au Maroc*, Rabat: Publications de l'Association pour la Recherche en Sciences Humaines.
Khondker, Habibul Haque, 1992, 'Internationalization, Indigenization and Globalization of Sociology', Paper presented at the Political Economy of the World System Section, American Sociological Association Meeting, Pittsburgh.
Kim, Kyong-Dong, 1978, 'Future of Social Science in Korea', *Korea Journal*, May: 22-32.
———, 1985, 'Republic of Korea', in *Sociology and Social Anthropology in Asia and the Pacific*, pp. 86-131, New Delhi: Wiley Eastern Limited & Paris: UNESCO.
———, 1991, 'Sociocultural Developments in the Republic of Korea', in Thomas W. Robinson (ed.), *Democracy and Development in East Asia: Taiwan, South Korea, and the Philippines*, pp. 137-54, Washington, DC.
———, 1994a, 'Reflections on the Non-Economic Factors in Korea's Economic Development', in Sung Yeung Kwack, (ed.), *The Korean Economy at a Crossroads*, pp. 41-56, Westport, CT: Praeger.
———, 1994b, 'Confucianism and Capitalist Development in East Asia', in Leslie Sklair (ed.), *Capitalism and Development*, pp. 87-106, London: Routledge.
———, 1995, 'The Korean Images of Old Age: A Glimpse of Verbal Culture', *Korean Journal of Population and Development*, 24(2): 173-79.
———, 1996a, 'Confucianism and Modernization in East Asia: Theoretical Exploration', in Josef Kreiner, (ed.), *The Impact of a Traditional Thought on Present-Day Japan*, p. 49-69, Munchen: Ludicium Verlag.
———, 1996b, 'Toward Culturally "Independent" Social Science: Illustrations of Indigenization in East Asia'. Paper presented to Korean Sociological Association-International Sociological Association East Asian Regional Colloquium on 'The Future of Sociology in East Asia', November 22-23, Seoul.
Kimble, George H.T., 1938, *Geography in the Middle Ages*, London: Methuen & Co. Ltd.
Kirzner, I.M., 1976, 'On the Methods of Modern Austrian economics', in E.G. Dolan (ed.), *The Foundations of Modern Austrian Economics*, pp. 40-51, Kansas City: Mo.: Sheed and Ward.
Kleden, Ignas, 1986, 'Social Science Indigenisation: National Response to Development Model and Theory Building', *Prisma*, 41: 27-38.
Kolakowski, Leszek, 1971, 'Althusser's Marx', in R. Miliband and J. Saville (eds), *Socialist Register*, pp. 111-28.
Kong, Lily and Victor Savage, 1986, 'The Malay World in Colonial Fiction', *Singapore Journal of Tropical Geography*, 7(1): 40-52.
Kosambi, D.D., 1965, *Culture and Civilization of Ancient India in Historical Outline*, London: Routledge and Kegan Paul.
———, 2002, 'Stages of Indian History', in D.D. Kosambi, *Combined Methods in Indology and Other Writings*, pp. 57-72, Compiled, edited and introduced by Brajadulal Chattopadhyaya, New Delhi: Oxford University Press.
Kroeber, Alfred Louis, 1944, *Configuration of Culture*, Berkeley: University of California Press.
Kumar, G., 1968, 'Servitude of the Mind', *Seminar*, 112: 39-66.
Kumar, Krishna, 1986 (ed.), *Bonds Without Bondage*. Honolulu: East-West Cultural Learning Center.

Kuwayama, Takami, 1997, 'Native Anthropologists: With Special Reference to Japanese Studies Inside and Outside Japan', *Japan Anthropology Workshop Newsletter*, September, 26-27: 52-56.

Kuwayama, T. & J. van Bremen, 1997, 'Native Anthropologists: With Special Reference to Japanese Studies Inside and Outside Japan', (Kuwayama-van Bremen Debate: Native Anthropologists), *Japan Anthropology Workshop Newsletter*, 26-27 September 1997, pp. 52-69.

———, 1997, 'Kuwayama-van Bremen Debate: Native Anthropologists—With Special Reference to Japanese Studies Inside and Outside Japan', *Japan Anthropology Workshop Newsletter*, September 26-27.

Kuznets, S., 1966, *Economic Growth and Structure*, London: Heinemann.

Kwon T'ae-Hwan, 1979, 'Seminar on Koreanizing Western Approaches to Social Science', *Korea Journal*, 19(11): 20-25.

Kyi, Khin Maung, 1984, 'Burma', in *Social Sciences in Asia and the Pacific*. pp. 93-141, Paris: UNESCO.

Lacoste, Yves, 1984, *Ibn Khaldun: The Birth of History and the Past of the Third World*, London: Verso.

Lamy, Paul, 1976, 'The Globalization of American Thought: Excellence or Imperialism?' *The American Sociologist*, 11: 104-14.

Laroui, Abdallah, 1980, *L'Etat dans le Monde Arabe Contemporain*, Louvain: Universite Catholique.

Lasch, Christopher, 1969, *The Agony of the American Left*, New York: Alfred Knopf.

Lashley, Karl S., 1923, 'The Behavioristic Interpretation of Consciousness', *Psychological Review*, 30(4): 237-72.

Lee Chong-Bum, 1979, 'Prolegomenon to the Indigenization of Public Administration', *Social Science Journal*, 6: 7-26.

Lee Jae-Yeol & Jung Jin-Seong, 1994, 'The Task of Education in Korean Sociology in Preparing for the 21st Century', in *Korean Sociological Association, Korean Sociology in the 21st Century*, Seoul: Moon-Hak-Kwa Ji-Seong-Sa. <In Korean>.

Lee, Rance P.L., 1992, 'Formulation of Relevant Concepts and Propositions for Sociological Research in Chinese Society', in Chie Nakane and Chien Chao (eds), *Home Bound: Studies in East Asian Society*, pp. 81-98, Tokyo: Centre for East Asian Cultural Studies.

Lee Su-Hoon, 1996, 'Wither Sociology in Korea? History, Reality, and World-System', Paper presented to Korean Sociological Association-International Sociological Association East Asian Regional Colloquium on 'The Future of Sociology in East Asia', 22-23 November, Seoul.

Lengyel, Peter, 1986, *International Social Science: The UNESCO Experience*, New Brunswick, New Jersey, Oxford: Transaction Books.

van Leur, J.C., 1937, 'Enkele aanteekeningen met betrekking tot de beoefening der Indische geschiedenis' [Some Notes Concerning the Study of the History of the Indies], *Koloniale Studiën*, 21: 651-66.

———, 1940a, 'Eenige aanteekeningen betreffende de mogelijkheid der 18e eeuw als categorie in de Indische geschiedschrijving' [Some Notes on the Possibility of the 18th Century as a Category in the Writing of the History of the Indies], *Tijdschrift voor Indische Taal-, Land-en Volkenkunde uitgegeven door het (Koninklijk) Bataviaasch Genootschap van Kunsten en Wetenschappen* 80: 544-67.

van Leur, J.C., 1940b, 'De Wereld van Zuidoost-Azië' [The World of Southeast Asia], in J.C. de Haan & P.J. van Winter (eds), *Nederlanders over de Zeeën: 350 jaar Nederlandsche koloniale geschiedenis*] *Dutchmen over the Seas: 350 Years of Dutch Colonial History*, pp. 101–44, Utrecht.

———, 1955, *Indonesian Trade and Society: Essays in Asian Social and Economic History*, The Hague: W. van Hoeve.

Lie, John, 1996, 'Sociology of Contemporary Japan', *Current Sociology*, 44(1): 1–95.

Lin, Nan, 1987, 'Sinicisation de la Sociologie: L'etape Suivante', *Revue Europeenne des Sciences Sociales*, 76: 127–39.

Line, Maurice & Stephen Roberts, 1976, 'The Size, Growth, and Composition of Social Science Literature'. *International Social Science Journal*, 28.

Ling, Mu, 1995, 'Beyond the Theory of 'Language Games': Huang Ziping and Chinese Literary Criticism in the 1980s', *Modern China*, 12(4): 420–49.

Linton, Ralph, 1955, *The Tree of Culture*, New York: Alfred Knopf.

Liu Kang, 1993, 'Politics, Critical Paradigms: Reflections on Modern Chinese Literature Studies', *Modern China*, 19(1): 13–40.

Lukacs, G., 1968, *History and Class Consciousness*. Cambridge, Mass.: MIT Press.

———, 1983, 'Tagore's Gandhi Novel: Review of Rabindranath Tagore, The Home and the World', in *Reviews and Articles* (trans.) pp. 8–11, Peter Palmer, London: Merlin.

Ludden, David, 2002, 'Introduction: A Brief History of Subalternity' in David Ludden, (ed.), *Reading Subaltern Studies: Critical History, Contested Meaning, and the Globalisation of South Asia*, Delhi: Permanent Black.

Mabogunje, A.L., 1980, *The Development Process: A Spatial Perspective*, London: Hutschinson University Library.

Madan, T.N., 1966, 'For a Sociology of India', *Contributions to Indian Sociology*, 9: 9–16.

———, 1977, 'The Quest for Hinduism', *International Social Science Journal*, 29(2): 261–78.

———, 1994, 'Images of India in American Anthropology' in T.N. Madan, *Pathways: Approaches to the Study of Society in India*, pp. 85–107, New Delhi: Oxford University Press.

Malo, Manasse (ed.), 1989, *Pengembangan Ilmu-Ilmu Sosial di Indonesia sampai decade '80-an*, Jakarta: CV Rajawali.

Mannheim, Karl, 1936, *Ideology and Utopia*, London: Routledge & Kegan Paul.

———, 1953, 'Structural Analysis of Epistemology', in Kal Mannheim, *Essays on Sociology and Social Psychology*, London: Routledge & Kegan Paul.

———, 1993, 'The Sociology of Intellectuals', *Theory, Culture & Society*, 10(3): 69–80.

Marriott, McKim, 1989, 'Constructing and Indian Ethnosociology', *Contributions to Indian Sociology*, 23(1): 1–39.

Marx, K., 1967, *Capital: A Critique of Political Economy*, Vol. 1., New York: International Publishers.

———, 1974, *The Grundrisse: Foundations of the Critique of Political Economy*, New York: Random House.

Marx, Karl & Frederick Engles, 1968, *Selected Works*, Moscow: Progress Publishers.

Matthes, Joachim, 1992, 'The Operation Called "Vergleichen"', *Soziale Welt*, 8: 75–99.

———, 2000, 'Religion in the Social Sciences: A Socio-Epistemological Critique', *Akademika*, 56: 85–105.

Maykovich, Minako K., 1987, 'Sociology in Taiwan', *International Review of Modern Sociology*, 17, 139–62.

McClelland, D.C., 1967, *The Achieving Society*, New York: Free Press
McKay, Donald Vernon, 1943, 'Colonialism in the French Geographical Movement 1871-1881', *Geographical Review*, 33(2): 214-32.
McTaggart, W. Donald & Duane Stormont, 1975, 'Urbanization Concepts in the Restructuring of Indonesia', *The Journal of Tropical Geography*, 41: 34-44.
McWilliams, Michael, 1995, 'Knowledge and Power: Reflections on National Interest and the Study of Asia', *Asian Affairs*, 26(1): 33-46.
Meillassoux, C., 1972, 'From Reproduction to Production', *Economy and Society*, 1: 93-105.
Memmi, Albert., 1957, *Portrait du Colonisé précédé du Portrait du Colonisateur*, Editions Buchet/Chastel, Corrêa.
——, 1967, *The Colonizer and the Colonized*, Boston: Beacon.
Mendoza, S. Lily, 2002, *Between the Homeland and the Diaspora: The Politics of Theorizing Filipino and Filipino-American Identities. A Second Look at the Poststructuralism-Indigenization Debates*, New York & London: Routledge.
Meyer, John W., 1987, 'The World Polity and the Authority of the Nation State', in George M. Thomas, John W. Meyer, Francisco O. Ramirez, and John Boli (eds), *Institutional Structure: Constituting State, Society, and the Individual*, pp. 41-70, Beverly Hills: Sage.
Meyer, John W. & Michael T. Hannan (eds), 1979, *National Development and the World System: Educational, Economic and Political Change, 1950-1970*, Chicago: University of Chicago Press.
Milbank, J., 1991, *Theology and Social Theory: Beyond Secular Reason*, Cambridge, MA: Blackwell.
Michaud, Gerard, 1981, 'Caste, confession et societe en Syrie: Ibn Khaldoun au chevet du "Progessisme Arabe"', *Peuples Mediterraneens*, 16: 119-30.
Misra, P.K., 1972, 'Social Science Researches in India: Their Relevance', *Journal of the Indian Anthropological Society*, 7: 89-96.
Mitchell, Timothy., 1991, 'America's Egypt: Discourse of the Development Industry', *Middle East Report*, March-April: 18-34.
Moghadam, Val, 1989, 'Against Eurocentrism and Nativism', *Socialism and Democracy*, 9: 81-104.
Mohanty, Chandra Talpade, 1984, 'Under Western Eyes: Feminist Scholarship and Colonial Discourses', *Boundary*, 2, 12(3): 333-58.
de Morga, Antonio, 1890/1991, Sucesos de las Islas Filipinas por el Doctor Antonio de Morga, obra publicada en Méjico el año de 1609, nuevamente sacada a luz y anotada por José Rizal y precedida de un prólogo del Prof. Fernando Blumentritt, Edición del Centenario, impression al offset de la Edición Anotada por Rizal, Paris 1890, Escritos de José Rizal Tomo VI, Manila: Comision Nacional del Centenario de José Rizal, Instituto Histórico Nacional.
——, 1890/1962, *Historical Events of the Philippine Islands* by Dr Antonio de Morga, Published in Mexico in 1609, recently brought to light and annotated by Jose Rizal, preceded by a prologue by Dr Ferdinand Blumentritt, Writings of José Rizal Volume VI, Manila: National Historical Institute.
Morawetz, D., 1980, 'Economic Lessons from Some Small Socialist Developing Countries', *World Development*, 8(5-6): 337-69.
van den Muijzenberg, Otto & Wolters, Willem, 1988, *Conceptualizing Development: The Historical-Sociological Tradition in Dutch Non-Western Sociology*, Dordrecht: Foris Publications.

Mukerji, D.P., 1945, *On Indian History: A Study in Method*, Bombay: Hind Kitabs.
———, 1946, *Views and Counterviews*, Lucknow: Universal.
———, 1955, 'Social Research', in K.M. Kapadia (ed.), *Professor Ghurye Felicitation Volume*. Bombay: Popular Prakashan.
———, 1958, *Diversities*, New Delhi: People's Publishing House.
Mukherji, Partha Nath, 2004, 'Indigeneity and Universality in Social Science', in Partha Nath Mukherji and Chandan Sen Gupta, (eds), *Indigeneity and Universality in Social Science: A South Asian Response*, pp. 15-65, Delhi: Sage.
Mukherji, Partha N., J. Aikara & C. Sengupta (eds), 1997, *Sociology in Southeast Asia: Heritage and Challenges*, Montreal: International Sociological Association Pre-Congress Volumes.
Mu Ling, 1995, 'Beyond the Theory of "Language Games": Huang Ziping and Chinese Literary Criticism in the 1980s', *Modern China*, 12(4): 420-49.
Mullard, Chris & Martin Brennan, 1978, 'The Malaysian Predicament: Towards a New Theoretical Frontier', *Journal of Contemporary Asia*, 8(3): 341-54.
Munshi, Surendra, 1979, 'Tribal Absorption and Sanskritization in Hindu Society', *Contributions to Indian Sociology* (ns), 13(2): 293-317.
———, 1988 'Max Weber on India: An Introductory Critique', *Contributions to Indian Sociology* (ns), 22(1): 1-34.
Myrdal, Gunnar, 1957, *Economic Theory and Underdeveloped Regions*, New York: Harper and Row.
———, 1968, *Asian Drama*, Vol. I. New York: The Twentieth Century Fund.
Nanda, B.R., 1989, *Mahatma Gandhi: A Biography*, Oxford: Oxford University Press.
Nandi, Proshanta K., 1994, 'Educational Culture in the Third World: The Lingering Colonial Connection', *International Review of Modern Sociology*, 24(2): 17-30.
Nandy, Ashish, 1983, *The Intimate Enemy: Loss and Recovery of Self under Colonialism*, Delhi: Oxford University Press.
———, 1994, *The Illegitimacy of Nationalism*, Delhi: Oxford University Press.
———, 1995, *Alternative Sciences: Creativity and Authenticity in Two Indian Scientists*, Delhi: Oxford University Press.
Naoroji, D., 1962 [1901], *Poverty and Un-British Rule in India*, Delhi: Publications Division, Ministry of Information & Broadcasting, Government of India.
Nasr, Seyyed Hossein, 1964, *An Introduction to Islamic Cosmological Doctrines*, Cambridge: Harvard University Press.
———, 1968, *Science and Civilization in Islam*, Cambridge: Harvard University Press.
———, 1980, 'Reflections on Methodology in the Islamic Sciences', *Hamdard Islamicus*, 3(3): 3-13.
———, 1981, *Knowledge and the Sacred: The Gifford Lectures*,. Edinburgh: Edinburgh University Press.
———, 1993, *The Need for a Sacred Science*, Surrey: Curzon Press.
Newby, Gordon D., 1983, 'Ibn Khaldun and Frederick Jackson Turner: Islam and the Frontier Experience', *Journal of Asian and African Studies*, 18(3-4): 274-85.
van Niel, Robert, 1960, *The Emergence of the Modern Indonesian Elite*, The Hague: W. van Hoeve.
Ocampo, Ambeth R., 1998, 'Rizal's Morga and Views of Philippine History', *Philippine Studies*, 46: 184-214.
Oommen, T.K., 1991, 'Internationalization of Sociology: A View from Developing Countries', *Current Sociology*, 39(1): 67-84.

Oommen, T.K., 1995, *Alien Concepts and South Asian Reality: Responses and Reformulations*, New Delhi: Sage.

Osunade, Adewole M.A., 1994, 'Community Environmental Knowledge and Land Resource Surveys in Swaziland', *Singapore Journal of Tropical Geography*, 15(2): 157-70.

Pané, Armijn, 1951, 'Indonesia di Asia Selatan: Sedjarah Indonesia sampai ± 1600' [Indonesia in Southern Asia: Indonesian History till ± 1600], *Indonesia*, 2: 1-36.

Parekh, Bhiku, 1992, 'The Poverty of Indian Political Theory', *History of Political Thought*, 13(3): 535-60.

Pathy, Jaganath, 1988, 'Emerging Frontiers of Anthropology from Third World Perspective', *Indian Anthropologist*, 18(1): 11-19.

Pels, Peter, 1994, 'Five Thesis on Ethnography as Colonial Practice', *History and Anthropology* 8(1-4): 1-34.

Pertierra, Raul, 1994, 'A National Imagination and the Social Sciences: Indigenization and the Discovery of the Filipino', *Jurnal Antropologi dan Sosiologi*, 21: 35-53.

———, 1997, 'Culture, Social Science and the Conceptualization of the Philippine Nation-State', Paper presented at the International Workshop on Indigenous and Indigenized Anthropology in Asia, 1-3 May, Leiden.

Peters, John D., 1990, 'Rhetoric's Revival, Positivism's Persistence: Social Science, Clear Communication, and the Public Space', *Sociological Theory*, 8(2): 224-31.

Pieke, Frank N., 1997, 'Is there Room for Cultural Anthropology in the People's Republic of China?' Paper presented at the International Workshop on Indigenous and Indigenized Anthropology in Asia, 1-3 May, Leiden.

Pieris, Ralph, 1969, 'The Implantation of Sociology in Asia', *International Social Science Journal*, 21(3): 433-44.

Pipes, D., 1983, *In the Path of God: Islam and Political Power*. New York: Basic Books.

Potter, Robert B. & Mark Wilson, 1990, 'Indigenous Environmental Learning in a Small Developing Country: Adolescents in Barbados, West Indies', *Singapore Journal of Tropical Geography*, 11(1): 56-67.

Potter, Jonathan, Margaret Wetherell & Andrew Chitty, 1991, 'Quantification Rhetoric—Cancer on Television', *Discourse and Society*, 2(3): 333-65.

Potter, Rob, 1993, 'Little England and Little Geography: Reflections on Third World Teaching and Research', *Area*, 25(3): 291-94.

Portes, A., 1976, 'On the Sociology of National Development', *American Journal of Sociology*, 82(1): 55.

Prakash, Gyan, 1990, 'Writing Post-Orientalist Histories of the Third World: Perspectives from Indian Historiography', *Comparative Studies in Society and History*, 32(2): 383-408.

———, 1992, 'Postcolonial Criticism and Indian Historiography', *Social Text*, 31/32, 8-19.

———, 1996, 'Who's Afraid of Postcoloniality?' *Social Text*, 14(4): 187-203.

PuruShotam, Nirmala, 1992, 'Women and Knowledge/Power. Notes on the Singaporean Dilemma', in K.C. Ban, A. Pakir and C.K. Tong (eds), *Imagining Singapore*, Singapore: Times Academic Press.

———, 1993, 'Caste: Woman. Occupation: Domestic Maid. Exploring the Realm of Foreign Full-time Workers in Singapore', in J, Ariffin (ed.), *Proceedings of the International Colloquium on Migration, Development and Gender in the Asean Region*, Kuala Lumpur: Population Studies Unit, University of Malaya.

———, 1998, 'Gender and the Middle Class Way of Life', in K. Sen and M. Stivens (eds), *Sex and Power in Affluent Asia*, London: Routledge.

Qadeer, M.A., 1974, 'Do Cities "Modernize" the Developing Countries: An Examination of the South Asian Experience', *Comparative Studies in Society and History*, 16(31): 266-67.

Raguraman, K. & Huang, Shirlena, 1993, 'Forty Years of Human Geography in the Journal', *Singapore Journal of Tropical Geography*, 14(2): 277-93.

Rahimi, Wali Mohammad, 1984, 'Afghanistan', in *Social Sciences in Asia and the Pacific*. pp. 21-51, Paris: UNESCO.

Rahman, Abdur, 1983, *Intellectual colonisation: science and technology in West-East relations*, New Delhi: Vikas Publishing House.

Rais, M. Amien et al. (eds), 1984, *Krisis Ilmu-Ilmu Sosial dalam Pembangunan di Dunia Ketiga*, Yogyakarta: PLP2M.

Ramstedt, Martin, 1997, 'Anthropology and the Nation State—Applied Anthropology in Indonesia', Paper presented at the International Workshop on Indigenous and Indigenized Anthropology in Asia, 1-3 May, Leiden.

Rana, Ratna S.J.B., 1984, 'Nepal', in *Social Sciences in Asia and the Pacific*. pp. 354-73, Paris: UNESCO.

Resink, G.J., 1950, 'Iets over Europacentrische, Regiocentrische en Indocentrische eschiedenschrijving', *Orientatie*, 37: 22-30

———, 1952-53, 'Passe-partout om Geschiedenschrijvers over Indonesie', *Indonesie*, 6: 372-79.

Rey, P.P., 1975, 'The Lineage Mode of Production', *Critique of Anthropology*, 3: 27-79.

Ritzer, George, 1988, 'Sociological Metatheory: A Defense of a Subfield by a Delineation of its Parameters', *Sociological Theory*, 6(3): 187-200.

Rizal, José, 1890/1962, 'To the Filipinos', in de Morga, *Historical Events of the Philippine Islands*, p. vii.

Rizal-Blumentritt, 1992, *The Rizal-Blumentritt Correspondence, Vol. 1*, Manila: National Historical Institute.

Rostow W.W., 1960, *The Stages of Economic Growth: A Non-Communist Manifesto*. Cambridge: Cambridge University Press.

Roy, M.N., 1971 [1922], *India in Transition and What do We Want*, Bombay: Nachiketa.

Roy, Rammohun, K. Nag and B. Burman (eds), 1945-48, *The English Works of Raja Rammohun Roy*, Allahabad: Calcutta Publishing House.

Rustam A. Sani & Norani Othman, 1991, 'The Social Sciences in Malaysia: A Critical Scenario', *Ilmu Masyarakat*, 19: 1-20.

Saberwal, Satish, 1968, 'The Problem', *Seminar*, 112: 10-13.

———, 1983, 'For a Sociology of India: Uncertain Transplants, Anthropology and Sociology in India', *Contributions to Indian Sociology*, 17(2): 301-15.

Said, Edward, 1979, *Orientalism*, New York: Vintage Books.

———, 1990, 'Third World Intellectuals and Metropolitan Culture', *Raritan*, 9(3): 27-50.

———, 1993, *Culture and Imperialism*, London: Chatto & Windus.

———, 1995, *The Politics of Disposition: The Struggle for Palestinian Self-Determination 1969-94*, London: Vintage Books.

Salazar, Zeus A., 1992, 'Introduction', in Remigio E. Agpalo, *Adventures in Political Science*, pp. xi-xiv, Quezon City: University of the Philippines Press & College of Social Science and Philosophy.

Dos Santos, Theotonio, 1968, 'La crisis de la teoria del desarrollo y las relaciones de dependencia en America Latina', *Boletin del CESO 3*.

———, 1970, 'The Structure of Dependence', *American Economic Review*, 60(2): 231-36.

Sarekat-Islam Congres, 17-24 Juni 1916 te Bandoeng, Behoort bij de Geheime Missive van den Wd. Adviseur voor Inlandsche Zaken dd. 29 September 1916 no. 226, Batavia: Landsdrukkerij, 1916.

Sarkar, P.R., 1967, *The Human Society*, Denver: Ananda Marga Press.

Sarkar, Benoy Kumar, 1937/1985, *The Positive Background of Hindu Sociology*, Delhi: Motilal Banarsidass. [First edition published in 1937 in Allahabad, reprinted in Delhi in 1985]

Schmutz, Georges M., 1989, 'Sociologie de la Chine ou Sociologie Chinoise?' *Revue Europeene des Sciences Sociales*, 27(84): 5-17.

Schutz, A., 1970, *Reflections on the Problem of Relevance*, New Haven: Yale University Press.

Scott, James C., 1972, *Comparative Political Corruption*, Englewood Cliffs, N.J.: Prentice-Hall.

Scott, Robert L., 1967, 'On Viewing Rhetoric as Epistemic', *Central States Speech Journal*, 18: 9-17.

Sen, Asok, 1987, 'Discussion: Subaltern Studies: Capital, Class and Community', in Ranajit Guha, (ed.), *Subaltern Studies V: Writings on South Asian History and Society*, pp. 203-35, Delhi: Oxford University Press.

Shaharuddin Maaruf, 1984, *The Concept of the Hero in Malay Society*, Singapore: Eastern Universities Press.

———, 1989, *Malay Ideas on Development: From Feudal Lord to Capitalist*, Singapore: Times Book International.

———, 1992, 'Some Theoretical Problems Concerning Tradition and Modernization Among the Malays of Southeast Asia', in Yong Mun Cheong (ed.), *Asian Tradition and Modernization: Perspectives from Singapore*, pp. 241-65, Singapore: Times Academic Press.

Sharifah Maznah Syed Omar, 1993, *Myths and the Malay Ruling Class*, Singapore: Times Academic Press.

Sharma, K.N., 1990, 'Western Sociology with Indian Icing', *Contributions to Indian Sociology*, 24(2): 251-58.

Shin Yong-Ha, 1994, 'Suggestions for the Development of a Creative Korean Sociology', in *Korean Sociological Association, Korean Sociology in the 21st Century*, pp. 15-30. Seoul: Moon-Hak-Kwa Ji-Seong-Sa, 1994. <In Korean>

Sidaway, James D., 1993, 'The Decolonisation of Development Geography?' Area 25(3): 299-300.

Siddiqui, Kalim, 1978, *The Islamic Movement: A Systems Approach*, Tehran: Bonyad Be'that.

Simons, Herbert W. (ed.), 1989, *Rhetoric in the Human Sciences*, London: Sage.

Singh, K.S., 1984, 'Colonialism, Anthropology and Primitive Society: The Indian Scenario (1928-47)', *Man in Asia*, 64(4): 399-413.

Singh, Yogendra, 1986, 'Indian Sociology', *Current Sociology*, 34(2): 1-150.

———, 1993, *Modernization of Indian Tradition*, New Delhi: Thomson.

Singhal, D., 1960, 'Some Comments on "The Western Element in Modern Southeast Asian History"', *Journal of Southeast Asian History*, 1(2): 118-23.

Sinha, Vineeta, 1997, 'Reconceptualizing the Social Sciences in Non-Western Settings: Challenges and Dilemmas', *Southeast Asian Journal of Social Science*, 25(1): 167-81.

———, 1998, 'Socio-Cultural Theory and Colonial Encounters: The Discourse on Indigenizing Anthropology in India', *Manuscript, Department of Sociology*, National University of Singapore.

Sinha, Vineeta, 1999, 'Making Harriet Martineau Visible in Androcentric Sociological Theory', Paper presented at the 3rd Asia Pacific Regional Conference of Sociology, Cheju City, Korea, 4-6 February.

——, 2001, 'Re-building Institutional Structures in the Social Sciences through Critique', in Syed Farid Alatas (ed.), *Reflections on Alternative Discourses from Southeast Asia*, Singapore: Pagesetters.

——, (forthcoming), 'Sankritzation', *Blackwell Encyclopedia of Sociology*, general editor, George Ritzer, Blackwell Publishing House.

Siti Hawa Ali, 1991, 'Western Theory and Local Practice: Implications for Social Work Education in Malaysia', *Asia-Pacific Journal of Social Work*, 1(1): 26-47.

Smith, A.D., 1986, *The Ethnic Origins of Nations*, Oxford: Blackwell.

Smail, J.R.W., 1961, 'On the Possibility of an Autonomous History of Modern Southeast Asia', *Journal of Southeast Asian History*, 2(2): 73-105.

Soedjatmoko, 1960, 'An Approach to Indonesian History: Towards an Open Future' (An address before the Seminar on Indonesian History, Gadjah Mada University, Jogjakarta, December 14, 1957), Ithaca, New York: Translation Series, Modern Indonesia Project, Southeast Asia Program, Department of Far Eastern Studies, Cornell University.

Spivak, Gayatri Chakravorty, 1987, 'Subaltern Studies: Deconstructing Historiography', in Gayatri Chakravorty Spivak, in *In Other Worlds: Essays in Cultural Politics*, pp. 197-221, New York & London: Routledge.

Srinivas, M.N., 1966, *Social Change in Modern India*, Bombay: Allied Publishers.

Srivastava, Vinay Kumar, 2000, 'Teaching Anthropology', *Seminar* 495. <http://www.india-seminar.com/2000/495/495%20vinay%20kumar%20srivastava.htm>

Stapel, F.W., (ed.), 1938-40, *De Geschiedenis van Nederlandsch-Indië*. 6 Vols, Amsterdam: Joost van den Vondel.

Storer, Norman, 1970, 'The Internationality of Science and the Nationality of Scientists', *International Social Science Journal*, 22: 80-93.

Stowasser, Barbara Freyer, 1983, 'Religion and Political Development: Some Comparative Ideas on Ibn Khaldun and Machiavelli, Occasional Paper Series. Washington, DC: Center for Contemporary Arab Studies, Georgetown University.

Sun Chung-Hsing, 1993, 'Aspects of "Sinicisation" and "Globalisation"', *International Sociology*, 8(1): 121-22.

Szymanski, Albert, 1981, *The Logic of Imperialism*. New York: Praeger.

Tagore, Rabindranath. 1919, *The Home and the World*, London: Macmillan.

Tarrant, J.R., 1980, 'The Geography of Food Aid', *Transactions of the Institute of British Geographers*, 5 (ns): 125-40.

Taylor, Charles, 1985a, 'Language and Human Nature', in Charles Taylor (ed.), *Philosophical Papers, Vol. 1.*, Cambridge: Cambridge University Press.

——, 1985b, 'Foucault on Freedom and Truth', in Charles Taylor, *Philosophy and the Human Sciences: Philosophical Papers 2*. Cambridge: Cambridge University Press.

Taylor, Peter J., 1989, *Political Geography: World-Economy, Nation-State and Locality*, Essex: Longman Scientific & Technical.

——, 1993, 'Full Circle or New Meaning for Global', in R.J. Johnston (ed.), *The Challenge for Geography: A Changing World, A Changing Discipline*, pp. 181-97, Oxford: Blackwell.

Taylor, M.J. & N.J. Thrift (eds), 1982, *The Geography of Multinationals*, London: Croom Helm.

Tham Seong Chee, 1971, 'Intellectual Colonization', *Suara Universiti*, 2(2): 39-40.

Thompson, E.P., 1963, *The Making of the English Working Class*, New York: Pantheon Books.

Tibawi, A.L., 1963, 'English Speaking Orientalists: A Critique of their Approach to Islam and Arab Nationalism', *Muslim World*, 53(3 & 4): 185-204 (First Part); 298-313 (Second Part).

———, 1979, 'Second Critique of English-Speaking Orientalists and Their Approach to Islam and the Arabs', *Islamic Quarterly*, 23(1): 3-54.

Tinbergen, J., 1967, *Development Planning*, London: Weidenfeld and Nicholson.

Tjokroaminoto, H.O.S., 1988, 'Islam dan Sosialisme', in Burhanuddin Al-Helmy, Syed Hussein Alatas, Suroosh Irfani and H.O.S. Tjokroaminoto (eds), *Islam dan Sosialisme*, Kuala Lumpur: Ikraq.

Toh Swee-Hin, 1983, 'The International Council for Educational Development: An Ideological Agency for World Capitalism', *Journal of Contemporary Asia*, 13(4): 409-31.

Toynbee, Arnold J., 1935, *A Study of History*, Vol. III, London: Oxford University Press.

Troeltsch, E., 1931, *The Social Teaching of the Christian Churches* 2 Vols., New York: Macmillan.

Trouillot, Michel-Rolph, 1991, 'Anthropology and the Savage Slot: The Poetics and Politics of Otherness', in Richard G. Fox (ed.), *Recapturing Anthropology: Working in the Present*, pp. 17-44, Santa Fe: School of American Research Press.

Tucker, Judith, 1987, *Women in Nineteenth Century Egypt*, Cairo: American University in Cairo Press.

Turner, Bryan S., 1971, 'Sociological Founders and Precursors: The Theories of Religion of Emile Durkheim, Fustel de Coulanges and Ibn Khaldun', *Religion*, 1: 32-48.

Uberoi, J.P.S., 1968, 'Science and Swaraj', *Contributions to Indian Sociology*, (ns) 2: 119-23.

———, 1974, 'New Outlines of Structural Sociology, 1945-70', *Contributions to Indian Sociology*, (ns) 8: 135-52.

Venturi, Franco, 1963, 'Oriental Despotism', *Journal of the History of Ideas*, 24(1): 133-42.

Vidyarthi, L.P., 1980, *Aspects of Social Anthropology in India*, Delhi: Classical Publications.

Walker R.B.J., 1981, 'World Politics and Western Reason: Universalism, Pluralism, and Hegemony', *Alternatives*, 7(2): 196-227.

Wallerstein, Immanuel, 1974, *The Modern World-System I: Capitalist Agriculture and the Origins of the European World-Economy in the Sixteenth Century*, New York: Academic Press.

———, 1979, *The Capitalist World-Economy*. Cambridge: Cambridge University Press.

———, 1980, *The Modern World-System II: Mercantilism and the Consolidation of the European World-Economy, 1600-1750*, New York: Academic Press.

———, 1996, 'Eurocentrism and Its Avatars: The Dilemmas of Social Science', Paper presented to Korean Sociological Association-International Sociological Association East Asian Regional Colloquium on 'The Future of Sociology in East Asia', November 22-23, Seoul.

———, 2003, 'Anthropology, Sociology, and other Dubious Disciplines', *Current Anthropology*, 44(4): 453-60.

Wallerstein, I., C. Juma, E.F. Keller, J. Kocka, D. Lecourt, V.U. Mudimbe, K. Mushakoji, I. Prigogine, P.J. Taylor and M-R. Trouillot, 1996, *Open the Social Sciences: Report of the Gulbenkian Commission on the Restructuring of the Social Sciences*, New Delhi: Vistaar.

Wang Gungwu, 2001, 'Shifting Paradigms and Asian Perspectives: Implications for Research and Teaching', in Syed Farid Alatas, (ed.), *Reflections on Alternative Discourses from Southeast Asia*, pp. 47-54, Singapore: Pagesetters.

Watanuki, Joji, 1984, 'Japan', in *Social Sciences in Asia and the Pacific*, pp. 281-295, Paris: UNESCO.
Weber, M., 1949, *The Methodology of the Social Sciences*, New York: Free Press.
———, 1958, *The Religion of India: The Sociology of Hinduism and Buddhism*, Hans Gerth and Don Martindale, trans. and eds., New York: The Free Press.
Wee, Vivienne, 1988, *Men, Women and Violence: A Handbook for Survival*, Singapore: AWARE and SAWL for the Task Force for the Prevention of Violence against Women, Singapore Council of Women's Organisations (SCWO).
Wee, Vivienne, Noeleen Heyzer, assisted by Aileen Kwa et al., 1995, *Gender, Poverty and Sustainable Development: Towards a Holistic Framework of Understanding and Action*, Singapore: Centre for Environment, Gender and Development.
Weeks, Priscilla, 1986, 'Rural Development and Social Theory Building in the Third World', *Philippines Sociological Review*, 34(1-4): 16-25.
———, 1990, 'Post-Colonial Challenges to Grand Theory', *Human Organization*, 49(3): 236-44.
Weimar, Walter B., 1977, 'Science as a Rhetorical Transaction: Towards a Non-Justificational Conception of Rhetoric', *Philosophy and Rhetoric* 10(1): 1-29.
Weiner, W.G., 1960, *On Gaming Limited War*, RAND Paper P2123.
Wiegersma, Nancy, 1982, 'The Asiatic Mode of Production in Vietnam', *Journal of Contemporary Asia*, 12(1): 19-33.
Wingens, Matthias & Ansgar Weymann, 1988, 'Utilization of Social Sciences in Public Discourse: Labeling Problems', *Knowledge in Society: The International Journal of Transfer*, 1(1): 80-97.
Worsely, Peter, 1964, *The Third World*, London: Weidenfeld & Nicholson.
Yang Choon, 1994, '21st Century Korean Society and Sociology Education', in Korean Sociological Association, *Korean Sociology in the 21st Century*, pp. 31-38, Seoul: Moon-Hak-Kwa Ji-Seong-Sa. <In Korean>
Yang, Kuo-Shu & Wen, Chung-I (eds), 1982, *The Sinicization of Social and Behavioral Science Research in China*, Institute of Ethnology Monograph Series B. No. 10, Taipei: Institute of Ethnology, Academia Sinica. <In Chinese>
Zaide, S., 1993, 'Historiography in the Spanish Period', in *Philippine Encyclopedia of the Social Sciences*, pp. 4-19, Quezon City: Philippine Social Science Council.
Zawiah Yahya, 1994, *Resisting Colonialist Discourse*, Bangi: Penerbit Universiti Kebangsaan Malaysia.
Zghlal, Abdelkader & Hachmi Karoui, 1973, 'Decolonization and Social Science Research: the Case of Tunisia', *Middle East Studies Association Bulletin*, 7(3): 11-27.

Index

Abdel-Malek, A., 42
bin Abdul Kadir, Munshi, Abdullah (1796-1854), 34-35; *Kesah Pelayaran Abdullah*, 35
abstraction/abstractions, 30, 47, 48, 49, 109, 122, 124, 134
academic colonialism/imperialism, 27-28, 31, 57, 58, 60, 74, 86, 87, 108, 112, 194, academic neo-colonialism, 70-71
academic dependency theory, 25, 32, 50, 53-54, 57, 80, 81, 104, 112, 131, 136-7, 139, 140, 148, 176, 190-91; definition, 58-61; demerits, 75-76; dependence on aid for research and training, 67-68, 75-76; dependence on ideas, 64-65; dependence on investment in education, 68-69; dependence on media of ideas, 65-66; dependence on technology of education, 66, 75; prospects of reversal, 73-75; structure, 61-70; technology, aid and investment, 54-55
advertising, 173
affinity, 139
Afghanistan: study of social sciences, 21
Afro-Asian society, 90
Afro-centrism, 110
Agus Salim, 128
aid for research and training, Third World dependence on West, 67-68, 75-76
Al-Attas, Syed Muhammad al-Naquib, 37-38, 95-96
al-'Azm, Sadiq Jalal, 108-09
Al-e Ahmad, Jalal, 50
Alatas, Syed Farid, 28, 31
Alatas, Syed Hussein, 28, 29, 30-31, 37, 38, 48-49, 52-53, 65, 72, 88, 112, 147, 163
Alavi, Hamza, 160
alienation, 134
alternative discourses, 33-39, 58, 112, 118, 170, 172, 173, 176, 187; and autonomous social science traditions in global social science, 190-91; critique, 106; cultural environment, 191; definition of, 80-89; marginal status, 105-06; obstacles to the emergence, 166-72, 190; prospects for, 190-91; teaching, 182-86; varieties, 83-89
American, *See* United States of America/American
Amin, Samir, *Eurocentrism*, 45
Anglo-American society, 90
Anglo-Saxon theoretical traditions, 25, 190
anthropology, 21, 23, 25, 32, 58, 62; indigenization, 83-84, 110-11; in the Third World, 21-22, 83-85
applied social science, 143-45
Arab, Arabs, Arabic, 42, 185; notion of man, 108-09; political economy, 43; social science, 172
arbitrariness of interpretation, 155
area studies journals, 72
Argentine: development and legitimation of geo-graphy as a discipline, 126
asabiyyah (group feeling), 117
Ashraf, Ahmad, 42
Asia Foundation, 67
Asian-centric history, 37
Asian diagnoses of the problem, 26-31

Asian Symposium on Intellectual Creativity in Endogenous Culture, Kyoto, Japan, (1978), 90
assumptions and reality, accordance, 141, 143; disaccord, 134-37
Australia: aid to Third World for education, 68; semi-peripheral social science power, 70
authoritarianism, 119, 137, 144, 160
authority, concepts of, 161
autonomous social science, autonomy, 83, 89, 104, 112-22, 139, 190-91
auto-Orientalism, 109-10
axiology, 88
Azerbaijan, Safavid mystical order, 187

Baharuddin, Shamsul Amri, 31
Bangladesh: social sciences, 21
Bastin, John, 37
belief systems, 181
Bennabi, Malik, 52
Béteille, André, 114, 115, 116
Blake, M.L., 28
Bodin, Jean, 179
Bombay University, India, 21
Book Translation Program, 67
Bose, Jagdis Chandra, 121
Bose, N.K., 27
bourgeoise, 99, 137, 160
brain drain, 69, 74
Brazil: academic dependency, 62
Britain, See United Kingdom
Buddhism, 130, 178, 180
Burma: social sciences studies, 21

Calcutta University, India, 21
CAMELOT Project, 58-60
capitalism, 45, 91, 115-16, 128, 130, 158, 188, 193
captive mind theory, 30-31, 33, 47-50, 53, 57, 73, 74, 108, 112, 122, 131, 133-34, 136, 137, 148, 151, 194; factorgenic and actorgenic analysis, 159-60; power and the discourses on development, 157-66
meta-analysis, 41-55, 123, 127, 135, 141-42; and its varieties, 40-41

Cardoso, Fernando, 192
Casal, Friar, 35
caste system, 118-21
Catholicism, 189
Cesaire, Aime, 33, 52
Chattopadhyay, K.P., 26
China, Chinese, 142; academic dependence, 68; culture and society, 110; indigenous anthropology, 85; Marxist sociology, 111; nationalization of social sciences, 101, 102-03; postmodernism, 129; social sciences studies, 22, 28; sociology, 22, 28, 168
Chinatown, North America, 43
Christianity, 26, 94-95, 138, 140, 178, 179, 180
civil society, 130, 142
Clinton, Bill, 192
colonial administration, colonialism, 22, 25, 26, 30, 38, 44, 57, 61, 85, 91, 126, 182, 191; colonial critiques, 51-52, 73; colonization, 191; colonized people, mindset, 51-52; psychological dimension, 51-52
communism, Communist, 84, 144
Comparative Studies in Society and History, 72
Comte, Auguste, 23, 26, 182
concept-formation and theory building, 118-22
conceptual irrelevance, 138
conceptualization, 30, 47, 48
Confucianism, 23, 119, 135, 137, 143, 144, 182, 193
Congress for Cultural Freedom, 68
conscientiousness, 191
consciousness, 35, 61, 142
conservatism, 24
Constitution, 116
consumer behaviour, 48
Contributions to Indian Sociology, 27
Contributions to Indian Sociology (New Series), 27
Coorgs, 120
core-periphery relationship, 55, 157
corruption, 162, 163, 184
counterism and proliferation of terminology, 77-78

creativity, 83, 118, 173; lack of, 24, 31, 32, 51
critical pedagogy, 57
cultural, culture, 85, 87, 91, 99, 121, 150-51, 173; borrowings between the Muslims and the Europeans, 185; dependency, 120; diversity, 111; environment in alternative discourses, 191; heritage, 119; homogeneity, 28, 109, 120; and ideology, 161-62; imperialism, 61; influences, 37; problems, 53; rootedness of theories, 119; terms, 179; vacuum, 122; voids, 192

Decision-making and policy implementation, 144
decolonization of knowledge/social sciences, 40, 57, 58, 81, 91-93, 105, 126, 139
deconstructionist theorists, 32
delinking, 103-04
democracy, 144, 148
demonstration effect, 48-49
demystification, 139, 143, 144
deschooling, 57, 104-05, 139
development discourse/theory, 43-44, 77, 165, 172; captive mind and power, 157-66; indigenization, 87; misspecification and neglect of pathologies, 164
development studies, 46, 48-49; factorgenic versus actorgenic analysis, 159-60, 164; imitation, and the need for alternative discourses, 147-51
Dhaka University, Bangladesh, 21
diffusionism, 92
disciplinary control of man, 156, 158-59, 174
discontinuity, 154, 156
discourses and autonomous social science traditions in global social science, 190-91
divide and rule, 58
dualisms, 44, 94
Dumont, Louis, 27, 116
Durkheim, Emile, 26, 52, 74, 105, 138, 177-78, 182, 183, 193

Dutch East India Company, 36
Dutt, B.N., 26

East Asia: lack of fit between Western theory and East Asian realities, 24
East-West dichotomy, 34
economic dependency and academic dependency, relation, 63, 75
economic imperialism, 48, 58, 60-61
economic power balance and academic dependency, link, 69-70
economic structure, economy, 91, 149-50
economic theory and policy, 44
economics, 23, 58; studies in Third World, 21-22
education, 50-51, 134
empirical studies and data collection, 143
endogenous intellectual creativity, 87, 90-91, 105
Engels, Friedrich, 135, 193
English Language Book Scheme, 68
environmentalism, 94
epistemological issues, epistemology, 88, 132-33, 172
equality, 116
ethnic and cultural prejudices, 64
ethnocentrism, 44, 110, 120
ethnography, 32
Euro-American social science, 25, 81, 121, 190
Eurocentrism in social sciences, 23, 26, 28-30, 32-33, 38, 44-45, 47, 50, 53, 57, 73, 81-82, 84, 90, 105, 106, 110, 121-22, 134, 136, 176, 186, 191; in curricula, 176-78; reversing via teaching, 179-82
European: discourses on non-Western societies, 32; dominance/political and economic superiority, 94, 176-78; as originators, 178; tradition of knowledge and indigenous systems of ideas, lack of continuity, 25
Evans, Grant, 110-11, 193
exclusion, 167
expansionism, 45
explanation, 30, 47, 48, 165
exteriority, 116, 156

external-cognitive, 47-50
external-institutional, 54-55

False consciousness, 30
Fanon, Frantz, 52
Fe Hsiao-t'ung, 121, 142
fetishism, 158
feudalism, 35, 113, 115
Filipinology, 101-02
Ford Foundation, 68
Foucault, Michael, 167, 169-70, 173-74; on discourse and power, 147, 151-57, 158
foundationalism, 100, on punishment, 173-74
France, French, 54, 60; anthropology, 62; aid to Third World for research and training, 67; institutionalization of social sciences, 64; intellectual dominance, 65; poststructuralism, 50
Frank, Andre Gunder, 192-93
Freire, Paulo, 51
Freud, Sigmund, 193
functionalism, 93
funding and policy formulation, 111

Gandhi, J.S., 125
Gandhi, M.K., 96-97, 105
Gandhian school, 23, 24
Garreau, Frederick H., 63
Gellner, Ernest, 181
gender, 185
geography, 21, 32, 58, 89, 124, 126; decolonization, 92; globalization, 93, 94; role in territorial acquisition and resource exploitation, 141
Germany, Germans, 22, 54, 60; aid to Third World for research and training, 67; institutionalization of social sciences, 64; intellectual dominance, 65
Ghose, Aurobindo, 24
Ghurye, G.S., 26
Giddens, Anthony, 104
global capitalism, 62
global division of labour in the social sciences, 56, 57, 70-73, 82, 94
global politics, 85

global system of exploitation, 92-93
globalization of knowledge/social sciences, 40, 58, 93-94
Gradated network, 121, 142
Gramsci, Antonio, 97, 119
Greek philosophy, 192
Greeks, 152
Guha, Ranajit, 97

Hagen, E.E., 49
Hasan Ali Soerati, 128
hidden curriculum, 50
hierarchy, 116
Hinduism, Hindus, 26, 116, 118-20, 178, 180, 189-90
historical continuity, 109
historical geography, 23
historiography studies in Philippines, 35
history, 58, 114-15; periodization, 98-99, 115
history studies in Third World, 22
holism, 116
Huang Ziping, 129
human sciences, 22, 23, 95-96, 152
humanism, 96
Hume, David, 118, 181
hybridity, 99

idealism, 117
ideas and media of ideas, 53-54, 64-66
ideological barriers, 121
Illich, Ivan, 50, 104
imitation, 57, 64, 147-48, 157, 161, 165, 194; negative, 162-63
imperialism, 157
imported models, 130
inapplicability, 136
India, academic dependence, 64-65, 67, 75; alternative discourses, 34; indigenization of anthropology, 83-85;—indigenization, 109-11; history, 114-15; social sciences, 23, 26-27;—failed to Indianize, 24; nationalization of social sciences, 101
Indianness, 109-10
indigenization of knowledge/social sciences, 33-34, 40, 57, 81, 83-89, 103, 139, 172-73

indigenous theories and concepts, 83
individualism, 116
Indocentrism, 36
Indology, 26
Indonesia, Indonesian, 29, 184; academic dependence, 67, 68; alternative discourses, 36; anthropology, 25; eighteenth century as a category in the history, 36; Indische Social-Democratische Vereniging (ISDV), 128-29; Indonesian Communist Party (PKI), 128; Islamization, 29; Sarekat Islam (Islamic Union), 128-29; social sciences, 112;—nationalization, 101-02
Industrial Revolution, 36
industrialization, 94
inequality, 53, 70-71, 184
inflation, 159
information technology, 99
Institute of Defense Analysis (IDA), 60
institutional impediments, 159
institutionalization of development, 165
institutionalization of social sciences, 64
intellectual creativity, 90-91, 105
intellectual dependence, 25, 126
intellectual division of labour, 85
intellectual imperialism theory, 30, 33, 52-55, 81, 84
intellectual socialization, 191
intelligentsia, 142
Inter-civilizational encounters, 185
internal-cognitive, 42-44
internal-institutional approach, 52-54
International Association of Philippinists, 35
International Institute of Islamic Thought and Civilization (ISTAC), United States, 95-96
international law, 61
International Monetary Fund (IMF), 76
international political economy, 61
international publications, 191
international social science community, 63
interpretation, 30, 47, 50, 155, 170
inter-state system, 157

investment in education, Third World dependence on West, 68
Iran, Iranian: irrelevance of imported models, 130; political economy and culture, Western dominance, 50-51, 117; revolution, 119; Safavid period, 117
Islam, Islamic, 26, 42, 78, 94-96, 108, 128, 130, 138, 140, 144, 178, 180, 182, 184-85, 193; economics, 77, 168-71; medieval European philosophy, impact on, 185; revivalism and imperialism, 185; socialism, 128
Italy: institutionalization of social sciences, 64

Jain, Rekha, 72
Japan, Japanese, 29, 60, 62; aid to Third World for research and training, 67; anthropology, 25; academic dependence on West, 69-70; colonization of China, 25; discrimination against in-house publications, 191; Meiji period (1868-1912), 22; social sciences establishment, 22, 69-70; sociology, 28, 109
Japan Foundation, 69
Java Sea Battle, 29
Java, Hinduization, 30
Jews, 189
Joshi, P.C., 125
Judaism, 189

Kabul University, Afghanistan, 21
Kakar, Sudhir, 90; *Shamans, Mystics and Doctors*, 91
kapwa, 142
Ketkar, S.V., 26
Ibn Khaldun, Abd al-Rahman, 23, 105, 117-18, 120, 161, 177-78, 182, 192; theory of development, 151; theory of state formation, 43, 83, 90, 117, 131, 142, 181
Kim Kyong Dong, 119, 143, 181
King Edward VII College of Medicine, Singapore, 22
kinship systems, 152

knowledge, 40, 80, 151, 155, 157–58, 192, 194; Islamization, 78, 95–96; role of language, 152–54; sacralization, 139; social bases, 132–33; three types, 112–13; non-Western sources, 117–22
Korea, Korean: social sciences, 23, 119, 143;—nationalization, 101; sociology, 28
Kosambi, D.D., 80, 114–15
kratonization, 112
Kroeber, Alfred Louis (1876–1960), *Configuration of Culture*, 44
Kuwayama, Takami, 62

laissez-faire principle, 62
language, 166–67; designative theory, 152–54, 170; an instrument of control in gaining knowledge, 152–54
Latin America, 62; academic dependence, 67
law and politics, 22, 116
van Leur, Jacob Cornelis, 29–30, 36, 101
Levi-Strauss, 152
liberation theology, 95
linguistics, 22, 58
Linton, Ralph, 44
literacy, 60
Locke, John, 153
Lokayata, 117
Lukacs, G., 158
Lutheranism, 189

Madan, T.N., 27, 44, 114
Madras University, India, 21
Malaya University, 22
Malay-Indonesian Archipelago, Islamization, 37
Malaysia, Malay, 55, 113, 184; academic dependence, 66, 68, 75, 76; backwardness, 35; colonialism, 30; ethnicity, 31; National Advisory Council for the Integration of Women in Development (NACIWD), 145; social sciences studies, 21, 34, 112; Women's Secretariat (HAWA), 145
male dominance, 130
Mandelbaum, David, 44

man-ecology relations, 23
Mannheim, Karl, 132, 142, 177
marginality, 99
Marriott, McKim, 91
Martel, Charles, 187
Marx, Karl, 26, 52, 74, 90, 105, 114, 132, 134, 136, 158, 177, 182, 183, 191–93
Marxism, Marxist, 34, 84, 100, 103, 111, 115, 117, 128, 150, 151
materialism, 26, 102
Matthes, Joachim, 179–80
medieval nominalism, 152
mediocrity, 135
Memmi, Albert, 52
metaphysics, 100
metatheory, 41, 64, 172, 181
methodology, 41; methodological concepts, 38; lack of attention to issues, 163–64
Middle East, 23
mimesis, 32, 64
mimetic irrelevance, 138
min-joong, 119, 121
minorities point of view, 32
modernity, 94, 99, 136, 174, 183; multicultural origins, 185
modernization theory, 92, 149–50, 161, 162, 164; pedagogical, 33, 50–51, 73, 131
de Morga, Antonio, 35; *Sucesos de las Islas Filipinas*, 29
Mukerji, D.P., 26, 27, 114–15
Mukherjee, Radhakamal, 26
Munshi, Surendra, 114, 116, 121
Muslims, 26, 96, 108, 167–69, 184–85, 192; social reality, 171
Myrdal, Gunnar, 147
mystification, 136

Nahraynianism, 188–89
Nandy, Ashish, 121
Naoroji, Dadabhai, 184
national integration, 32
National University of Singapore, 22, 182
nationalism, nationalist consciousness, 26, 98
nationalization of knowledge/social sciences, 40, 58, 101–03, 111, 139

nation-state, collapse, 99
natives, 137, 140
nativism, 85, 108–12, 170, 194
neo-colonialism, 93
Nepal: social sciences studies, 21
Netherlands Indies: Eurocentrism, 29–30; social science power, 70; social sciences studies, 21; aid to Third World for research and training, 67
neutrality, 173
Nigeria: academic dependence, 67
nihonjinron (theories of Japanese people), 28, 109
non-economic variables, 124
non-governmental organizations (NGOs), 144–45
non-Western sources of knowledge, 117–22
normalization, 100, 155, 156, 158–59, 160, 162–64, 171–74; as Westernization, 164–66
North Africa: sociology, decolonization, 93
North America, 55; aid to Third World for education, 68
North-South divide, 63
Nueva Ecija, Philippines: irrelevance of imported models, 130, 136

obfuscating convolutions, 135
objectivity, objectivism, 36, 133
Occident, 26, 109; Orient divide, 26, 43–44
ontology, 109
Oommen, T.K., *Alien Concepts and South Asian Reality*, 90–91
Open the Social Sciences project, 38
Orientalist discourses, Orientalism, 26, 32, 33–34, 38, 42–44, 45, 47, 50, 53, 57, 73, 81–82, 108–10, 116, 121–22, 130–32, 134, 137, 144, 176, 186, 191, 194
originality, lack of, 133–35, 139
orthodoxy, 189
Ottoman, 184; social system, 130–31; Turks, 187
overpopulation, 77

Pal, Bipin Chadra, 24
Pandey, T.N., 72
Pané, Armijn, 36
Park Chung-Hee, 89
parochialism, 88, 93
passive consumption, 50
pastoral nomadism, 130
pathological process, 165
patriarchy, 130
Persian, 184
phenomenology, 89
Philippines: concept of 'self' and Others (*Kapwa*), 142; cultural perspective, 30; education system on American lines, 22; Eurocentric epistemological legacy, 35; history, 35; indigenization movement, 35; indigenization of psychology, 83–84; irrelevance of imported models, 130, 136; nationalization of social sciences, 101–03; social sciences studies, 22, 23; Spanish colonization, 29
Philosophy of the Social Sciences, 71
Plato, 151
Pocock, D.F., 27
policy formulation, 173
policy implementation, 145
political economy of social sciences, 57, 94, 99, 100, 117, 124, 129, 158
political emancipation, 25
political imperialism, 48, 60–61
political science studies in Third World, 21–23
politico-economic domination, 84
politics, 135
polycentrism, 126
positivism, 26, 77
post colonial theory, post-colonialism, 45–46, 98–100, 132–33, 137, 139–40, 160
post-modernism, 135
poverty, 40, 148, 173, 184
power relations, 141; inequality, 150
problem-setting, 30, 47, 48
production, 115, 117; Asiatic mode, 90, 115, 134, 182; shift to economic system, 99
Progressive Sociologists Network, 193

Protestant, Protestantism, 130, 135, 137, 140, 179, 180
provincialism, 45
psycho-cultural theory of capitalist development, 193
psychology, 89
psychology studies in Third World, 21, 22, 35
public opinion polls, 129
publishing industry, foreign aid, 67; Western dominance, 65–66

qizilbash, 187

Raffles College, Singapore, 21–22, 38
Ramanujan, Srinivasa, 121
RAND Corporation, 60
Rangoon University, Burma, 21
rationality, rationalism, 26, 169–70
Raychaudhuri, Tapan, 72
recontextualization, 103, 111
redundance, 134–35; of development studies, 160, 164
reification, 158
relative autonomy, 135
religion, religious, 179–80, 188–90; heterogeneity, 189; oscillation theory, 118; prejudices, 45
reversal principle, 156
rhetorical theories of social science, 46–47, 73, 76–77
Rizal, José (1861–1896), 29, 35, 52, 74, 105, 178, 182
Rostow, W.W., 149
Roy, M.N., 184
Roy, Rammohan (1772–1833), 26, 52, 183
rural-urban dichotomy, 162

Saberwal, Satish, 72
sacralization of knowledge/social sciences, 94–100, 139
Saddikni, Georges, 108–09
Safavid Sufi movement, 187
Safi al-Din, Sheikh, 187
Sahlins, 32
Said, Edward, 42–43, 45; *See also* Orientalism

Sanskritization, 120–21
dos Santos, Theotonio, 63
Saran, A.K., 27
Sarkar, Benoy Kumar (1887–1949), 26, 52, 74, 118, 178, 182–83
scientific colonialism, 62
Seal, B.N., 26
secularism, 95
secularization, 149, 162, 168
self-reliance, 101–02
semantic analysis, 38
Seminar, 27
semiological ontologies, 152–53
servitude of the mind, 28
sexuality and power, 155–56
shared identity, 142
Sharia'ati, Ali, 52
Sharifah Maznah Syed Omar, 38
Sierra Project, 60
Singapore: alternative discourses, 38; social sciences studies, 21, 28; feminist alternatives to mainstream sociological discourses, 29
Singh, Yogendra, 26, 27, 125
Sinha, Surajit, 72
Sinha, Vineeta, 29, 38, 182, 183
sinicization, 102–03
social cycle theory, 118
social change, 90, 119
social ethics, 95
social identity, 142
social movements, 99
social organization, 165
social reformation, 26
social sciences: in context of colonial expansion, 25; defining the problem, 31–33; need for meta-analysis, 55–56; theories, rhetorical, 46–47;— a typology of meta-analysis, 41–55;— need for universality and levels of relevance, 193–95; as a Western phenomenon, 22–25
sociology, 58, 89, 120, 142; of education, 134; of knowledge, 40, 151
sociology studies, in Afghanistan, 21; in Bangladesh, 21; in Burma, 21; in Philippines, 22
South Korea, 89

Southeast Asia: hoe, 49; state of knowledge, 29
spatial dualisms, 44
Special Operations Research Office (SORO), American University, Washington, 58-59
Spencer, Herbert, 26; *Principles of Sociology*, 22
spirituality, 95
Srinivas, M.N., 27, 120-21
state, 32; formation, 43, 83, 90, 117, 131, 142; and individual, relationship, 95; and society relations, 24
statecraft, 91, 119
statehood, 165
structuralism, 99, 101, 152
subaltern groups, 140
subaltern studies, 97-98, 106, 119, 140
subject-object dichotomy, 176-77
subjectivity, subjectivism, 36, 152
subjugation, 58
succinctness (non-redundancy), 139, 143
Sufism, 38
swadeshi, 97
swaraj, 101-02
systems of utility, 165

Tagore, Rabindranath, 105; *The Home and the World*, 34
Tahmasb I Shah (930-984 AH), 187
Taiwan: nationalization of social sciences, 101, 102, 103; recontextualization, 111
Talmud, 189
tauhid (Unity of God), 96
Taylor, Charles, 173
Teaching, of alternative discourses, 182-86
Teaching Sociology, 182, 183
technical-economic rationality, 170
technology of education, Third World dependence on West, 66, 75
terminology, proliferation, 77-78
territorial identity, 126
tertium comparationis, 180
textualism, 189
Thailand: academic dependence, 68

theory, theoretical perspectives, 32, 41, 142-43
Theory and Society, 72
Third World, 22, 40, 42, 44-48, 52, 57, 83, 94, 99, 104, 139; academic dependency, 54-55, 61-71, 73, 76-77; call for autonomous social science, 89; British parochialism, 53; development discourses/theories, 152, 159, 172-73; lack of indigenous theories, concepts and methods, 23-24; imitation of West, 57, 64, 147-48, 157, 161-63; social sciences, 73, 113, 116, 151, 169; relevance and irrelevance of Western social science, 123-45, 161, 192, 193-95
Tinbergen, 49
Tjokroaminoto, H.O.S., 128
de Tocqueville, 52, 182
topical irrelevance, 138-39
topography, 23, 77
Torah, 189
Toyota Foundation, 69
transformations, 130-31
Tri Chandra College, Nepal, 21
Turkic Shi'ite rule, 187-89
Turkish social science, 21, 23
Turkomans, 187
two-gap model of development, 159

Uberoi, J.P.S., 27, 72, 148
underdevelopment, 44, 92-93, 100, 124, 149-50, 159, 165, 185
unemployment, 150-51
United Kingdom (British), 54, 60; aid to Third World for education and research and training, 67, 68; anthropology, 62; institutionalization of social sciences, 64; intellectual dominance, 65
United States (of America)/American, 22, 54; aid to Third World for research and training, 67; anthropology, 62; Central Intelligence Agency (CIA), 68; Defense Department, 58; educational system, 22; foreign policy, 45; institutionalization of social sciences,

64; intellectual dominance, 65; sociology, 22
universal, differentiation from particular, 161-62
universality of Western knowledge, 83, 88
universalization of social science, 83, 102, 193-95; and indigenization, 83-88
urbanization, 161-62

values, 115, 132, 138
Varna model, 118-19, 120
verstehen, 37
Vietnam; academic dependence, 68
Vivekananda, 24

Wallerstein, Immanuel, 64
Wang An Shih, 52
Wang Gungwu, 38
Wang Anyi (*Xiaobao Village*), 129
Weber, Max, 26, 37, 52, 74, 105, 116, 129, 132, 134, 137, 144, 163, 177-78, 182, 183, 190-93
West, Western, 105, 183; anthropological theory, 84; colonial powers, 57; concepts, 108, 151; consciousness, 151; culture/tradition, 36-37, 69, 92, 170-71; development theories/discourse on development, 149, 166, 174; dominance/influence, 31, 48-49, 53, 69, 120, 166; economic system, 148; educational system, 24; representation of Indian society, 28; individualism, 34; intervention, 44; journals, prestige value, 31; knowledge, 80, 95-96, 110, 113-14;—constructive critique, 114-17; mindset/psychology, 35, 43; monopolistic control, 61; point of reference, 129-30; post-enlightenment thought, 23; ideology of postmodernism and postcolonialism, 98; social science models, 32, 47-48, 86-88, 102, 108, 147, 118, 121, 157, 167-69, 172, 192;—ethnocentric biases, 54, 64;—relevance and irrelevance to Third World, 123-45, 161, 192, 193-95; notion of society, 172; spatio-cultural origins, 40; superiority, 43, 48-51; theory, recontextualization, 103;—and non-Western realities, 34, 128; university education, 190; values, 166
Westernization, 162, 164-66, 168
Windelband, 37
World Bank, 76
world-system, 62, world-system theory, 150

Yanagita Kunio, 182
ying-yang, 119, 143

About the Author

Syed Farid Alatas is Associate Professor at the Department of Sociology, National University of Singapore, where he has been since 1992. He obtained his PhD (1991) from Johns Hopkins University and has previously lectured in the Department of Southeast Asian Studies, University of Malaya (1989–92). Besides being published in journals such as *Current Sociology, Teaching Sociology, Antropologi Indonesia* and *The European Legacy*, he has previously published two books—*Democracy and Authoritarianism: The Rise of the Post-Colonial State in Indonesia and Malaysia* (1997) and *Asian Anthropology* (co-edited with Jan Breman and Eyal Ben-Ari) (2005). He is currently working on a book in the area of Muslim revival and another project on the Ba'alawi sufi order.